The Arabs

THE ARABS

Their History and Future

by

JACQUES BERQUE

Translated by

JEAN STEWART

With a preface by

SIR HAMILTON GIBB

FREDERICK A. PRAEGER, *Publishers*

NEW YORK · WASHINGTON

BOOKS THAT MATTER

Published in the United States of America in 1964
by Frederick A. Praeger, Inc., Publishers
111 Fourth Avenue, New York 3, N.Y., U.S.A.

Second printing, 1965

Library of Congress Catalog Card Number: 64-19954

Printed in Great Britain

Contents

Illustrations

Illustrations in the Text

There is a map of the Middle East on pages 22–23

Preface

This book is a watershed in the study of the contemporary Middle East by Western man. To say this is not to belittle the product of a generation of Western students of the region, of political scientists, sociologists and economists. But Jacques Berque, orientalist by heredity, sociologist by training, all of whose life has been spent in intimate contact and close working relations with Muslims, brings to his study an equipment that is literally unique in this field. It is an exciting book but not one to be read quickly and easily. It is complex, even at times obscure, because the Middle East is complex and obscure. It is aware of the contradictions within Middle Eastern society and lays them bare, without seeking to resolve them or presuming to prescribe for them in any but the most general terms. Above all, it is keenly sensitive to the rôle of the unseen factors in Arab life and thought, the symbolic and the 'irrational', which so often confound the theories and expectations of social and economic experts, and to the strange power that resides in the hypostases of the Arabic language and Islam, united in the charismatic 'Word'. To grasp its significance is the most difficult task that confronts the pragmatic student of the Arab world; but those who have experienced it in whatever degree know—as mystics know of the Divine—that without an understanding of its potency there is no reality.

For this reason the book is authentic in a profound sense and at different levels. It is based on personal experience and observation by an eye trained to notice, an ear tuned to rhythms and inflections. At the same time, their impressions are checked against an astonishing range of data and studies published by Arabs themselves, in Egypt, Syria, Lebanon and Iraq, as well as of pertinent materials in journals and newspapers. Earlier Western studies, too, are not neglected, though never permitted to challenge the primacy of the approach from within. Finally, all these materials are sifted and ordered with a powerful sense of the seamlessness of the web of life. Outside forces may strive to pull it apart, and newer looms may force it into new patterns, involving it in a continuous process of adjustment. But Jacques Berque is no idolizer of the past; he sees it in its proper function as an experienced living force whose effects persist under the newer structures which both displace it and draw sustenance from it; hence even 'the present is not to be interpreted too closely in the light of events'.

There may be readers who will feel aggrieved that nothing is said, except in casual references, about bedouins, and little about villagers and peasants, although these consitute the overwhelming majority of Arabs. If there be such, they have surely mistaken the purpose and axis of the whole study. The author himself, in one passage, defines his work as 'a study chiefly attentive to evolutions, movements and attitudes'. He focuses therefore on the points of growth, of interaction, and of dislocation. These are to be found primarily, and at diverse levels, in the urban and urbanized populations, whence they radiate into other sectors more or less widely and deeply. Before critics charge Jacques Berque with being interested only in 'townees', let them take the trouble to consult a bibliography of his writings.

Much the same may be said of another notable omission from this book, because more closely related to its general subject: the development of legal institutions, not so much in the sense of the enactment of new codes, but rather in respect of methods and ethos in their administration. Since not the least remarkable among Berque's earlier writings have been studies of legal institutions and their functioning, the omission is clearly deliberate. And in this case not because legal institutions are regarded as secondary in the contemporary evolution of the Arabs, but (this at least is my assumption) because they demand a special study of their own, long, intricate and delicate, and it is clearly better to say nothing than to generalize from fragmentary—and not infrequently dubious—data.

It is but natural, however, that with such riches presented to him the reader should want more. The academic professional, on the other hand, will appreciate the book's quality more especially for its restraints and the numerous suggestions it throws out for further research in sociological and economic fields. That all such future research, if not actually starting from this book, will be forced to reckon with its insights, is a major cause for gratitude that it is now generally available, in this revised edition, in English. One may dispute its findings on specific points and details, but even the most arid theorist will disregard it only at his peril.

HAMILTON GIBB

English Publisher's Note

This translation has been done from the second French edition, and it embodies a number of recent corrections and alterations made by the author. Many of the transliterations of Arabic words in the French original would have been confusing for English readers and so they have been modified accordingly. The French term 'Orient' has been translated as 'Middle East' where it refers to the Middle East and not to the whole of the Eastern world.

straight from their context of feeling, from which they must not be abstracted, any more than the history of the Middle East can be detached from its visible landscapes.

The phenomenal accuracy I have thus aimed at not only implies lacunae in the scene covered, but also carries its own intrinsic risks. Seeking objectivity on the level of facts and ideas, I frequently grasped, as was inevitable, only a sort of personal relation between an Arab East thus arbitrarily delimited and a West whose definition also required some reservations.

This is the West as it has appeared in contemporary Arab history for the past century or more, from the first Franco-British impact to the rivalry of the great blocs. The West, bringing its machines and its language, pillaging the East and, at the same time, awakening it, destroying and also constructing, exercising attraction and yet arousing hatred. Tsarist Russia, protector of the orthodox, shared this rôle, as does Soviet Russia today, that champion of a policy which, although competing with that of the Atlantic powers, is derived none the less from the same technological civilization.

No doubt the history of events, and even social history, would need to introduce substantial distinctions between these partners. Even an attitude of positive neutralism can no longer envisage the U.S.S.R. as the sole counterpoise to the American drive, as one of two weights in a balance analogous to that which the Ottoman Porte had long maintained between the Powers. Behind the great political figures there have now emerged conceptions of the world, practical attitudes which influence these peoples from within, despite or unbeknown to traditional diplomacy. Finally, black Africa on the one hand, the humane ideals of Bandung on the other, and the impressive example of China from the East now appeal to the subtle Arab mind and whet Arab hopes.

But a work like the present one, concerned with internal developments, can confine itself to the forces which have become one with the Arab East and which, within it, participate in a fundamental evolution where events only gradually make themselves felt. In any case, it is the intimate criterion of the Arabs' conflict with the outside world, a conflict which arouses their emotions and opinions but which involves the deepest levels of reality, that has dictated my choice.

I could never have achieved this interpretation had I not enjoyed the benefit of that of the late Louis Massignon. That admirable *shaikh* would have recognized where I have followed him, or contradicted him, or both at once. In all three cases, I am deeply in his debt.

On a more practical level, my thanks are due to those who enabled me not merely to visit the Middle East but to live in it, and sometimes to live its life; to U.N.E.S.C.O., thanks to which I spent a long time as educational expert in the Middle Delta; to the Minister Tharwat 'Ukâsha who, after the distressing happenings at Port Said, allowed me to enjoy once more the welcome of eternal Egypt; to M. de Bourbon-Busset, then Director of Cultural Relations at the Quai d'Orsay, who had entrusted me with the duty of founding a school for the study of modern Arabic in the Lebanese mountains; to the touching hospitality of the village of Bikfaya, and to that of the Lebanese University; to Dr. 'Aqrâwî, then Rector of Baghdad, who during a difficult period ensured my reception in his country; to Maître Ẓâfir al-Qâsimî, who brought me the friendship of Damascus; to the family of the Mahdi, who gave me so magnificent a welcome in Khartoum.

These acts of kindness, and many others, have enabled me to spend, since 1953, the greater or the better part of my time amongst the Arabs, and to form there friendships which will be mentioned here and there in these pages. Of course I have not been able to name them all. Let me simply say that I should never have dared to describe the evolution of these societies without the manifold exchanges, cross-checkings, contributions, criticisms and encouragements lavished on me by my Eastern colleagues, collaborators, students and companions.

To my wife Lucie Berque, who has been my companion on journeys through an East so rich in hope, I owe the drawings that perpetuate certain memories.

In Paris, the fruitful dissatisfaction, the constantly stimulating researches of the *École des Hautes Études*, Section VI, and its staff, the encouraging companionship of Marcel Bataillon and Fernand Braudel, and sympathetic exchanges of opinion with Régis Blachère—to name only a few—have greatly helped the conception and accomplishment of my work. My collaborator, Mlle M. N. Devaux, has kindly checked my references.

While gratefully acknowledging such help, I must claim entire responsibility for my own statements and judgements. Not without some anxiety; for ten years of acquaintance with the Arab East, even ten years of constant interest and active participation, are not enough to justify such wide-ranging views. It would have been more prudent to present my investigation in the shape of disconnected details. This alone, in the opinion of many, would have been legitimate. I should thus have been on safer ground to offer my incomplete observations and interpretations. But the method would have been no better basically. A grasp of detail follows only from a view of the whole, or rather the two can only be understood in the light they throw on one another. And moreover, in my admittedly premature attempt to grasp the historic essence of the Arabs, could I neglect that element latent in their impulse towards unity, that nostalgia for completeness, which requires the study itself to see things as a whole? I had no alternative but to adjust my method, and indeed my whole exposition, to so fundamental a *fact*.

It is true that such a judgement, although central to my enquiry, can scarcely be offered to the reader with equal confidence in all its aspects. I feel that the view of the world which many Arabs hold even today, and the evolution of which seems to me responsible for the present changes in their society, down to the merest detail, has its roots and its sponsors in a remote antiquity. But this is merely a hypothesis, the control of which would require the exploration of little-known realms: Arab philosophy, pre-Islamic civilization, Eastern and Mediterranean antiquity, an exploration which lay beyond my aims or my capacities. On this point, then, I defer to specialists in these fields.

On the other hand, believing that such a view of the world is postulated by observable reality, and that variations of it, with their particular historical conditionings and effects, can be recognized during the recent period, I willingly submit my theory to discussion by well-informed observers and by the people directly concerned.

If I venture to offer a broad explanation it is because this seems to me in conformity with the new function of our studies in this field. The time is past when orientalism could play the part of conscience-saving auxiliary or learned pathfinder for economic and political expansion. Today, it must integrate itself with the developments it seeks to understand, and serve them by analysis and comparison. And perhaps, in my case, there is an additional sense of privilege and responsibility, since I feel myself, in Cairo and Beirut, almost a member of that intelligentsia, which is all the dearer to French hearts in that it is so often linked to France by the use of our language, by many impulses of sympathy and, alas, by too many disappointed hopes.

Not that my country always represents, to Eastern minds, the touchstone or the adversary. It had never wholly been either. Besides the regions of the Arab world which our ideas had never, or only faintly, affected, due to the fact of their remoteness or of colonial competition, there is an increasing number of others for which Americanism now represents the West. More profoundly, more validly than through this division which is after all only a division of influences, the Arab spirit today maintains or restores a self-sufficiency, an autonomy of sensation and expression of which no external system, however enriching, should ever have sought to deprive it.

Could this be a sufficient motive for the foreign enquirer, feeling himself initially suspect, and bound to take infinite precautions for fear of wounding sensitive susceptibilities, to abstain from offering his theory? On the contrary, his contribution will seem all the more opportune as the Arabs recover their spontaneity.

If then I venture to submit to them an analysis of their contemporary history, it is in the hope of submitting it to history's judgement. The more criticism it arouses within these countries, the better it will have helped those it aims at serving to make progress in self-study. Though suffering from the disadvantage of emanating from a foreigner, it will enjoy, correspondingly, the advantage of detachment. Its fortunes, for good or ill, are after all those of a new orientalism, at once disinterested and committed.

Shall I, after pleading in favour of my venture, have to justify its expression? As an Eastern proverb says, 'one may lie to one's enemy but never to one's friend'. God forbid, my Arab friends, that I should weaken by unconditional approval the sympathy aroused by your impressive re-entry into the history of men and things. What you are doing, or rather what you are, is significant enough to have earned you the historian's frankness. You have made mistakes, you have shown weaknesses, just like ourselves.

May this strengthen the bonds of brotherhood between us.

Damascus, 10 *November* 1959

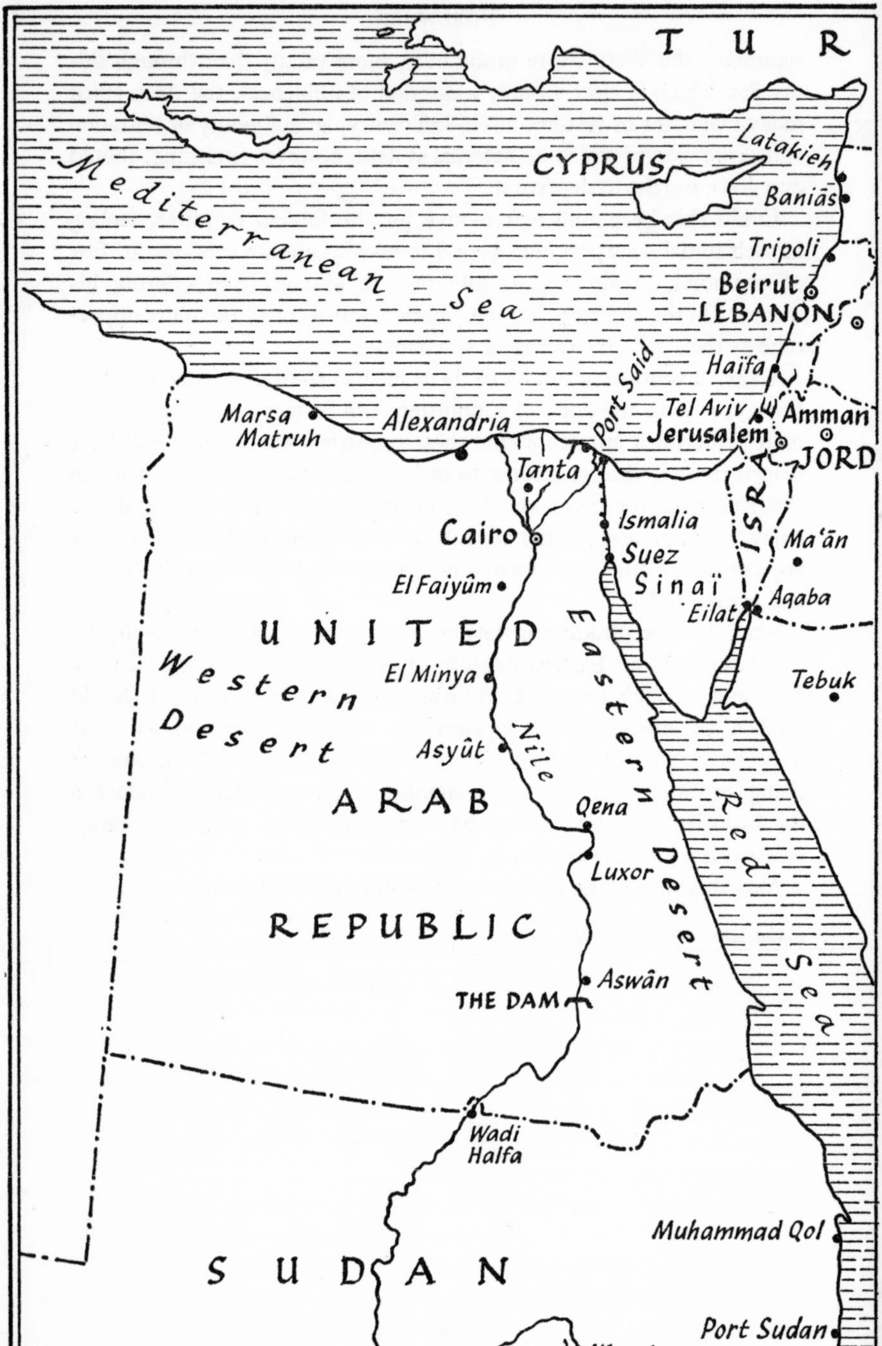

TUR
Mediterranean Sea
CYPRUS
Latakieh
Baniās
Tripoli
Beirut
LEBANON
Haïfa
Tel Aviv
Amman
Jerusalem
JORD
ISRAEL
Port Said
Marsa Matruh
Alexandria
Tanta
Cairo
Ismalia
Suez
Sinaï
Ma'ān
Aqaba
Eilat
El Faiyûm
UNITED
ARAB
REPUBLIC
Western Desert
Eastern Desert
El Minya
Tebuk
Asyût
Nile
Qena
Luxor
Red Sea
Aswân
THE DAM
Wadi Halfa
Muhammad Qol
SUDAN
Port Sudan
Khartoum

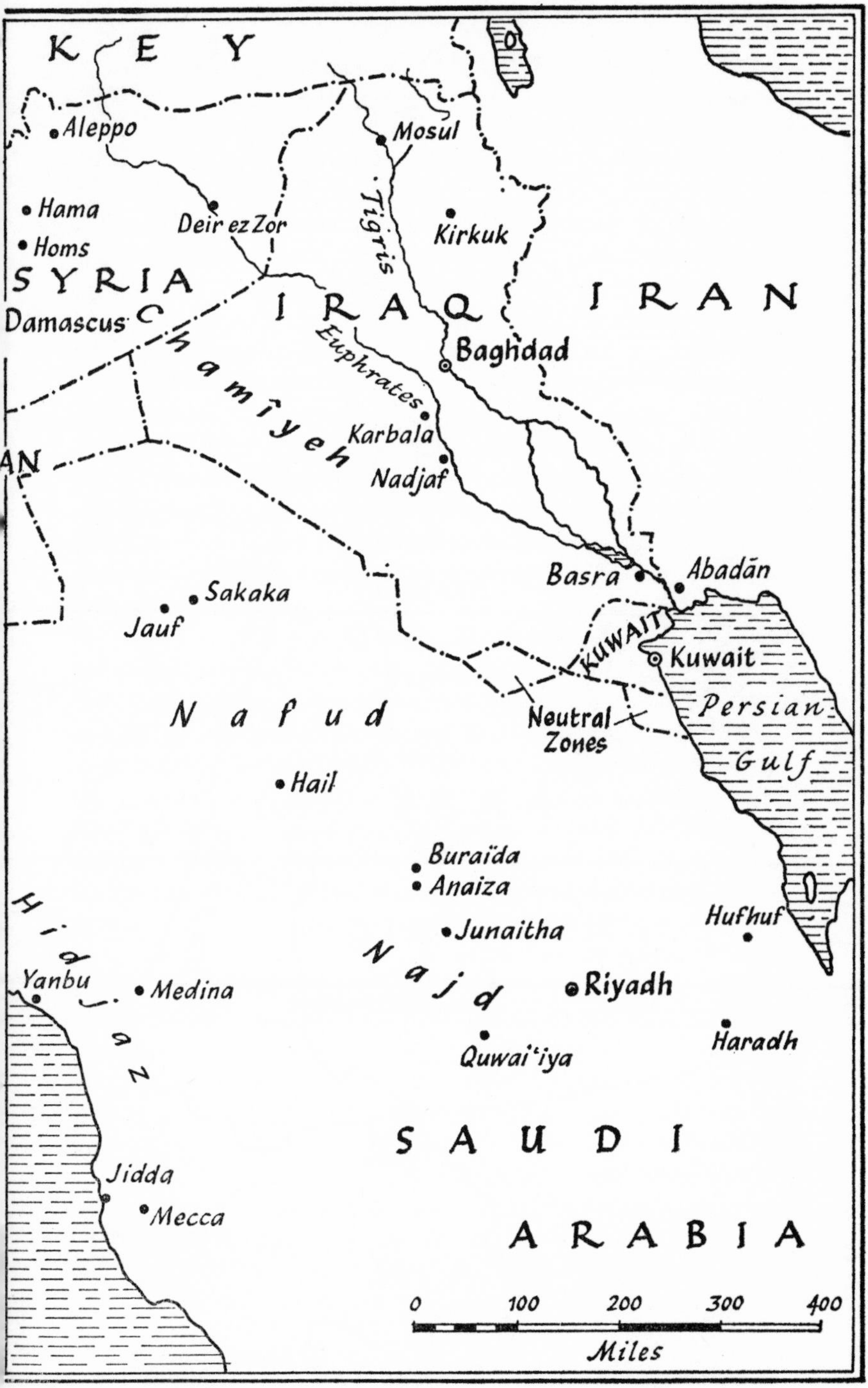
KEY
Aleppo
Mosul
Hama
Homs
Deir ez Zor
Tigris
Kirkuk
SYRIA
IRAQ
IRAN
Damascus
Chamiyeh
Euphrates
Baghdad
Karbala
Nadjaf
AN
Basra
Abadān
Sakaka
Jauf
KUWAIT
Kuwait
Persian Gulf
Nafud
Neutral Zones
Hail
Buraïda
Anaiza
Junaitha
Hidjaz
Hufhuf
Najd
Riyadh
Yanbu
Medina
Quwai'iya
Haradh
SAUDI ARABIA
Jidda
Mecca
0
100
200
300
400
Miles

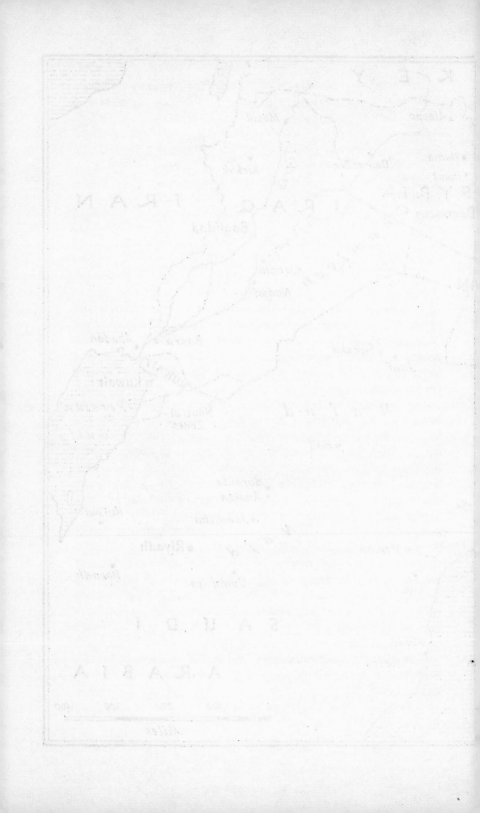

CHAPTER I

The Disruption of Traditional Man

If the East is the home of the Word, it is also that of the men by whom the Word is treasured and multiplied. And nowhere is man's social being composed of such a wealth of contradictory aspects. The splendour of the past, the sufferings of the present, the call of the senses and of the absolute, the harshest interdicts and the most ardent impulses are found there contrasted or mingled, sincere or sincerely imitated. In their synthesis, which may be either beneficent or disastrous, contradictions are accumulated and incongruities become law. This is one of the most characteristic features of the Arab East. Here the eternal and the transitory, the sublime and the trivial, the rage to live and loyalty to what is basic are found united in a gesture, a comment, a landscape. The immediate fact betokens an enduring truth. Here both the mystical and the historical interpretation of events find confirmation, for a symbol implies both a transcendental ethic and the present trend of the community. Hence it happens that the most instinctive actions as well as the most mechanical ones, utilitarianism as well as disinterestedness, maintain their connection with the ideal and invoke the sanction of authoritative sayings and great figures. Thus in times of struggle and doubt the meaner elements in Eastern life are redeemed, whereas its nobler elements betray their weakness. The whole of life here oscillates between the heraldic and the practical. Its evil and its riches lie within a totality which embraces the unexpected. By a permissible play on words we may relate *tawassul*, 'intercession', and *tasalsul*, 'chain' or 'sequence'. A symbol, in the Arab East, serves above all to proclaim completeness and continuity.

The Qadîm: *the 'Old' or 'Organic'*

Now this continuity and completeness rebel against themselves. *Rabî' yatadawwar*, 'Convulsive Springtime', is the title of a story by a Syrian writer.[1] The Arab Renaissance hopes to remain faithful to itself even while rejecting its heritage. During the colonial period the Arab world had been burdened with its own heritage together with that of others, and had seen them sometimes as its natural destiny, sometimes as machinery imposed by a foreign power. Today it seeks to remake everything. It ventures on its revolution inspired by determinism and the quest for liberty. It is thus going through one of those critical phases which our own societies experienced before it; they too, in the second half of the nineteenth century, had faced the necessity of self-renewal. They had laid away the past in its purple shroud. They were resolved to become something new. Utopian socialists went beyond the question of 'the organic' versus 'the critical' in their plea for a final synthesis and reconciliation.

To the Arabs the *qadîm*, the old, so violently abused by the partisans of the *jadîd*, the new, implies 'the organic'. Traditionalists are wont to contrast living traditions with decayed traditions; we may define the *qadîm* as the reverse side, now decayed, of something that might be called archetypal. Something which was once great, and which many of us feel to lie at the base of Arab attitudes, as many Arabs cultivate it within themselves. Whence the strange attraction they exercise over us. It is not exclusive to adepts in tradition, nor to aesthetes such as T. E. Lawrence, although many are led to Orientalism by one or other of these paths. Others again, with whom I am more in sympathy, appreciate the Arabs' great shout of liberty, the fervour with which they seek to take their place in modern life. Louis Massignon saw the Arab world as one of the realms of the Absolute. In fact, at the present time, in everything they do the Absolute conflicts and competes with history. It contradicts it and, at the same time, lays the foundations for it. And here we recognize that symbolic quality of the Arab East, which is related to the close involvement of facts and values, the upsurge of the new from the old and the compromise between the one and the other.[2]

[1] Fû'âd Shâ'ib, *Ta'rîkh Jurḥ*, Damascus, 1944.

[2] Even so systematic a study as that of Daniel Lerner, *The Passing of Traditional Society*, Glencoe, 1958, fails to grasp the reciprocal relations of present and past, revolution and authenticity; which somewhat invalidates his probing research. On the other hand this specific heterogeneity is realized by many Middle Eastern writers: for instance 'Izzat al-Nuṣṣ, *Arab Teachers' Review*, Damascus, April 1950, p. 527; unpublished thesis on Syria (1951), p. 273; *Review of Syrian Broadcasting*, no. 74, 19 Sep. 1956.

This intimate connection either persists unbroken or else is shattered into opposites. The conflict, in the Arab East, shows the disruption of the symbol; it explains and realizes the symbol even while it profanes it.[1] Arabs of the inter-war generation would not have opposed the new to the old with such ferocity had they not felt the clash within themselves, in their own ambiguity.

The Arabs have spoken much ill of their *qadîm*, such as four centuries of the rule of Sultans had made it. They had to admit its continuity with a metaphysical tradition. The old system was guilty, in the last resort, of having 'deserved' colonization and compacted with it to some extent, and has therefore earned accumulated blame due to the Arab people's reaction not only against those who had subjugated them but against that part of themselves that had submitted. A more balanced judgement will reconsider the verdict. It is easy today to denounce the collusions of ancestral Islam with foreign powers; but it had fought bravely in an earlier phase. Present-day poetry, enamoured of free verse and the irrational, rightly condemns the rhetorical writers of the nineteenth century; can it boast a wider audience than these traditional bards? Moreover in the minds of the Arab people, even if not in their expressed opinions, ancient habits linger on unaffected by imported political forms. There is nothing surprising about this persistence. Tradition, even if decayed, is never utterly renounced. The *tajdîd*, the 'renewal', proceeds from it even while it rejects it. Should we ascribe success to the modernism which assumes responsibility for the struggle for emancipation, or to the permanent factors which provoke and sustain the revolt? It would be hard to give an answer. Many Arabs, at all events, are asking themselves the question.

However, the present essay will obviously not be devoted to a paradoxical rehabilitation of the *qadîm*, but to revealing the characteristics which confer on many attitudes and types, today despised as old-fashioned, their astonishing power of resistance, and doubtless of persistence too. And in any case their meaning.

Classical Damascus

Where can we study the old and the new better than in Damascus, that significant city?[2] Let us climb the Qasyûn and see the town at our

[1] See on this point my discussion with Gabriel Bounoure, 'Destin de l'Arabisme', *Lettres Nouvelles*, 1962.

[2] This analysis owes much to Damascan writers: the excellent descriptions of Kurd 'Alî, *Khiṭaṭ al-Shâm*, vols. v and vi, 1925–28: memoirs like those of Fakhrî al-Barûdî, *Mudhakkirât*, Damascus, 1951, 2 vols.; collections of speeches such as those of Luṭfî al-Ḥaffâr, *Dhikrîyât*, Damascus, 1954, 2 vols., and

feet, hectic, gifted, constantly renewed. It has overflowed its medieval rectangle; a long suburb has shot out southward, the Maidân, which points the way towards Mecca for the pilgrim. It has flung out another limb towards the enchanted mountain, the very Qasyûn from which we are looking down at it, and from which we behold some of the panoramic sites of history and human thought: at our feet the tomb of the Andalusian Ibn 'Arabî, behind us the crypt of the Seven Sleepers with its seven *qiblas*.[1] The city also spreads towards the North-West and towards the West, where a monumental avenue welcomes the visitor from Beirut. But these two accretions date from after the first world war. Let us ignore them and turn back to the early years of this century in search of facts and attitudes which are more unmistakably charged with antiquity.

Let us picture the city of that earlier generation against which the men of the *Thaura* rose in their youth (now themselves grown old and subject to assault from newer forces). Damascus, encircled with groves, seems an oasis, or more precisely a granary, in the heart of a vast orchard; a place where things are stored and transformed. The landscape is expressed, in the most physical sense of the word, by the ingenious artisan. Apricot oils and pastes carry the sweetness of the Ghûṭa to all corners of the Islamic world. In 1890 there were 3000 looms employing 20,000 weavers, producing those stuffs that make the name of Damascus famous: silks, *quṭnî* (cotton) and that striped rustic cloth, the *dîma*,[2] which was widespread throughout the Middle East and had even penetrated Anatolia and Macedonia in face of German competition. Damascus is still living on the fruits of its savings. Its bourgeoisie displays great commercial activity. Its business connections cover the whole Ottoman empire. It still provides a starting-point on the road to Mecca. In a typical jumble of piety, bargaining, luxury and pleasure, crowds equip themselves for the annual rite, seeking sustenance for body and soul. The Mosque of the Umayyads and countless sanctuaries provide blessings from the past to safeguard the troubled present. The city achieves and proclaims concord between men and things, nature and human life.

Shukrî al-Quwatlî, *Majmû' al-Khuṭab*, Damascus, 1957; finally the analysis of Jamîl Ṣalîba, which rightly stresses the importance of poetry, *al-Ittijâhât al-fikrîya fî bilâd al-Shâm*, Cairo, 1957. Among European descriptions one of the most sensitive is Gertrude Bell's.

[1] L. Massignon, *Revue des Études Islamiques*, vol. xxii, 1954, pp. 87 ff.

[2] Edmond Bulaybal, *Taqwîm Bikfayyâ*, 1935, pp. 195 ff. studies the history of the industry in connection with this centre of rural craftsmanship.

Meanwhile there has been a period of decline. During long centuries the city's original unity had disintegrated into districts.[1] Each self-contained group tended to uphold its own interests and virtues according to a patriarchal code of honour which owed much to the Bedouin model; the latter, both through its poetic tradition and its geographical importance, forced itself on the city. A slow but continuous process of urbanization of the nomad, noticeable particularly in the Maidân, penetrated with ever-greater persistence from the outskirts to the centre of the town and affected the bourgeois districts themselves. From pride and from avarice, these stood out against anything that might alter their nature. Under the Turkish administration, the rights and organization of citizens, suppressed *qua* institutions, survived only in events and in customs. True, autocracy was met with abstention or with open revolt; the city's chronicle displays the whole gamut between the two extremes. Damascan cunning often won the day over Ottoman diligence. But, at this period precisely, the game was felt to be unproductive. Behind and against the reformism of the Young Turks there began to appear an Arab reformist movement. The dissatisfaction peculiar to the Syrians had the backing of an impressive academic tradition. But now, for the first time, it strove to develop. Already a 'committee spirit', *rûḥ al-takattul*, was in the air. In certain cafés, fiery orators who were destined to go far, such as Luṭfî al-Ḥaffâr, began to extol what is today known as Arabism. They were keenly aware of the degradation of the present, for which they blamed the vices of the past. And, in a characteristically bourgeois phenomenon, which was to dominate the whole nationalist movement between the wars, they combined the most urgent fervour, the most inventive spirit of intrigue with loyalty to class and civic values. Hence the interest of the works written by some of them, such as Kurd 'Alî or Fakhrî al-Barûdî, when, with mingled affection and bitterness, they look into the heart of their city.

They condemn, above all, traditionalism in religious belief. In the days of their youth religion played an overpowering rôle.[2] The year consisted of phases of secular life, calm, dreary, rigidly restricted, but interrupted on the occasion of innumerable festivals by moments of vehement social activity and excitement: ceremonies such as the *fiṭr*, (breaking of fast), return journeys after pilgrimages, *nudhûr* (votive celebrations) and confraternal synods. Added to these were various

[1] See on this point Sauvaget's authoritative analysis, *Revue des Études Islamiques*, 1934, pp. 422 ff.

[2] Kurd 'Alî, op. cit., vol. vi, pp. 284 ff.

family rites. Funerals, for instance: interminable visits, crowds forgathering at the home of the head of the household, *'amîd al-usra*, who is almost the chief of a clan. A marriage is the occasion for a whole drama, or rather a tetralogy: the greater the family's nobility, the longer lasts the quest for a suitable partner—a year, at least, for any self-respecting house. Relations and neighbours unite in a busy series of visits, receptions, enquiries, processions and delegations. What matters, of course, is not the physical or moral attributes of the individual but the alliance between two families; it is another way of periodically confirming the unity of the city.

Not until 1930, it would seem, did beauty begin to count in the marriage market.[1] Undoubtedly this shocked the older generation as a symptom of the depravity of the age. The young, meanwhile, were shaking off the supremacy of social and religious rules. For in this charming but conventional milieu, individuality was crushed, impulse repressed. Hypocrisy and ignorance predominated. The lowly fawned on the great in order to subsist. From childhood, a young aristocrat was surrounded by flatterers; his early upbringing was entrusted to ignorant and obsequious domestics. True, he soon took part in the warfare between children of different districts. But this precocious taste of military glory did not compensate for the deficiencies of his education. The instruction provided by traditional establishments (although these had benefited by a first reform under Midḥat Pasha) remained authoritarian and narrow. A son never dared speak directly to his father. When he had something to ask him he had to call on some family friend as intermediary. The writer to whose memoirs I am indebted for several of these details can only remember receiving a single kiss as a child, when he was half asleep.

There were no clubs for culture or sport. An adolescent could only frequent cafés, most of which were of an old-fashioned type. Knowledge of the outside world was so limited there that when one day a portrait of Hugo was displayed at Dimitri's café on the Place al-Marja, most of the patrons mistook him for the president of the Parisian Mineral Waters Manufacturers! Shadow-theatres and the one-act plays of Karagöz certainly did little to raise the level of entertainment. Sometimes a *ḥakawâtî*, a popular story-teller, in some great public

[1] Al-Barûdî, op. cit., vol. i, p. 64. Naturally there is an element of paradox in the observation. Shaikh 'Alawân in the seventeenth century had already condemned such 'novelties' (cf. *Majallat al-majma' al-'ilmî*, Damascus, vol. xxxii, 1957, pp. 327 ff.).

competition, would recite the tale of the Banû Hilâl or of King Baibars, which evoked widespread emotion but which fostered a chivalric moral code centuries old, bearing no relation to reality. Apart from these popular pleasures there was nothing but the 'Tiâtro', where Egyptian music could already be heard, and the performances of *chanteuses*, some of whom, including a number of Jewesses, had an unsavoury reputation.

To so restricted an existence an outlet might be found in the study of advanced sciences. But these could only be glimpsed through the narrow windows of tradition. Oratory was still feeble;[1] on Fridays the *khaṭîb* merely read a sermon, invariably the same one. Public speaking became widespread only with the revolution of the Young Turks, some of whom did not disdain to harangue the poorer suburbs; sometimes with unfortunate consequences, for public opinion in these districts, torn between respect for notabilities and fear of swashbucklers, was slow to accept general ideas. Traditional scholars derived their prestige from such implications rather than from any intellectual fecundity of their own. Many of them, through the exercise of memory and of a concentration unknown in our own day, attained to a sort of wisdom that proscribed all vain agitation, even that of speech. Respect for the written word reduced them to silence. Of one of them, a contemporary historian says significantly: 'Despite his profound immersion (*tabaḥḥur*) in the knowledge and secrets of Arabic he wrote no work of literature or philology that can be quoted. Like most of the ulemas of his day he considered that learning is a treasure enclosed within the pages of ancient books. Scholars must discover these treasures by diligent enquiry, study and patience. Science consists only of trying to understand what the men of old have left us. . . .'[2] When in 1908 Shaikh Rashîd Riḍâ made his innovatory speech urging believers to go back to the fountain-head of the *sîra* (traditions about the Prophet's life), another *shaikh*, Ṣâliḥ al-Sharîf al-Tûnsî, interrupted him to defend the worship of saints and intercessors. There was a great to-do, and the disturber was arrested. But the chief of police was forced to set him free, in face of public demonstrations. And he himself only owed his safety to the intervention of an *abâḍây*, a swashbuckler, from the Qanawât district. This indicates the extent to which the champions of the past drew their strength from urban opinion.

[1] Id., ibid., p. 64.

[2] Sâmî al-Kayyâlî, *al-Ḥaraka al-adabîya fî Ḥalab* (dealing in fact with Aleppo), pp. 162 ff. (with reference to Bashîr al-Ghâzî, 'kadi of kadis', 1857–1921). But many similar figures are to be found in Damascus.

Such a milieu, stifling as it already seemed to some of its sons, contained, nevertheless, enduring energies. Since the balance of its constituent parts dated from time immemorial, each element within the whole, taken separately, withstood innovation. The most conflicting sorts of behaviour formed an organic whole and compensated one another. The reformist, after all, serves as counterpoise to the traditionalist, according to an age-old game already played by Ibn Taimîya. Artisans abused but helped one another. Only on rare occasions did the exploitation of the poor by the rich provoke revolt. The whole town, although torn by inner animosities, would unite to defend one of its nobles against the Government. People were concerned only with day-to-day affairs, yet the pressure of another world was felt on all sides. Fencing, horse-riding, country excursions—*sîrân*—according to a tradition so highly organized that special committees saw to its maintenance among the working class, all these brought fresh air into this splendid but narrowly confined way of life. This tyrannically regulated system reached its apogee with a certain type of elegant city-dweller. A bourgeois might spend much of the night in the summerhouse, *qunâq*, set up for that purpose within his garden, sheltered so to speak from the intimacy of family life. There he would receive his coterie of friends, men of the same age and tastes as himself and almost all connected by marriage; there, over a cup of bitter coffee, they would talk about hunting, chess or pigeon-breeding, and also about the news of the day, consisting largely of a survey of society's doings, studded with family names and well-worn recollections.

Such a society finds an end in itself. It rejoices in itself. It practises being what long centuries have taught it that it is. Its completeness, its harmony with an impressive setting and an inexhaustible chronicle, make its strength and its spell. Even its miseries, born of subjection, mercantilism and phariseeism, cannot overshadow its nobility. Moreover it conceals within itself the ferment of its own transformation. The unheard-of events which were to shake the Arab East from the time of the Young Turks' revolution were to upset conservatism to the advantage of the Renewal. But in a city like this the immemorial has such enduring power that the old balance did not immediately succumb. Only since the emancipation, and as a result of violent contact with facts and ideas come from afar, have the civic community and the human type of Damascus begun to lose something of their finality. Even today, in spite of the many municipal and national revolutions, continuity persists. The nobility of the urban scene and that of the city's way of life, an obstinate adherence to the proud tradition of the Golden Age combined with stirring visions of the future, the highest standards in speaking, eating, praying or making love, all contribute to the city's individual character, to its *style*. But this contains, indeed fosters within itself, the forces that will shatter it. Stubborn in asserting itself, it delights in self-contradiction. Whence this uneven history, all made up of impulsive movements and revisions, which would break the patriot's heart if it did not fill him with pride.

Such an individual way of life obviously resists any attempt to abolish it. Not that it is averse to innovation. Quite the contrary. It consists precisely in the contending alternation, or ambiguous compound, of old and new. We may speak of Classicism where the conflicting elements so subtly balance and compensate each other. In Damascus, Arabism reaches its highest point of perfection. But its academic character is the price it pays for this superiority. For Damascus is also the least romantic of capitals. It is not by chance that the instrument it provides for the new modes of feeling and expression is the *lugha*, the classical Arabic language, more highly cultivated and refined here than elsewhere, with its infinite capacities and its subtle taboos. Is this why a form as typical of modern times as the novel finds few adepts here, whereas it flourishes in Cairo,[1] and why Damascus, capital of the Arabic language, is not also the capital of the new Arabic literature? It seems as if its more highly integrated, more self-sufficient system and way of life are better fitted to resist what is in many respects only a disturbance inflicted by outside forces, or at least what will seem so until it has been profoundly assimilated and adopted as a patriotic weapon.

The Eternal Bedouin

Damascus provides one of the exemplary types of such integration, which is deeply bound up with *'urûba*, Arabism. Here, the fact that it is also bound up with the complex life of a great city and with a learned and religious culture might make one question how far it is a natural characteristic. But this integration, this plenitude, also strike us in other parts of the Arab world, where such associations are lacking.

A Sudanese *sharîf* was telling me of the life led by his grandfather in a remote corner of the Dongola, towards the middle of the nineteenth

[1] Is this because Egypt offers clearer examples of the evolution of a new type of bourgeois? See the interesting studies of L. Goldmann.

century. He lived solely on milk products and shared the booty of the chase among his vassals. His life was governed by a strict ritual. He had four wives, all chiefs' daughters, and had intercourse only once a month. He was to reach the age of a hundred and fifty. My interlocutor, while still a youth, at the time of the Great Mahdi, met one of the wives. Not being related to her by blood, he made bold to ask her if this conjugal moderation had satisfied her. And the old lady replied, with magnificent shamelessness: 'O my son, one of his embraces was worth twenty of yours. . . .'

Similar stories might be collected from among the desert nomads in the hinterland of Damascus. Apart, that is to say, from the moderation, for the Bedouin is full of fierce vitality. Several of the figures in *Revolt in the Desert*—the *sharîf* Shâkir, old Nûrî Sha'lân, for instance—illustrate this regal type long after the days of pre-Islamic poetry. The fact that these were used in the interests of British politics and aestheticism must have weighed heavily on the Arabs. It does not invalidate the burning authenticity of what happened in 1916. The type we find there, seen through the meshes of an Intelligence Service intrigue and coloured by the sensual imagination of an Oxford don, is the pre-Islamic hero, the restless wandering nomad, 'his camel's parasite'[1] maybe, but whose avid generosity, uneven courage, crafty loyalty and impulsive calculatingness make him one of the most touching of human figures.

Such a man differs from the men of the Industrial Revolution in his muted quality. His *wijdân*, his life-pulse, will not be expressed effusively. It is revealed merely by gestures or songs which are both passionate and dry, tumultuous and still. It blossoms at ground level, restrainedly. It's as though a carpet were spread in the unsheltered desert; beneath it, you can feel growing plants, crushed, and the unevenness and heat of the soil: all the fierce upsurge of nature held down under an ornamented surface. An impulse rising from deep down seems to deny itself as soon as it reaches the light, and shrivels up into pattern and colour. This renunciation is also a form of Classicism. Herein the Bedouin differs from the barbarian. The whole man, with his consciousness, his sexuality, his way of life, his adherence to a certain natural and social milieu, illustrates a system.

And how can we describe him when he becomes a poet, when reaching the summit of his system he attains attitudes which, right up to our own day, in Islam and outside Islam, have never lost their appeal?

[1] Was this remark made by Weulersse or by Doughty, that admirable connoisseur?

Ḥâjj Zâyir is an example.[1] He is considered the greatest popular poet of Iraq. His poems, which have only recently been collected, had been familiar on all lips for a whole generation. After his death he appeared in a dream to some fanatical Shî'ite believer. But when he was questioned about the favours of the imam Ḥusain he would confine himself within the laws of *sirr*, 'the secret'. In his case it was the secret of poetry. The harmony between the collective faith, his personal experience and the fame of his verse revealingly sums up the place and the period. Inspiration came to him amidst his brothers, after a gathering at which they had shed many tears over the sufferings of 'Alî. What stirred him then, says his biographer, was 'love and loyalty', *walâ*! Let us add: unanimity. Naturally, he improvised. He poured out mystic stanzas as profusely as the elegant obscenities directed at some passing girl. During the later period of Turkish rule he was mobilized and stationed in Qaṭar. There his sorrows found vent in moving verse that drew his comrades round him and touched the heart of his commanding officer; he was allowed to go home. He joined up again in 1914, which furnished the occasion for heroic paeans. Unfortunately the British attacked Basra. The intellectuals led the defence of their country against the unbeliever. The poet, who had denounced the retreat of the Turks, was obliged to hide for a while at Kufa. Then he reappeared in Baghdad. In the mosque of Ḥaidar he beheld the whole populace assembled while a Sayyid exhorted them to holy war. This was too much for Ḥâjj Zâyir. 'He grew excited by the people's excitement,' *tahayyaj min hiyâj al-nâs*, and once again broke into improvisation. Noble feelings, in a noble setting. But such an idealized portrait is incomplete. Our hero was subject to passions which his biographer relates indulgently. On his return from Qaṭar he lived for a while peacefully with the youth al-Hâdî. Then his friend was found murdered. The poet was under strong suspicion of the crime. It provided him with yet another theme for some fine verse. And the biographer compares him to another poet who had reacted in similar fashion after the double murder of his friend and his mistress, whom he had surprised in amorous conversation; he killed them both, burned their bodies, and made of their ashes two vases from which he drank alternately, uttering nostalgic elegies.

The incredible remoteness of such an attitude from any morality based on religion enables us to gauge the prestige enjoyed by Bedouin poetry, which could appeal, above and beyond morality, to a natural code, as it were from before the Fall, in which impulses, desires,

[1] Muḥammad Bâqir al-Arwânî, *Dîwân al-Ḥâjj Zâyir*, Najaf, 1957.

revenge and avidity contained within themselves their own redemption. The next step is 'immoralism', and this is quickly taken. By a paradoxical route, Baudelaire and Rimbaud reach the Arabs of today through the Bedouin tradition.[1] This shows the enduring significance of a theme which has mingled with that of Islam, and has, in the case of Ḥâjj Zâyir even been akin to religious emotion of a dramatic sort, but which in itself has nothing to do with religion.

Sometimes, of course, popular poetry dwells on gentler slopes. Above all, it casts off the glamour of adventure, while renouncing wider horizons. It bestrides, paradoxically, the whole distance between the shepherd and the ploughman. Without forfeiting any of its ideals it gives them each a different and almost opposite realization. It is full of the gnomic wisdom of the peasantry.[2] This is the case in Lebanon, in Mesopotamia, and above all in Egypt where village inspiration was subtly adapted to the culture of the Azhar. So much so, indeed, that for a long time the ancient University provided a home for the literature of the countryside. However, I need not further stress the importance of these questions, which today, in Egypt itself, are satisfactorily recognized in academic studies and in official policies. Let me merely say that here too, here more than elsewhere perhaps, men of the humblest status, knowing only the simple hardships and joys of toil, display a completeness which neither urban culture with its passion for pious traditionalism or for Western modernism, nor the growing hardship of the economic situation has hitherto discouraged.

A Greek of the Underworld

This type may rightly be described as Islamic. And yet it derives from an Eastern or Arab original anterior to Islam. But it has become incorporated with Islam in such a way that it cannot easily be dissociated from it. It would need close analysis to discover beneath, and in opposition to, the culture and moral code of Islam this close unity between man and the world. For despite its tenet of 'innateness', *fiṭra*, a transcendental faith cannot entirely accept nature. Its theology, its laws,

[1] The 'bohemianism' of the Palestinian poet al-Tall seems to form the connecting link. *Naurî*, 'gipsy', is given as synonym of *badawî*, 'bedouin'. A Beirut magazine of *avant-garde* poetry, *al-Shi'r*, has recently devoted a feature to the study of pre-Islamic poetry which provides a wealth of parallels to modernist writing.

[2] I have dealt summarily with this question which I have studied fully elsewhere and which is beginning to be fairly familiar.

steeped in Aristotelian rationalism, set subject against object, good against evil, the determinate against the indeterminate—they are strongly coloured by the culture of the city, which can be a distorting as well as a refining influence. The well-educated man learns to take for granted, and sometimes to repress, the teaching of his fathers, even while he savours its charm. On the other hand mysticism asserts itself against legalistic piety, reviving the sense of man's wholeness. Plotinus is invoked to correct Aristotle. After ten centuries of conflict between the separating factor, *furqân*, and the ancient ideal of unity, the reformist movement calls simultaneously, in the name of tradition, *sunna*, for a return to the sources of faith and an active reconciliation with a living universe.

Hence conflicts and discrepancies, undoubtedly. But it is surely possible that the very latest developments, the appeal to the masses, the unprecedented interest in spontaneous art, the rehabilitation of the things of the people, in short the whole impulse towards democracy, may derive their strength from a nostalgic longing for unity, may tend, through revolt, to a revival of harmony. This is understandable. The modernist movement may rebel against traditionalism, *taqlîd*; it does so partly in the name of tradition. The struggle would not be so moving were it not in many respects a struggle with the Angel, in other words the struggle of a man divided against himself. Certain features of the old attitude can be retraced by noting, in the biographies of the present generation, the persistent power of the undying past. Here we see one of the most unexpected characteristics of the 'renewal', *tajdîd*: it implies, in so many respects, restitution. For many Arabs, revolution means restoration. And this remains the case so long as a too decisive renewal of ideas and things has not deprived the ancient system of its capacity to evolve while still maintaining its balance.

Such a break occurs at the point when a society's relations with the outside world alter in their direction and in their potentialities. And indeed the Arab only attains modernity, morally and materially, at the cost of a crisis the result of which is to strengthen his hold on reality. His civilization, as can still be observed well into the twentieth century, was far too natural to dominate nature. Unlike industrial society, it failed to gain possession of nature because it formed part of it. This privilege, or this misfortune, is clearly and continually displayed in the attitudes I have described, and above all in the poetry that celebrates them, whose tender 'freshness', *ṭarâwa*, the modern Arab still treasures, unless he chooses rather to seek it in the songs of the 'unlearned', *ummîyîn*—the name itself is revealing.[1]

The charm of proximity, of immediacy which Hegel ascribed to the Greeks through whom, he says, 'the spirit itself comes down', was shared by traditional Arab life. This divine simplicity which the Greeks have from the outset, by their aesthetic communion with the world, also constitutes the secret—for other reasons and in a different manner—of any 'Islamic' way of life. A Greek statue of the best period seems to have grown of itself under the chisel, it is detached neither from Nature, which it perfects, nor from man, whom it exalts. To the same extent, although in other ways, in Islam, traditional life had a quality of wholeness; it was free from original sin, in harmony with itself, and favoured by God. It gave a kindly welcome to instinct, repressing only that which served as vehicle for forbidden things, *ḥarâm*: risk, interest, fornication. Hence it possesses, as did Hellenism, a secret that we have lost. Greek sculpture on the one hand, Islamic behaviour on the other, are two symmetrical triumphs of human 'immediacy'.

But any study of the types of Islam, as seen in its present quarrels and its past harmonies, must take into account a new figure, participant in a conflict between East and West which is no longer merely philosophical but also historical. When the Arabs rebel against their past, the Colonial era is both the object and also the motive force of their revolt. Their passionate self-assertion cannot, for many reasons, be dissociated from the West. Now their hatred of the past is also, as we have seen, a restoration of the past, in so far as it implies a striving for authenticity. *Nahḍa*, 'raising up again', *ba'th*, 'rebirth', even *salafîya*, 'respect for the past, the ancestral': all these words, describing attempts of varying nature and success, have at least their aim in common: the recovery of something lost. If, then, we accept the Arabs' invitation to impugn their past, even while reinstating it, we shall discover that, long centuries ago, their conflict with Europe was almost as essential a part of their lives as the present conflict is a part of their Renaissance.

Such an observation, which is by no means soothing—quite the contrary, since we find ourselves challenged by ancient tradition to a contest, or rather to an exchange—acquires concrete significance from the existence of the Mediterranean. And by this I do not mean only a

[1] An epithet of the Prophet's, translated as 'the uninstructed' or 'the spontaneous' (i.e. not yet touched by preaching, not knowing what Allah has revealed). Modern Arabic wrongly, but suggestively, translates *ummî* as 'illiterate' whereas it doubtless means 'natural', 'integrated'.

geographical zone which seems to have imposed on the societies that border it a kind of structural alternation between South Bank and North Bank. Nor even a common treasury in which the Arabs have dipped throughout their history, by means of Alexandrian or Syrian translators. But an essential place, even though it is limited in space and time: the undivided East-West of the pre-Socratic age. For there are no doubt many places and periods at which the two partners have met, transformed, and inspired each other. But nowhere, in my opinion, is light more clearly thrown on the conflict between ourselves and the Arabs, and between the Arabs and themselves, than in that study of attitudes towards the world made by an ancient Greek, a forerunner of many of our present ideas.[1] To gain a profounder understanding of the traditional Arab both from a historical and a philosophical point of view, we should no longer follow the way of Abraham[2] but that of Heraclitus.[3]

If we consider that the Arabs combine that adherence to the transcendental which is of the essence of the Jewish message, with a wholeness—almost a sense of immanence—in their lives, we shall see the identity of what they call *ṣabr* or *riḍâ'*, the virtues of patience, connivance, with the Greek *homologia, harmonia.*[4] The Arab, like the Greek, whatever his theology may imply, clings close to Nature. And with the coming of Islam he still clings to it, while at the same time acknowledging the almighty power of God. This conjunction of attitudes which may seem to us contradictory was to prove a source of argument to Arab philosophers, a source of anxiety to Arab mystics. But it has served as a practical way of life right up to our own day. Neither decadence nor subjection[5] has robbed the Arab of his privilege of living an integrated life. He might well say with Heraclitus, if it were not such a horrible impiety, that 'man's temperament is identified with his share in the divine' or again that 'if Being were all smoke, man would be all a sense

[1] K. Axelos, *Heraclitus*, 1962.

[2] 'Abrahamism' certainly provided Orientalists with the most specific explanation of Arabism and Islam hitherto at their disposal. Cf. L. Massignon in 'The Three Prayers of Abraham', *Dieu Vivant*, 1949, no. 13, pp. 15–28. Cf. also Y. Moubarac, *Abraham dans le Coran*, 1958.

[3] Significantly studied by another great Eastern thinker, Shri Aurobindo, *Heraclitus*, Lyons, Paul Derain, 1951.

[4] Heidegger, *What is Philosophy?* Paris, 1957, p. 24. Cf. Papaioannou, 'Nature and History in the Greek Conception of the Cosmos', *Diogenes*, 1959, no. 25, pp. 1 ff. Consider the term *sawî*, 'harmonious' (T. Burckhardt) or 'fulfilled' (R. Blachère) describing the man who appears to Mary (*Koran*, XIX, 17, 18).

[5] Nor yet the teaching of Gnostics or Neoplatonists.

of smell', so strongly felt is the harmony between man and the cosmos: and not only on the level of a philosophical aphorism or a mystic intuition, but on the level of behaviour.

Traditional Islamic society appears as a compact sphere where reason, transcendence, the world as perceived through the senses, a sort of visceral happiness in short, correspond to one another in a system which is subtly described by Avicenna's illuminism, or the 'scattered soul' of Averroes, but which also finds confirmation in everyday life. We can still feel this typical Arab quality, however alien we may be from it, in the gestures of the common people as much as in the serenity of the sage. In such a system, or rather according to such an attitude to life, the concrete is only a symbol, but the idea has a material taste. Neither the intellect nor the body are divorced from their transfiguring values. In spite of an obsessive assertion of Divine transcendence, there is formed a whole nexus of solidarity, bounty, fervent exchange between person and object, interalliance between all things.

Yet such wisdom is only revealed to us today in ruins, at the close of a long decadence and amidst the bitterness of conflict. A society wasted by political servitude and economic insecurity, a reactionary scholasticism and the ravages as well as the teachings of the Western world had, by a simple reversal, transformed the Arabs' adherence to the cosmos into fatalism, *qadarîya*, their serenity into inertia, their 'global' quality into complacency. This is inherent, too, in *taqlîd*, devout conformism. On the eve of his Renaissance or his Revolution, what fills the Arab thinker with distress is to see his great past inverted in cruel parody, his privilege made abject. The traditional Arab is still a Hellene. But in disharmony with the world, challenged by the history of other races, relegated to humiliating tasks, and, in a word, cast back into the mire, he has become a Hellene of the underworld.[1]

The New Fitna

His universe, which had found its expression in a certain sort of wisdom, of art, and of attitude, has burst asunder. Our generation has witnessed the explosion. Let us run through old numbers of *al-Hilâl*, those of 1910 for instance.[2] Revolutionary as they are in

[1] Arab 'hellenism', in a different sense, is a theme treated by Ṭaha Ḥusain, Taufîq al-Ḥakîm, etc.

[2] *al-Hilâl*, Cairo, vols. xix and xx (1910–11). We find here: a documentary study of the Yemen; an obviously inspired article on 'The Resurrection of Arabic Literature by Order of the Egyptian Government' (pp. 220 ff); notes on 'Beirut Revisited'; a study of Tripolitania; the Sanûsî; an epistle of Shauqî to

intent, they reveal when we compare them with recent numbers of the Beirut review *al-Âdâb* the tremendous distance travelled by Arab feeling and expression. Thought is divorced from living experience. Consciousness, increasingly exacting and tortured, has lost its cosmic sense. True, it has gained, in exchange, nature and history, both at once. A fruitful but a painful development! The original unanimity of the Moslem world had been broken by the quarrel about the devolution of the caliphate—the *fitna*. Today we behold the wisdom of tradition being disrupted by the necessity of adaptation to the world of others. A gulf is growing between those elements whose closeness made up the unity of ancient times. This feeling of emptiness is the *qalaq*, the *angst* of the present generation of Arabs,[1] which dominates their writing and their actions. For today's problem is that, to adapt himself to others, to reconcile himself with a world which has been re-created by the machine in the name of imperious causalities, traditional man has to repudiate himself in many respects. He can only readjust his being, so to speak, by *disadhering*. Hence his disquiet. He can only achieve self-mastery by regaining his esteem in others' eyes, but also divorcing an essential part of himself.

How is this rupture to be endured? Through a prodigious impulse of the collective will. This is what the Arabs once called *nahḍa*, 'raising up'; they now call it *thaura*, 'revolution'.[2] Let us consider the word. The reference to antiquity being ever-present, what they seek is a recovery rather than a creation. And the long subjection endured over the past few centuries emphasizes still further the backward-looking element in what is, or should be, only a forward movement. They are acting under the impact of the industrial world. If they still retain, despite their increasingly radical transformation, their nostalgia for the old order, if the wisdom transmitted by Islam seems to them today like a lost Paradise, everything happens as though their society, hitherto innocent

the Red Crescent; recollections of a journey to Rhodes; finally a mystical love story, 'Fatât al-Qairawân', the only strictly literary item in this review, subsequently to symbolize even in its excesses the literary trend of the Arab world (cf. an unpublished thesis by Maḥmûd Fakkâr). On the intellectual tendencies of the time, the *Revue du Monde musulman*, vol. xii, is very well informed.

[1] Cf. what I have said about it under this title in the *Revue des Études Islamiques*, 1958. As'ad Razzûq, '*al-usṭûra fî 'l-sh'ir al-mu'âṣir*', *Âfâq*, Beirut, 1959, p. 53, quotes from modern Arabic poetry some fifty expressions ceaselessly recurring to describe this anxiety.

[2] The word *thaura* is in this sense a neologism. It suggests an effervescence on which a Syrian existentialist, Muṭâ' al-Ṣafadî, has laid great stress in a recent book, *al-Thaurî, wa'l-'arabî al-thaurî*, Beirut, 1961.

of Adam's transgression, had been dealt this blow by the West, with all its infinite repercussions. Colonization and expansive capitalism seem to have played in the Arab world, and indeed throughout the Eastern world, the part played amongst ourselves by original sin!

The fact that this sin, whose consequences they suffer, came to them from abroad has given rise to enduring resentment, and has tinged with horror the attraction of the foreigner. But they are well aware that in order to repair the damage done by history they must plunge boldly forward into history. Only can they do it without ruining themselves? Hence their attempt to counterbalance adaptation to others with self-assertion. They maintain the struggle, and will continue to do so, less by mobilizing material forces than by a strategy of symbolism. It is true that these symbols are borrowed more and more from the world's history—independence, democracy—and that they derive fresh vigour, in the East, from the increasing appeal to popular energies. Such societies get their strength from their heroic tension, or from the unanimity of the *umma*, the Islamic nation. Even in their planning, they seem in many respects to be transposing into the economic sphere an old theological centralism.

But this process itself is being relegated into the past by another, newer one. Faced with the choice between what is ideal and what is effective, between heaven and earth, these nations turn more and more towards the second alternative. In order to get into line with others, they repudiate the powers of the symbol to acquire those of the object. They tend therefore to escape from those very symbols through which, and in spite of which, we have first to understand them.[1] Thus many ambiguities are disappearing among the Arabs of today. A rearrangement is taking place between the rival, but united, forces governing their lives. It affects their actions, their feelings, their situations, their persons. This general movement obeys a definite rhythm.

Although it certainly eludes any chronological definition, we can none the less distinguish in it several phases.

From the first phase, their traditional state of harmony with the world, of complete undividedness, the Arabs have been uprooted by the necessity—at first imposed on them and later deliberately chosen—of controlling nature and taking the initiative in history.[2] This second phase is represented politically by struggles for independence, socially by the mutation of the group, materially by industrialization,[3] aestheti-

[1] See Chapter II. [2] See Chapter III.
[3] See the central chapters of this book.

cally by a renewal of sensibility.[1] Finally—the third phase—an increasingly critical attitude,[2] the stronger surge of ideas and forces hitherto repressed both by internal standards and by outside forces, so that once the threshold of independence has been crossed, fresh problems break out.

[1] See Chapters X ff. [2] See Chapter XIII.

CHAPTER II

Variable and Invariable Factors

At Baghdad, in the summer of 1958, I made my way to a piece of waste land between a graveyard and a hospital. Some children showed me, close to a dusty palm tree, a quadrangular wall of rammed clay surmounted by a cupola through which ran a telegraph wire. All around was a used car dump. Contorted chassis, scrap iron waving in the air, like a surrealist nightmare, adorned the cenotaph of al-Ḥallâj, the 'martyr of Islam'. This neglect is perhaps deceptive; at that very moment, in a Baghdad newspaper, the scholar Bahjat al-Atharî was indicting the man who so many centuries ago dared to identify himself with the essential Being: *anâ 'l-ḥaqq*. The dilapidation of the site did not protect him from the enduring resentment of the orthodox. Around his tomb lay heaped up the silt of our machine civilization, which here, as bereft of its own values as the memory of al-Ḥallâj was of any material garment, displayed a grotesque artificiality and complication. The ancient East, represented by a saint, acknowledged its regretful self-renunciation and, at the same time, its adherence to the industrial world; in an extreme and derelict form, it is true: the underside, almost the caricature of what, elsewhere in this country or in other Arab countries, an authentic surge of modernism was trying to create. And yet all around, a revolution was in process. The themes and conflicts of the day thus impinged upon the desolate terrain of al-Ḥallâj.

The East-West Conflict Again

We are here made aware of a unique conjunction of time and place: the very thing that stirs one in any historic study of the Arabs. Their ambiguous originality endures and welcomes the assault of the vast universe, in a planet in process of assembly, where ideas and things press on them from every side. Hence the dramatic conflict between their personality and the unification of the world.

Between the two world wars, many of them chose to put the problem in terms of a geographical classification, accompanied by a distinction between the East, as the realm of the spirit, and the West, as the realm of matter and of imperious causality—involving moreover a psychological hierarchy which allotted certain layers of the soul to mind and others to matter. We may note in this connection the views of such men as Taufîq al-Hakîm, Aḥmad Amîn, and Ṭaha Ḥusain. The issue is still being debated, for in a recent publication, dealing with intellectual trends in Hama, Jamîl Ṣalîba, Dean of the Faculty of Pedagogy in Damascus, devotes several pages to it.[1]

Professor Muḥammad Mubârak, in a speech made on the day of the constitutive union of the United Arab Republic, declared: 'Western civilization is deprived of the light (*al-nûr*) which might clarify the problem of humanity for it; and Western psychology has shown its essential (*dhâtî*) incapacity, its egotism and moral backwardness. It has proved unable to assume the role of spiritual teacher in this world.' Contrariwise, such a task and such a dignity belong to the East. Truly, a very literary classification! Jamîl Ṣalîba is far too much of a philosopher to restrict himself to it. He has no difficulty in tracing a whole current of idealism in the West. The fact is, of course, that no society is either idealist or materialist in the sociological meaning of these words. All societies are materialist and idealist at once, although in different forms and proportions. However, these specious dichotomies, as expressed by Eastern writers, have an interest as evidence of feeling and experience, and many of our own thinkers have assented to them.

The most sceptical analyst has to admit it: an archetypal element still persists in the Eastern world. A whole school of modern thought has sought there, and has found, or thinks it has found there, an enduring message. It discerns in Islam, particularly in Arab Islam, a tradition less impaired than elsewhere, even though buried under the silt of centuries and warred against by Western civilization. Gérard de

[1] Jamîl Ṣalîba, *al-Ittijâhât al-fikrîya fî bilâd al-Shâm*, Cairo, 1958. This antithesis has been frequently elaborated by Eastern apologists for the East; see the scathing comments of Von Grünebaum in his 'Attempts at self-interpretation in contemporary Islam', I and II, *Approaches to Group Understanding*, New York, 1947, particularly with reference to Ḥusain Haikal. It is only fair to mention that other writings by Muḥammad Mubârak show a more liberal point of view.

Nerval recognized in the landscapes of Egypt a secret part of himself and the appeal of a long-lost family, 'a humble and heavenly family whose eyes', he says, 'sought mine with gentle compassion'.[1] Guénon, in 1912, turned to Islam rather than to Hinduism. Through initiation he became connected with certain shaikhs of orthodox line, for instance Shaikh 'Ulaish, Grand Mâlikite of Cairo, who had already 'converted' a Swedish painter. (This Hageli was a strange figure, known in Islam as Brother 'Abd al-Hâdî. A generation ago, he became one of the first interpreters of Ibn 'Arabî.)[2] 'Ulaish professed to be the great teacher of Shâdhilite mysticism in Egypt. How much of his teaching has passed into the book devoted by Guénon, in 1924, to a study of the East-West antithesis? At that time, the *Cahiers du Mois* were conducting an enquiry into what they called 'the appeal of the East'. Doubtless Arab students who happened to be in Paris at this period may have been influenced by these discussions; and perhaps also by Guénon's later book, *La Crise du Monde Moderne* (1927). Here we find some highly subversive ideas about industrial civilization. A paradoxical synthesis was then being formed of such notions with Spengler's catastrophic theory of history and the anti-colonial views of the Left, to which we must also relate the anti-rationalism of the between-war period.[3] François Bonjean describes Guénon,[4] about 1927, holding forth in his drawing-room. 'I can see him still, tall and thin, brimming over with sincerity as he faced his opponents. The sight of this Westerner stubbornly defending the heritage of the East against his amused Eastern listeners was both piquant and impressive.'

We must allow these Eastern listeners their amusement, and also perhaps a touch of irony. For now, as we gather from some of their pronouncements, most of them envisage the conflict differently from Guénon. We ourselves may value the objective exactness of Guénon's analysis of the archetypal element in the East, and also the way it communicates a certain spiritual intensity. But his choice would appear to Eastern activists, as to ourselves, tainted with the cult of the past, with

[1] *Aurélia*, Jose Corti, p. 26. Cf. Nerval's letter to Gautier reproduced in *La Tour Saint-Jacques*, nos. 13–14, 1958, p. 51. The choice of the title *Héliopolis* by Ernst Jünger is no accident.

[2] We must also include in this group the Italian orientalist In Sabato.

[3] Correctly assessed by Henri Lefebvre in *Critiques de la Vie Quotidienne*, vol. i, 1958, pp. 130 ff. But we must also recognize its subtle connections with Asiatic thoughts, stressed by Mircea Eliade.

[4] P. Chacornac. *La Vie Simple de René Guénon*, edit. Traditionnelles, 1958, p. 85. P. Naville, in 1926, attacked the excessive use of the 'myth of the East' made by the Surrealists.

traditionalism, with *taqlîd*, although he would undoubtedly have rejected the charge in horror. The new generation might perhaps accuse him of providing too vegetarian an ideal for their youthful appetites!

Sign and Object

The galleries of the Vatican dazzle us by the splendour of their display of objects: ivories, planispheres, paintings, statues; matter is here triumphant—mastered by artists, exalted by believers and mystics, but always subtly opposed to the incorporeal. Here the soul is made flesh, truth becomes tactile, made of the same stuff as landscapes and human faces. Contrast with this the mosque of the Rock, at Jerusalem, in its formidable bareness, and, even more, the Ka'ba, focus of the whole world, the place of the black stone, with its implied renunciation of material things. Mecca: the Rome of the world of signs.

The concept of a sign or symbol suggests, to one who speaks Arabic, the splendid word *âya*.[1] In the Koran, God says: *Sa-nurî-him âyata-nâ fî' l-âfâq*, 'we will let them see our sign on the horizon'. This sign, this primordial testimony, arising amidst the desert, condemns matter. The Latin *signum*, 'mark by which a thing is known', whence 'relief', 'graven image', takes concrete form as a statue, whereas *âya* takes spiritual form as the Word. It is true that our medieval period also conferred spiritual meanings on *signum*:[2] the mark by which Christ is recognized (sign of the Cross), language of certain orders. Such is the sign of the bell that marks the various stages of the Liturgy, just as the muezzin summons believers to prayer; and we can see how, both at Fez and at Granada, symmetrically, these antagonistic signs provoked controversies, whose violence amazes us today, between the prevailing faith and that of a dissenting minority. At such a distance in the past, moreover, the contrasts seem less sharp than those which some thirty years ago divided Islam, withdrawn in religious contemplation, from the West, seeking like Alberich to master the world. Now, once again, the differences tend to diminish between a West grown self-critical and an Islam in process of modernization. Clearly they belong, in the main, to history, which modifies values and forms. We shall try to circumscribe and explain what is specific and irreducible about them, rather than base misleading definitions upon them.

Christianity has its Apostolic symbol. According to Ruffinus, the

[1] *Lisân al-'Arab*. q.v.

[2] Daremberg and Saglio, Freund, Du Cange, q.v.; the latter dictionary notes 17 meanings of the word!

Apostles chose the term *symbol* to describe their rule because in Greek it means both *initium*, principle, and *collatio*, agreement. St. Augustine illustrates the concept by the suggestive analogy of a sign of recognition between traders.[1] We might also say between comrades, or conspirators, or initiates. Complicity, more or less secret, is implied: the symbol is an instrument. The 'traditional' interpretation represses the social element, whether secular or ecclesiastical, as far as it can, and insists only on 'the impulse towards holiness'.[2] But this is to distort the meaning of the Greek prefix *sun*, which modern sociologists, on the contrary, tend to stress. Mircea Eliade's thesis[3] emphasizes the instrumental aspect of the symbol. In his view, symbols, precisely in so far as they are religious, escape from history, or at least are only indirectly connected with it. Rather, they spring from man's original involvement with the cosmos. And thus they have been transmitted to us in concrete form, as images, words, objects, with the East playing a major part in this transmission.

At the other extreme, we may refer to the sociologists. Guvritch's method is well known, and that conceptual lucidity of his which might become too rigid but for the live and dynamic quality of his thought. He defines symbols as social signs which are both inadequate and mediatory.[4] They are related to a whole which is vaster, in mass or in quality, than their own substance as instruments or even than the minds to which they are addressed. It is from this whole (here conceived of as social, but it might also be called transcendental) that they derive their emotive and evocative force. Their richness is counterbalanced by their inadequacy to say things clearly. They cannot provide such exact information as logical speech. As a corollary, words can assume, in prayer or in art, a symbolic value almost in inverse ratio to their practical value as instruments of communication.[5]

Linguistics, which distinguishes two registers, that of the significant medium and that of the thing signified,[6] allows one to develop this

[1] *Dictionary of Christian and Liturgical Archaeology*, q.v. Cf. also, for Islam, Margoliouth's article in the *Encyclopedia of Religion and Ethics*.

[2] R. Alleau, *De la nature des symboles*.

[3] Mircea Eliade, *Images et symboles. Essai sur le symbolisme magico-religieux*, Gallimard, 1952.

[4] G. Gurvitch, *Vocation de la sociologie*, 1950, pp. 75 ff.

[5] The pragmatic aspect of linguistic communication has been examined by Henri Lefebvre, 'Besoins et langage', *Recherches et dialogues philosophiques et économiques*, 3, I.S.E.A. (Institut de Science Économique Appliquée), Paris, 1958.

[6] Cf. Saussure, *Cours de linguistique générale*, Payot, 1955, pp. 98 ff. But this distinction strikes one today as somewhat sketchy.

point of view. Any spoken formula, for instance, includes the vocal element which conveys the meaning, and the meaning conveyed, which both communicates information and arouses emotion. Between these two elements, classicism maintains a skilful balance. Modern poetic methods disturb it. 'I noted the inexpressible. I pinned down raptures', says Rimbaud. Whereas Racine's poetry might be represented as a splendid isosceles triangle where everything is balanced: verbal music, intellectual communication and suggestive power.[1] It is to the latter that we are most sensitive today. Through our aesthetic emotion we seek to share in all those values which surpass the individual, the practical and the rational: great waves of social unanimity, impulse towards holiness, descent into the unconscious. What is true of poetry is also true of the other arts, and even, in a less privileged fashion, of words, gestures and things. Everything within us and around us can take on meaning as soon as the thing, the gesture or the word lose their common consistency and become the means of access to something deeper and fuller. The very inequality of the communication gives the symbol greater force. The poverty of the instrument, for all conscious and practical purposes, confers on it, by a sort of crystallization, the essence of its power.

The meaning of the Arabic word *ramz*[2] is, indeed, something almost immaterial: a whisper, a silent movement of lips or eyelids, an allusion, an inflexion. With the ambiguity that is characteristic of the language, this profound word can assume the most diverse hues, leaning alternately towards good and evil in its implications.

What, for instance, is meant by a *rammâza* or *ghammâza*, for the two words are used in the same sense? A woman who makes herself understood without speech, by fluttering her eyelids for instance in invitation or acquiescence; possibly a flirt who gives her answer by the pressure of her finger-tips or in some such fashion, but who in any case avoids the use of language, that dangerous medium. But exactly at the antipodes from these emotional values, a *rajul ramîz al-ra'î* is the wise man, disdaining speech, expressing himself by allusive maxims or perhaps solely by a silence pregnant with wisdom, *ṣamt al-ḥikma*, or by his expression or his gait.

[1] And this, in other words, is poetry precisely through that return to the original (anthropological, if you like) undividedness between the various 'functions' which our analysis arbitrarily isolates in language—wrongly, according to Heidegger, *Letter on Humanism*, Aubier, p. 79; Heidegger spoke truer than he realized, where Arabic is concerned!

[2] On all these words, see *Lisân al-'Arab*.

Another word, in more current use today in the sense of 'token' or even 'slogan', *shi'âr*, has a disconcerting wealth of meanings in the old Arabic language. Lexicographers, rightly or wrongly, connect it with *sha'r*, 'hair'. It can also mean a grove, a shady place. Or else, by that sort of sensuous transference which is so characteristic of this civilization, one's most private garment and hence the intimate secrecy of one's body. Another derivation: the mark imprinted on a victim, so that when a king was killed in pre-Islamic Arabia, it was said: *ush'ira*, 'he has been marked', he has received the symbolic wound, the bloodstain that lifts him into a realm of legendary slayings and tragic responsibility. *Shi'âr* means, finally, a watchword or war-cry. All these meanings, by stressing what makes a thing *different*, lead to its symbolic meaning, that is its significance of something fuller and deeper.

By another route, such terms as *wasm* or *sima* lead there too. They refer to the emblems of pastoral life. The nomads make an incision on the ear or shoulder of their animals to show that they belong to a certain flock. An individual is distinguished by such physical signs. The *wasîm*, the man of good family, the thoroughbred, carries his genealogy in his face; such meaningful beauty was highly thought of by the Arabs of old.

We may pass over *'alâma*, too self-conscious, indeed artificial, for our purpose, and go back to the amazing word I have already quoted. The verses of the Koran follow one another in a panting rhythm where each sentence constitutes an *âya*. Lexicographers further define *âya* as a form of punctuation in the recital of psalms. Other interpretations concern individuality, that miracle of identity contained within every being; thus one can speak of *ayât rajul*, a man's 'personality', or say that some group of men have gone 'as a body', *kharajat al-qaum bi-âyati-him*. In this concept of entirety and completeness, we find one, at least, of the things that sociologists and theologians, strangely united on this point, recognize in a symbol.

The Symbolic East

This richness of vocabulary has implications which are not contradicted by Eastern life today. Here are a few random illustrations.

In July 1958, Sayyid 'Abd al-Raḥmân, son of the Sudanese Mahdi, was in Geneva, undergoing treatment for his heart. In his room, with its gleaming enamel and all the luxurious bleakness with which our industrial civilization surrounds the sick, the old man was resting. Behind him, by the window, hung a golden sword, which had belonged to the man who defeated Gordon. The *sayyid* took the emblem with him, he told me, every time he left his country. In this case the symbolism was deliberate.

Less easy to interpret is the red flag that waves over the mosques of Karbala, as though to illustrate the view that Shî'ism is Islam's permanent revolution. But it has a deeper meaning, being connected with a language of colours which Iranian mystics have subtly expounded. Man, says al-Samnânî, is ruled by seven centres, each having its own colour; green representing Muḥammad and Shi'ism, black representing Jesus, and so on.[1]

But such speculations are superfluous. Symbols are everywhere visible in a Muslim town. Its whole life is planned symbolically, with the call of the muezzin, the thronged streets on a Friday, and the many district sanctuaries, oratories and mausoleums grouped around the central mosque. If we look close we see that the domes of these buildings are related to the vault of heaven as their quadrangular bases are to the earth, by an inverse symbolism to that of Indo-European nations. The arabesque, too, is symbolic. In its design and its material it implies far more than it expresses. Here the traditional artist draws his inspiration from the very complication of the lines. Their interlacing presents the spectator with an enigma whose solution, over and above all literal meaning, postulates the ineffable. Even when used in the most ordinary circumstances, for a letter or a contract, Arabic writing is more suggestive than informative. Its structural division into consonants and vowels awakens correspondences in every sphere, musical as well as mystical. And for this reason the spoken language offers only the mutilated skeleton of written Arabic, almost a mockery of it. The concrete semantics of the dialect contradict the ontological semantics of the *lugha*, the priestly idiom, and are therefore repudiated by nationalist movements, which derive from the Classical speech not only their Panarabian interconnections, but even more, a source of exaltation through mutual rivalry. This is a burning issue of the day. It is not pure aestheticism to ascribe such a rôle to the solemn framework, and the means of communication by writing and speech, that provided Arab nationalism, at least in the period between the two world wars, with its most powerful means of recruitment.

In order to gain a foothold in modern history, the Arab East has had to become one vast symbol.

[1] H. Corbin, *L'imagination créatrice dans le soufisme d'Ibn 'Arabî*, Paris, 1958, p. 46.

The Synoptic East

It still strikes one thus today, despite its increasing industrialism and its trend towards the things of this world. By a paradoxical coincidence, the message sought and found in the East by mystics and poets from Suhrawardi to Nerval, a message of ancient truth conveyed through its tradition, its outward aspect, its very substance right to our own day, is visible even to the most profane observer. The reporter's description here confirms the historian's syntheses and the initiate's meditations.

In any Eastern city there is a blatant discrepancy between the categories of life and of things, a sort of telescoping of past ages and present-day levels of existence. Alexandrinism persists round the corners of narrow lanes, on café terraces, in the dusty, pearly mornings and the orgiastic dusks of Sîdî Bishr. Others besides the poet Cavafy[1] have felt it. All Eastern cities are 'citadels of memory' in that they exalt the sordid, profane the august and sacred. In every modernist movement or *tajdîd* there is an element of such profanation, which the foreigner is apt to misinterpret. Thus Baghdad, nowadays, is a city where the past testifies and yet mutilates itself. Great geometrical avenues cut through mazes of brownish mortar, contrasting violently with domes of blue Persian tiles but harmonizing with the great metal bridges built by Krupp for the Common Market. Another contrast strikes you sharply when you visit the Arab Museum. This occupies a former annexe of the Mosque of al-Mirjân, from which it is separated today by the Avenue al-Rashîd. It is a dark twilit house, full of silent richness. And when you pause for breath, between two rooms, and look out of the window, you see Bank Street, where today all the banks congregate as once the money-changers congregated. And you can gaze alternately at the exquisite ceramics from Samara on the shelves and, close by, at the steel and reinforced concrete pillars of a showy capitalism.

You have the same impression if you look over to Cairo from the Gezireh. This embankment has entirely altered during the last few years. It has become an outlet for the suburbs, and is completely overgrown with popular refreshment booths. I happened to be there recently. In front of me I saw an irregular façade of houses lining the right bank.

[1] Translated into French by Marguerite Yourcenar, Gallimard, 1959; into English by Rae Dalven, Hogarth Press, London, 1961.

And one cannot, in any study of 'alexandrinism', dissociate Cavafy from the astonishing observations of Lawrence Durrell.

All possible styles reigned there simultaneously, telling of a long succession of periods and fashions. A few old patrician dwellings, with mouldings and arabesques, belong to the Italianate fashion current in Egypt at the beginning of this century. Semiramis was of this sort; but the more recent hotels, the new Shepheard's and the Hilton,[1] have carefully purged away all ornament and practically all local colour. To your left, the building of the Arab League; another rises on the extreme right, towards Roda, brandishing aloft, like a flaming *shi'âr*, an aggressive neon sign for Coca-Cola. Meanwhile, however, on the bank, just opposite the Club, you can still make out a *santon*, a statuette, obscurely connected with the Nile. The big buildings have swallowed it up. The offices that surround it, on the Maspero Quay, happen to be occupied by representatives of great engineering firms: apparatus for measuring engine pressure, composition of alloys, etc. . . .

It is impossible to over-stress such antitheses, which are the very stuff of the present-day Eastern world. Tripoli is a further example. From a small garden full of aubergines on the left bank of the mountain stream Abû 'Alî, I can see before me the hill of Qubba, with its fantastic outline of daringly overhanging rocks and curved minarets. A perilous erection of reinforced concrete tramples cheerfully on the remains of medieval Islam: an Islam of carved lintels, shadowy streets, curious wooden turrets from which women peep out. Behind me is the Frankish district, climbing up the Abû Samrâ hill towards St. Giles' castle. On the left, around the Tell, modern Tripoli radiates in broad avenues, where active industry—oils, soaps, confectionery—tells of the renewed pact between the city and its countryside of olive and orange groves.

So, too, Aleppo, which Yâqût celebrated for its profusion of vegetables and the vast plain, rich in appanages, spread out around as far as the eye can see. The citadel, which still calls itself Abraham's, towers above an immense square of buildings that unfold on either side of it like the two valves of a shell. This division goes back far into the past. On the Western side one is still aware, under the layout of the streets, of Hellenistic geometry, oddly revived by modern town-planning. To the East there is an Asiatic tangle of streets: a medieval legacy, as are the huge *sûqs* or markets. The Turkish period lingers sumptuously in the patrician dwellings with their polychrome marbles and their cool patios through which flow artificial waterfalls, beautifully called *salsabil*. And the modern town, by its intensive industrialization as well as by its

[1] Since writing these lines I have seen the completed Hilton; I could offer a good many criticisms of this grandiose example of *wagon-lit* aesthetics.

proud vitality, tries to prove itself worthy, by challenging it, of its unfathomable past.

Not, indeed, without difficulty. The contrast of periods and tendencies, the disproportion between memories and hopes and the drab norm, give to everything in the Arab East a significance, an index and landmark, which it does not intrinsically possess. That is why one can still walk about there in our own period in the spirit of Gérard de Nerval; unless one walks about as Director of the I.B.R.D.![1] The same is true, to a greater or lesser extent, in other societies. But nowhere do such staggering contrasts bestow such high significance on things experienced, or inflict such crushing comparisons on present-day realities.

Nostalgia, hope, precariousness, such are today the three dimensions of Arab life. That is why everything that is said and done in the Arab world, behaviour, speech, things themselves assume in turn the contrary qualities of intimacy and solemnity. There is an element of tragedy here, but an element of comedy as well. This double register of feeling and interpretation involves the Arabs themselves and whoever tries to explain the Arabs, in misunderstandings and surprises. The critic is apt to resort to antitheses, unless he indulges in one or other of two opposite attitudes: either suspect flattery or ill-founded spite.[2] Or both at once. And in fact this twofold attitude only reflects, in other people, what the Arabs feel about themselves: ardent optimism or hopeless pessimism. Or both at once. Hence their uncertainties, too often unintelligible to the outsider.

Where psychology fails to account for such a phenomenon except by antitheses—cunning and violence, nobility and rapacity, the habit of bargaining and the visionary faculty—semantic analysis may be more ambitious. If the Don Quixote[3] of the Middle East surprises you with a knowing wink, while Sancho, the plump sensual townsman, is capable of dying a selfless hero's death,[4] we should be wary of such oppositions, which have too often been fostered and exploited by outsiders in their own interests.

[1] International Bank for Reconstruction and Development.

[2] No names need be mentioned here.

[3] After all, *Don Quixote* itself illustrates that conflict between the symbolic and the concrete which, at certain moments, affects certain nations more than others. . . .

[4] Whence the somewhat comic surprise of foreign powers on witnessing the fierce combativeness displayed, in spite of accepted 'psychology', by such city-folk as the bourgeois of Damascus or members of the Cairo parliament. At such times, it is the Bedouin warrior who is facing the wrong way, i.e. against the course of history; he loses his significance, and his supporters lose their way.

The provisional explanation, at any rate, is that the Arabs, in their actions, in the setting of their lives, amid the vicissitudes that beset them, derive a virtue peculiar to themselves from confronting their present sufferings with the vastness of their past and their future. Everything within them, through them, around them, takes concrete form in deeply moving symbols: a source both of strength and of weakness in their modern adventure.

The Historic East

Until they gained their independence, the Arab countries had asserted themselves by rebelling against the very thing which principally maintained Western expansion: the economic element. The analyses of Claude Lévi-Strauss[1] have shown us the three levels at which exchange went on: through women, through words, through goods. For more than half a century, with increasing urgency, Islam had defended itself by means of its demographic luxuriance, an elementary life-force overriding all barriers, and of its linguistic renaissance, which allowed a sense of unity to spread from the Atlantic to the Persian Gulf. Was this not a form of insurrection, so to speak, of the two humbler levels of exchange against the economic level, the appanage of more highly developed countries?

Now the Middle East is striving increasingly to attain this third level. For that is where the competitions of present-day life take place, as it well knows, having been both the victim and the prize of these. Such a tendency, and the conflict to which it appertains, alter the terms of the problem. And they can only be opposed to one another thus at the cost of a somewhat misleading simplification. True, the variations in the interplay between an incoercible vitality, an oratorical emotionality and an economy which, although increasingly restrictive, fosters credulous hopes, offer a convenient hold to the interpreter of the Arab world today. Yet it is only provisionally, and for the sake of clarity, that one must distinguish in these societies the respective importance of the two forces, mistakenly but conveniently contrasted by the traditional concepts of mind, *rûḥ*, and matter, *mâdda*. Let us imagine them for a moment as if they sprang from two rival sources, every creature and every thing in these countries resulting from their interaction. At the very least, this simplifying view will derive some value no longer merely from the Arabs' own conception of themselves, but from the historical

[1] Who will forgive me for borrowing this 'working model' from his valuable work.

movement which is involving this society, with its illustrious past and its powerful religious individuality, in a difficult struggle of adaptation to the mechanized world. At the two extremes we see: on the one hand a concrete power, hitherto the sole prerogative of the West, which appears to those who are subjugated by it as ungenerous, unlawful and even senseless; on the other, an idealism that rebels against oppression, yet covets material reconquest. Thus, in 1956, did millions of Arabs interpret the Suez conflict. In fact the 'cowardly threefold aggression' came as a sequel to the nationalization of the Canal, as did the latter to the refusal to grant credits for the Dam, which implied a promotion to the economic sphere. They rose not merely in the name of justice, but in order to gain access to their adversary's plane—that of concrete achievement. Such a position seemed to them no less 'realistic' than moral. Hence its powerful appeal, which cannot be explained away as the fervour of frustrated idealism.

And yet much in Arab behaviour, more than in our own, seems influenced by emotion and an ethical sense. Although the conflicts between dogma and modernity have lost their virulence, they are still latent. Tensions of another order, for instance that provoked by irredentist patriotism, replace them in many cases. In 1956 Syria denounced an export agreement concerning corn from the Jazîra as a protest against the Algerian affair; the 'triangular' operations that ensued cost the fellah dear, but political idealism was saved. Beirut aerodrome had difficulty in saving Air-France, source of substantial profits, from the effects of the boycott (1957). An Egyptian economist has categorically stated that the material elements of economic growth must be repudiated if they are incompatible with justice. Of course this rigorism comes to terms, in practice, with objective facts—the need for credits, techniques and equipment—through which the foreigner, once more, makes his power felt. Moreover it conflicts, or co-operates, as the case may be, with irrational forces, to which it resorts, without great faith maybe, to arouse the fervour of the crowd, but which often lead it astray or disfigure it. This gives to Arab behaviour its mixture of naivety and cunning, surprising to the unwary observer, and too often lucrative to the native or foreigner who knows how to take advantage of it.

Arab Individuality and World Factors

In its striving towards the economic and technical spheres, which dominate the world, the Arab East remains true to itself. Whoever, whether as scholar or as man of action, approaches it from without, whoever among its own national reformers tries to affect it from within, is conscious of a highly individual character.

Analysis, in any case, must refrain from summary judgements and prescriptions. While refusing to consider Arab society as predominantly picturesque, imaginative and irrational, we must notice that many other societies (even those that invented positivism) are prone to flights of fancy. A recent American study entitled 'The Fabulous French'[1] pointed out the same propensity for myth-making, among the French, that strikes one in the Arab world. It is a question of degree rather than of nature. We must therefore distinguish, in the present-day activities of the Arabs, between what is concrete and rational and what springs from an enthusiastic but sometimes wrong-headed idealism. We should gauge and measure, rather than attempt to define. In a word, we must assess the variable factors which invalidate any law. Now many of these, belonging to the ancient foundations of these societies, display the permanence of invariable factors.[2]

As a matter of fact, are things so very different in our own countries? Economic research has long ago given up assuming simple relations between 'economic man' and the market. It no longer believes in cut-and-dried determinism, or in so-called normality. It has developed in the same direction as human geography, which now denies any direct conditioning of man by his environment, but speaks of exchanges between society and nature. Thanks to this new school, to which many French thinkers belong, psychology now plays a part, and an important part, in economic science.[3] Psychology, with its varied subdivisions, unhesitatingly invades the sphere of the irrational itself. Actually, the movement had begun long ago. Vilfredo Pareto sought to reduce economics to a rational, mechanistic science. But, let us not forget, he wrote a 'sociology' to study those famous 'residues' and 'derivations' which were held to account, to a large extent, for human actions. Keynes, who has so greatly influenced our contemporaries, also refers to collective dispositions. He attributes to these a primordial rôle in the functioning of his 'independent variables'.[4] And what are we to say of

[1] *The Atlantic*, June 1958. Cf. also Lüthy, *La France à l'heure de son clocher*.

[2] This valuable concept is borrowed from L. Massignon's great study on 'La poussée de l'Islam,' *Encyclopédie Française*, vol. xx, 1959, ch. vii., pp. 11, 20, 35.

[3] Cf. particularly the pioneer article of A. Piatier, 'Economie et sociologie', *Revue des sciences morales et politiques*, 1957, pp. 5 ff.; and the penetrating study of man and myth by the geographer Le Lannou in *Le Monde*, 29–30 June 1958.

[4] For a precise exposé see James, *History of Economic Thought in the Twentieth Century*, which I have frequently consulted.

the analysis of those phenomena that we modestly call 'growth phenomena', and that others ascribe to 'underdevelopment'? Here the psychological, cultural, human element plays the principal rôle. On this subject I can only refer to the decisive studies made by François Perroux. These finally dispose of the myth that economic behaviour is guided by the 'rational' laws of the market, of competition and profit.[1] Such behaviour, whether 'Eastern' or 'Western', involves innumerable factors. It oscillates constantly between the practical and the symbolic. Everything about it is both significant and utilitarian.

Yet these two elements are differently adjusted in each case. Through its predilection for what is *differential* in men and things and moments, may not social history recover that specific Arab quality which is inadequately accounted for by either the psychological or the economic approach?

Issuing from a colonial system to enter the field of nationalist rivalries, the whole of the Middle Eastern world escapes from the usual laws of the market. It had suffered not so much from economic laws, strictly speaking, as from situations forcibly imposed. Today it intends to withdraw from them in the same way. For what François Perroux has called the economy of domination it seeks to substitute, if I may coin a term, de-domination. Its motive is to recapture its own, or even to take lawful prizes; we might find many indications of this in its recent history: nationalization of Suez, Egyptianizing of the banks, pressure on oil companies, etc. In this sense we may say that, in a world moving towards uniformity, the Arabs maintain their individual demeanour. Amongst them, up till the present, the symbol has tended to beget the fact rather than to be supported by it. The wish to *be* something is more powerful than the wish to *do* something. In any case it precedes it. Whence the strange spectacle of an emancipation that goes from assertion to realization, from the superstructure to the base. It first asserts its political nature, then seeks to attain economic and social being, and thus justify or, in other words, prove worthy of itself. On July 22nd, 1958, President Nasser devoted an important speech to the relations between Egypt and the world. Very significantly, he pleaded urgency and unpreparedness as an explanation for dealing only with foreign policy, postponing to a later occasion any analysis of home affairs,

[1] As well as Perroux's classic pages, see Gottfried Eisermann, 'Sociologie de la connaissance et théorie économique', *Cahiers internationaux de sociologie*, xviii, 1955, pp. 17 ff. and an enlightening discussion of these problems by F. Bourricaud, in his Introduction to *Eléments* . . . by Talcott Parsons, Plon, 1955, pp. 12 ff.

particularly economic questions. To a sociologist, this would seem to be treating these factors in the wrong order. But Middle East opinion demands this sort of thing. The Lebanese essayist Muḥammad Wahbî notes the contrast, on this point, between East and West. The West, he says, reserves its realistic rapacity and machiavellism for its foreign policy, while its internal policy appeals to high principles. The reverse is true in Arab countries. Cunning and greed are rife in internal affairs, whereas in external relations Arabs profess a generous idealism which is often hoodwinked.[1] By a corollary, these countries attain political independence in the reverse order to their internal readiness for it. The first of them all to be emancipated was the Saudi Arabian kingdom, hitherto the least affected by modernity, then Iraq, which had not experienced the Nahḍa, the renaissance, then Egypt,[2] finally Syria and Lebanon, the latter the most profoundly steeped in Western culture, the least illiterate, the country with the highest individual incomes and the most markedly European character.

To be sure, it would be far-fetched and paradoxical to pursue in detail these inverted parallels between the West and the Arab East, which seems to be going through a sort of Victorian era of decolonization. But there is some truth in the picture. It is due to the rôle—both constructive and repellent, at all events determining—played by the West in this history which today is taking place through and against the West. Hence a profound conflict of identity. Hence a basic ambiguity: that of the notion of *qaumîya*, so obscure as to defy exact definition. Patriotism? Racial exaltation? Nationalism? It was thus interpreted at the Third Congress of Arab Writers (1957) by the Sudanese Muḥyî al-Dîn Ṣâbir:

'*Qaumîya* is not an ethnic concept, but a struggle aiming at realizing the ideal values of industrial civilization, and notably those which are the most equitable in political, economic, social and cultural spheres. It is also an aggregate of common vital interests, and a common destiny,

[1] Muḥammad Wahbî, *Azmat al-tamaddun al-'arabî*, Beirut, 1956, p. 96.

[2] In an interview with *Al-Ahrâm*, 2 July 1959, Nasser asserted the primacy of economics in amazingly categorical fashion. He went so far as to say that the Revolution of 1952 had preceded its own structuration, which was still to be achieved. In the West, no doubt, democracy is political before being economic or social. It has not come 'on its head', to quote a famous phrase, but according to an obvious context of economic preparation. It is possible, however, that this precedence of 'the head', i.e. feeling and ideology, is inherent in any state of revolutionary tension. The subsequent measures taken by Egypt, notably in July 1961, are aimed at giving the Revolution an economic content and foundation.

which are now being recognized throughout the Arab world, but which spread beyond its borders, since these interests and this destiny remain linked with those of the whole contemporary world.'[1]

Similarly, in an extremely acute, though necessarily circumspect, article, a Syrian intellectual sought to extend the isolationist notion of *turâth*, 'cultural heritage', to a broader concept of human effectiveness: this seemed to him essential for any real involvement in the modern world. Thus braving prejudices and alibis, he had discovered a profound truth.[2]

Qaumîya, then, is the effort of the Arabs to adapt themselves to other nations, while remaining faithful to their own individuality. It matters little that the conflict is not always clearly defined or felt. This urgent, if contradictory, impulse brings us to the heart of the reality that we are studying. It goes beyond the contrasts of the present day and that portion of truth which they reveal, and explains many of the characteristics through which I have sought a preliminary approach to the Arab people, through a twofold confrontation of the specific with the universal, and of the historic with what belongs to the sphere of religion. By a fortunate coincidence, at the very moment when the French edition of this book was being printed, there appeared the lucid book by Qusṭanṭîn Zuraiq entitled: *Naḥnu wa-ta'rîkh*, 'History and Ourselves'.[3] An obvious binomial? Each of the two terms must act henceforward on the other. In particular, what is to become of 'ourselves'?

[1] Muḥyî al-Dîn Ṣâbir is French-educated. We may quote as symptomatic of the same preoccupations: Kamâl Yûsuf al-Ḥâjj, *Fî'l-qaumîya wa'l-insânîya*, Beirut, 1957; Muḥammad Wahbî, '*Urûba wa-insânîya*, Beirut, 1959. The great poet Sa'îd 'Aql, in his lecture *Mushkilat al-Nakhba fî' l-Sharq* (1954), appeals to the younger generation to extend their patriotism from their nation to the whole world.

[2] Ḥâfiẓ al-Jamâlî, *al-Wafâ' li'l-mîrâth al qaumî*, Damascus, 1960.

[3] Beirut, 1959.

CHAPTER III

Towards an Economic System[1]

Rashîd Street cuts right through the *sûqs* of Baghdad. In many such towns modern planning has, in general, superimposed an angular order on the curvilinear order of the past. And yet in these *sûqs* the streets have always intersected at right angles, as if the Hellenistic model, from Latakia to the further end of Morocco, had uninterruptedly dictated the plan of markets. I was wandering, then, amidst these geometrical labyrinths where, as at Bâb Zuwaila in Cairo, there still linger the old skilled craftsmanship and the ornate tradesmen's stalls of former days. But all of it is threatened and jeopardized by the growing banality of the world. True, in several corners of these market-places there can still be seen the mausoleums of those whom the Shî'ite faith considers as 'agents' of the hidden Mahdi, his *wukalâ'*.

[1] The chapters of this book devoted to economic questions are entirely based, as will be seen, on local sources and on first-hand impressions. However, I cannot omit to mention here the first general accounts which have helped to elucidate this complex matter: Ch. Issawi, *Egypt, an Economic and Social Analysis*, 1957, and *Egypt in Mid Century*, 1950; Doreen Warriner, *Land and Poverty in the Middle East*, 1948; the lively and well-informed work of J. and S. Lacouture on *L'Egypte en mouvement*, 1956; the valuable (unpublished) lectures by Prof. A. Philip, given after his journey to Egypt in 1959; finally the useful, if somewhat belated and entirely official, documentation of the U.N.O. *Reports*. In this field the Arabs themselves have begun to provide valuable documentation, to which I have freely referred. I have made constant use of the *Economic Bulletin* of the National Bank of Egypt, the remarkable Syrian review *L'Economie et les Finances de la Syrie et des pays arabes*, and the *Supplement économique de l'Ahram*; these are referred to, respectively, as *Ec. Bull.*, *E.F.S.P.A.*, and *A.S.* The unusual and extensive character of this documentation, concerning a period fertile in political and social change, would present disadvantages for a specialized economic enquiry, which the present work is not. These disadvantages can, on the contrary, prove assets for a sociological study concerned with permanent factors as much as with historical changes.

I saw two of them, where men and women were weeping aloud. And I visited a merchant next door. He had lived a long time in Japan. His conversation was equal to that of any other tradesman in the most cosmopolitan market-place. And I contrasted his experienced alertness, his knowledgeable shrewdness with those scenes of piety and grief. What transition led from one to the other? How could such a man, while lamenting the death of 'Alî, cope so efficiently with his business affairs?

Formerly much of the trading hereabouts was done by Jews. When they left, they had to be replaced. Curious laws decided the distribution of these substitutes. Goldsmiths were recruited mainly from among the Mandeans, whose fame was legendary. Chaldeans became hotel managers. Shî'ites took over a large proportion of businesses, particularly banking, which they shared with other minorities, while the Sunnites assumed as their right certain functions connected with governmental tradition and initiative. It would be most interesting to study these replacements in detail, in Baghdad and in other Eastern cities. Elsewhere the Egyptianizing of society offers similar opportunities for research at this very moment.

In these countries, as in our own, a group *is*, above all, that which sets it apart from the rest: its origin, its rites, its attitudes, and in many cases a certain type of labour. The substitutions which took place in Baghdad, showing us with the clarity of an experiment the reaction of groups with old-established qualifications in an operation of economic readjustment, illustrate both the importance of the differential element in determining individuality, and of the permanent element in the evolutionary process. And this small corner of the East was not alone involved. The French visitor, by contact with these places and these people, also felt within himself and concerning himself these differences and constant factors, and the subtle bond between them.

According to a summary but necessary classification, the lament of the faithful at the mausoleum of the *wukalâ'* belongs to the realm of religion and symbolism, whereas the tradesman's behaviour is 'modern' and 'realistic'. But in him, as in ourselves, these strongly contrasted values balance one another and amalgamate. Only the time factor and the material circumstances are different, between ourselves and him, as also between the groups within his own society. However, we must take a wider and more distant view, and leave for a while the behaviour of individuals or communities to consider the Arab East as a whole. For these variations have been dictated by broad historic options, some of them deliberate. As the East has attained its present character, with all its idiosyncrasies, after long self-scrutiny, one of the first steps we must take in order to understand it is to examine the moral attitude it has assumed towards economic questions.

Ethics and Economics

We were jolting over a dusty road from Baghdad to Karabla. My companion in the car was a leading Shî'ite magistrate of the Supreme Court of Appeal.[1] Although of purely local education, he had acquired, either through the intermediary of Egyptian jurisprudence or by reading translations of French works, a relatively broad outlook. The conversation turned naturally to the lot of those landless peasants who, on the bank of one of the *jadâwil* (canals) that branch out from the river, cultivate the land that bears a strangely Latin name, *rustâq* (*rustica*?)[2] A crushing primitivism, an immemorial destitution were cruelly obvious all around us, the more shocking by contrast with the exuberance of nature, flinging up its palm trees in these irrigated corners. Before us was Karbala, with its traditionalist piety surrounding its golden domes. How was the bond between all these ancient things to be broken? Or rather, how was the vital sap which could bring new life to be drawn from their ancient depths?

And my companion explained to me how Shî'ite law was tending to renovate itself to meet the demands of modern life. Insurance? Insurance implies risk. And they get round the question of *gharar* (risk, gamble), the subject of so many prohibitions according to the strict moral code, by considering insurance not as profit on a gamble, but purely as an expression of solidarity. This is a respectable concept, subject to no ban. Then there is the question of expropriation; for the State to seize an individual's sacred property in the public interest would be a grave infringement of religious law. But a subterfuge enables them to assert that the State acts on this occasion as mandatory for the legitimate owner. There is no change of ownership, but a return to the *umma*, the Muslim nation, for the good of the community. Interest itself, that taboo of taboos, is 'admitted', *ijâza*, by shrewd lawyers, by identifying it with the profits of a limited liability company, which the law allows. Only it is no longer called by name, *fâ'ida*, or as the ancient authorities describe it, *salaf jârr naf'a*, 'a loan with interest', but 'gain', *rabḥ*,

[1] Aḥmad Jamâl al-Dîn, *al-Waqf*, Baghdad, 1955; *al-Istimlâk*, Baghdad, 1956.

[2] Cf. *contra*, J. Fück, *Arabîya*, tr. Denizeau, Paris, 1955, p. 168, who ascribes a Persian origin to this word.

istirbâḥ, 'pursuit of gain', and the whole thing remains perfectly harmless. By similar methods it has proved possible in many Muslim countries to liberate and restore to economic circulation the *waqf* or mortmain. Legislators in Iraq, like those in Tunis or Egypt, had to face the problem of the *auqâf dhurrîya*, pious mortmain, which debarred a whole category of real estate from the market. In any case, the magistrate told me with a laugh, as the *waqf* in this form is itself a *ḥîla*, a subterfuge, there was nothing wrong about eluding it by other subterfuges.

Of course, I was dealing with an enlightened mind. There is no reason to suppose that the theologians of Karbala, who were about to offer us such Biblical hospitality, would have followed him on all these points. Still, he was expressing the dominant tendency. It cannot be said that the conflict between dogma and modernism offers insuperable difficulties to the Muslims in the economic field. Only it has spread, almost everywhere, from being a doctrinal controversy, basic because it involves two opposite views of the world, to affect manners and morals. Arab society is hesitant between a choice of attitudes, rather than actually divided by them.

A commonplace often repeated in the West as well as in the East is the contrast between the Arabs' traditionalism, their fatalism, etc. and our cult of activity. These conceptions are held not only by Western teachers; witness the recent work of Dr. Sa'd Mâhir Ḥamza, an Egyptian economist then teaching in the Sudan: 'Economic Growth and Social Stagnation: a contrast and a contradiction.'[1] A glance at this work shows it to consist of an analysis of the mental conditions underlying this contrast between the two worlds. The East displays a deliberately negative attitude, due to excessive stress on the spiritual. The author finds it hard to express his view without offending religion. He therefore uses circumlocutions. He devotes one chapter, for instance, to 'ritual idealism', *rûḥânîya,* as an obstacle to economic development. He denounces many vestiges of the past among his contemporaries, whether cultural, political or psychological.

He is perhaps over pessimistic. Almost everywhere the things he inveighs against are commonly considered as characteristic of a past to be abolished. In fact these realities, for they are real, are daily weakening in their social and moral influence. For an increasing number of groups, these are the very things against which they rebel, and in spite of which they want to act.

By a curious development, the rule tends to become the anomaly,

[1] *Al-Tanmîya al-iqtiṣâdîya wa'l-jumûd al-ijtimâ'î, ta'âruḍ wa-tanâquḍ.*

1. Old houses overshadow a narrow alley, mistrustfully keeping their secrets to themselves. Street in Baghdad.

2. Cosmopolitan and rural: a view of Beit-Shabâb, Lebanon, village of the poet Rîḥânî. (Drawing by Lucie Berque.)

to be confined to social exceptions or geographically remote regions. The scorn or the scandal aroused in this connection by the primitivism of the Yemenites, by Saudi Arabian rigorism or by reactionary propaganda such as that of the Muslim Brotherhood, show that the conflict itself has in general ceased to be related to a moral code laid down by law. But it retains certain psychological effects, like the draughtsman's hesitancies blurring the boldness of his line.

The interaction of heterogeneous attitudes provides a wealth of curious illustrations. The Syrian law of 1962, revising agrarian reform, used the ban on interest as an argument for cutting down certain compensations. An Egyptian engineer calculates the loss involved by the annual sacrifice at Mina, and advocates the cold-storage of this meat; thus passing from the theme of *kaffâra*, or expiation, to that of the fight against malnutrition. Apparently the idea goes back to Hudâ Sha'-râwî, progressive in this sphere as in others. . . . Aḥmad Bahâ' al-Dîn deplores the disillusionment of youth faced with a too successful revolution, and seeks instead to rouse their enthusiasm for economic progress. A tradesman offers a lottery ticket as a bonus to his customers: the lucky winner will get a free pilgrimage to Mecca; thus something essentially impious is combined with lucre and devoutness.

But there have been more far-reaching developments. Side by side with the florescence of the Shâfi'ite *fiqh* in Egypt and the Shî'ite *ijtihâd* in Iraq, the new economic trends have begun to find their formulation in the Arab East: still, perhaps, too meekly following the lessons they have learnt, but all the more interesting as reflecting a generation or two of local teaching.[1]

Economic sciences made their first appearance in Egypt with a translation of Leroy-Beaulieu: the apogee of a classicism which seems very old-fashioned today. Concurrently, the Anglo-Saxon conception asserted itself, and for a long time Todd's manual reigned in rivalry with that of Leroy-Beaulieu. Meanwhile there had grown up a flourishing Law School, fostered by the Faculty of French, and a School of Advanced Commercial Studies, which became the Faculty of Commerce. The latter drew its inspiration both from France and from Britain. During the 'twenties the Miṣr group proved themselves somewhat sketchy theorists, but dauntless experimenters. At the same time the

[1] The facts are quoted from a report made by Dr. Wahîb Misîḥa to the U.N.E.S.C.O. Congress at Damascus, 1954, on the teaching of the social sciences. 'Social and economic sciences in advanced education'. Since then, planning has brought about much theoretical and practical progress.

doctrinal influence of Dr. Aḥmad Muḥammad Ibrâhîm was felt. His importance as a teacher restored to the French school the position it had somewhat lost. The best contemporary economists, 'Alî Grîtlî, 'Abd al-Mun'im al-Qaisûnî, 'Abd al-Mun'im al-Rifâ'î, have all had a British training. But in the latest efforts displayed by the Economic Organization or the Planning Committee, with Ismâ'îl Ṣabrî 'Abd Allâh for instance, or Ibrâhîm Ḥilmî 'Abd al-Raḥmân, the researches of the French school have been closely studied and to a certain extent put into practice.

What interests us in all this is not a futile academic quarrel, but the way in which the work of the London School of Economics, and that of F. Perroux, O. Lange, Nurkse, Gunnar Myrdal, Timberghen, Ch. Bettelheim and A. Piatier contribute, although by different routes, to an analysis of underdevelopment, and the encouragement to original research which their work provides: the only way, for the East, to avoid both scruples and depression, scruples inspired by lingering habits of dogmatism and a depression too often encouraged by orthodox analyses. It is possible to interpret in this sense the two words associated in the title of a book by the Lebanese economist Anîs Sâyigh, *al-Khubz wa'l-karâma*, 'bread and honour'; honour is, and always will be, for these countries as for others, respect for personality, in terms of which all other forms of progress are appreciated.

No wonder then if, despite so many inequalities both in relation to the outside world and between the participants themselves, the Afro-Asian Conference held at Cairo from Dec. 8–11, 1958, should have recommended an organization which is remarkable less for its offensive or defensive character than for the attention paid to concrete information.[1] The word 'study' recurs a dozen times in its recommendations. This trend towards the concrete struck foreign observers at the last Planning Congress.[2] After this there seems little justification for devoting a whole book, as does Dr. Sa'd Ḥamza, to the 'contrasts and contradictions' which still spring from rival attitudes. The positive line must win the day, here as elsewhere, on pain of death. But what survives, what must survive—and on its survival all positive construction

[1] Anglo-Franco-Arabic brochure recording the Recommendations of the Congress of 8 Dec. 1958. Cf., as a sequel to this Congress, the Afro-Asian Colloquy on the Common Market held at Brussels, 27–29 May 1959, presided over by Prof. Abel. Cf. also the brochure *The Arab Financial Institution*, Cairo, 1958, and a report from the Arab League delegate, Dr. Muḥammad Rifâ'at at the Brussels Colloquy, 1961.

[2] *Ahrâm iqtiṣâdî*. 15 Jan. 1962. The same impression was felt at the Third Arab Oil Congress, ibid., 15 Oct. 1961.

depends—is an individuality which the economists' first task must be to bring to light.

Risk

The Arab world, as a whole, belongs to a semi-arid zone, and this, in spite of the varying types of climate due to a greater or lesser proximity to the sea and to temperate or tropical influences, has had a marked effect on the whole of its history until the present day. Its general background consists of agriculture and stock-breeding in equal proportions, with wide divergences of type such as that between the camel-breeder of the Sahara or the Nejd and the cereal-grower of the Syrian plains, and the peasant of the Nile region. For in the case of the herdsman, as in that of the tillage farmer, there is no *causality* about their system. The play of natural forces determines the growth of plants and beasts, while man's efforts are unable to introduce any noticeable variations.

Against this vast, insecure background the traditional favoured cities, Fez, Damascus, Cairo, Aleppo, Baghdad stand out in mercantile opulence and intellectual splendour. Speculative usury dwells here, as well as a moral code based on barter. Their liberal-minded citizens now bow to the scrupulous rules of Islam, and now display all the shrewdness of the money-making tradesman. In either case risk is equally shunned.

Islam dreads gambling, whereby capital bears fruit spontaneously. Growth, *numuw*, in Islamic opinion, implies a dangerous impurity which only the canonic levies, *zakât*, can redeem, and which in any case it seeks severely to restrict. In these old trading societies there is a constant swing between two attitudes: one, that of orthodox moralism, disapproves of everything in commerce which savours, however indirectly, of long-term transactions, in which exchange ceases to be immediate. For an immediate deal between individuals is that approved of by Islamic law. At the other extreme we have speculation. The practice of usury and stock-jobbing gain in extent what they have lost in orthodoxy. Hence so many moral conflicts and controversies within society, and perhaps also within individual souls. No doubt, as we have seen, conflicts and controversies have lost much of their dogmatic harshness since the day when Shaikh 'Abduh attempted to make his specious adjustments between the strict law and evident practical necessities. But it cannot be said that nothing of it still lingers in modern attitudes. Even today, one hears of certain bank accounts whose depositors never claim the interest due to them: which does not displease the banker!

In Egypt, as in Syria,[1] the mechanism of insurance has had great difficulty in establishing itself. A historic study of this institution would reveal in these countries a strange reluctance on the part of local capital to invest in it. And the reforms of 1957 in Cairo, of 1959 in Damascus found this sphere still mainly under the control of foreign companies. On the whole, the citizen becomes involved in it only through a series of State interventions, and almost against his will.[2] Even the authoritarian planning in which several of these countries are at present engaged is liable to be interpreted, as we shall see, as resulting from a traditional repudiation of risk.

One of these countries, it is true, remains the champion of liberalism. It is a land for big investments and great adventures. But what sort of investments and adventures? Let us examine a few cases. An enterprise, at its outset, appeals for foreign funds. It starts off with massive loans. Then gradually, with a sort of stealthy prudence, nationals take over. This was the case with an active aviation company in which Lebanese capital gained the majority only at the end of a long evolution, which in fact eliminated the risk factor. And this is true also of other firms in Beirut. They make use of credit, true, but according to highly individual methods.

To begin with, they borrow on the strength of their personal contacts, their lavish spending, their family connections. It might be said that in certain milieux, marriage is sometimes only a union between Stock Exchange reputations and financial hopes: hopes which are often realized, but may equally be disappointed. For sudden aggrandizement implies a rapid fall. Family triumphs may last twenty or thirty years. They are subject to the shocks of history, but they also take advantage of its opportunities. And with what scheming shrewdness! Everything is grist to their mill: relief fund for famine-stricken mountain-dwellers, the installation of the French mandate, its fall, war with Israel, the Suez crisis, the triangular operations necessitated by the breaking-off of official relations between certain countries, and so forth. Many fortunes seem to have been acquired miraculously, 'by parthenogenesis', as M. Teilhac wittily remarked.[3]

I was recently walking past a block of flats in al-Ḥamra, near Ra's-

[1] On the history of insurance in Egypt, *Ec. Bull.*, 1950, III, pp. 167–8 and Feb. 1959; *The Economic and Political Review*, Cairo, Dec. 1957.

[2] *E.F.S.P.A.*, July 1958 and Feb. 1959.

[3] Whence the subtle interconnection, in the way of life of these families, between gentilitial or religious traditionalism, and a broad cosmopolitan outlook in money matters.

Beirut. Some friends of mine wanted to know who owned it; they were shown a man in baggy trousers sitting on a little straw stool, such as market-gardeners once used. He was keeping watch over the door of his house. He could not get used to feeling himself a house-owner. When anyone tried to rent a flat he would reply: 'No, I'm in no hurry!' His new-found rich man's pride objected. He could not yet clearly realize that his houses would bring him in money. Glory, for the time being, was enough for him. But the prospective tenant would lose nothing by waiting. . . .

'Is the price real?' wonders one of my correspondents,[1] and adds this profound comment: 'A mentality of wealth has been created, which is as important as wealth itself.' We are here dealing with things at third-hand, or even more remotely. The symbol is evidently far more potent than the thing itself. And how far these speculators are from entrepreneurs' capitalism! By all the laws of logic, bankruptcy should be the penalty for such a state of things. But if there was one bankruptcy there would be fifty or a hundred. This society would disintegrate, chainwise.

It subsists, then, by virtue of its complexity, one might even say by virtue of its fragility, which involves so many human factors that economic laws can be defied. Through mercantilism it seeks that self-completion that other Arab societies seek through planning. Some of its businessmen may be mere speculators in the Western sense of the word. But their enterprise safeguards itself against failure by bonds of family and of faith, by national and international solidarity, so that finally the whole structure is maintained by its very inextricability. And this is all to the good, for it brings out many qualities of skill and loyalty. But will it last? Many people, in Lebanon itself, are asking themselves this question.

Things

Every human society has its material context, on which it acts, which acts upon it, and which consists, empirically, of *things*. The *Lisân al-'Arab*, usually so explicit, merely says: 'A thing, *al-shai'*, needs no explaining.' Unfortunately this is not the case. But avoiding philosophical speculation, let us confine ourselves to history.

In relation to present-day Arab societies, 'things' means, first, objects

[1] These are numerous, and my information is also based on much direct personal observation made in this hospitable country. I take this opportunity of saying how much my study of Lebanese society owes to my conversation with so many kind friends.

seen against that background of Nature that implies human effort, Nature with its privilege of spontaneity and fertility. And at the opposite pole, objects flowing into the 'under-developed' countries in the shape of industrial articles manufactured elsewhere. The opposition between the two aspects is immediately apparent: Nature on the one hand, manufacture on the other. And on both sides, the Arabs have long endured frustration. Geographically divided or confined, by forces which they repudiate, they do not fully exploit their own terrain. As regards manufacture, they still lag behind the foreigner; they are too often considered, by others, merely as 'markets', or sources of raw materials or labour reserves, or inversely as unemployed and underfed masses, dangerously liable to become subversive.

Moreover, at the present time, even on the theoretical plane, they have begun to reproach themselves for too subjective and emotional an attitude. In newspaper articles, in speeches, at congresses, they contrast that objectivity which is requisite and which they call *mauḍû'îya*, with their excess of sentiment. Are they justified in this? Is not their concept of objectivity somewhat over-mechanical, 'scientific' and abstract? Modern science and technique are not so arid as this. It was not by chance that the industrial revolution coincided in time and place with the Romantic revolution. Romanticism gives life to the 'inanimate object' which, meanwhile, the workshop transforms. Advanced techniques assume an intimate understanding of the laws of matter, and may be only another form of sensitivity towards things. Perhaps the industrial worker is really more 'natural' than the craftsman. . . .

An inventory of Mediterranean Islam at periods or in regions unaffected by machine civilization would certainly reveal its relative poverty in material things, both in Bedouin life,[1] where it is disconcerting to the ethnographer, and in city life;[2] the vigour of creative craftsmanship declined after the beginning of the fifteenth century.[3] Art, which is among the traditional components of these societies, and one of their liveliest ideals, disdains the figurative. It prefers the subtleties of the arabesque to the imitation of the concrete. A few months ago, at Khartoum, I admired some exquisitely carved figures—some in ivory, some in ebony—displayed on the pavement; but they were flat

[1] Cf. de Boucheman, *Matériel de vie bédouine en Syrie* (1934) and the catalogues undertaken by the excellent Maghrib review *Arts et Techniques*.

[2] Probably because the *floor* is the basis for Muslim furniture; importance of carpets. Cf. Henri Seyrig, *Syria*, 1957, pp. 373 ff. summarizing Kurt Erdmann's book.

[3] G. Wiet and L. Hautecoeur, *Les Mosquées du Caire*, vol. i, 1932, pp. 80 ff.

silhouettes, even though sculptured. The artist had conjured away their solidity as though he begrudged or feared his own creation. Even today, among the children who weave the tapestries of Ramses Wîṣâ Wâṣif, at Ḥarranîya near Cairo, the Copts are remarkable for lively representation, the Muslims for geometrical ornament. Is this pure coincidence or reversion to type? Let us leave that to psychologists to decide, and turn for a decisive argument to the language. This Arabic language is a gift from on high. Here, more than elsewhere, is Heidegger's saying justified, that language is 'the home of Being'. And the *Nahḍa*, the Arab renaissance, seeks rather to safeguard this hallowed classicism than to promote dialects. It thus proceeds inversely to the evolution of Romance languages. But in so doing it opts for signs rather than for things, and moreover seeks, by reinstating signs, to assert its hold on things. I shall return to this later.

Finally, the Arab countries have suffered from a long political inertia. Until the great transformations of our own day, they have endured a universe imposed by others, rather than taken active possession of their own universe.

In what may be called the traditional phase, the number, form and character of objects reflected one-sided power relationships. Egypt produces cotton, but gets its cotton goods from Manchester. Lebanon grows mulberry trees, but silks from Lyons have found their way into the wealthy homes of Fez and Aleppo and have become an integral part of luxurious furnishings and women's dress. As for metal, even today a walk through the *sûqs* of Baghdad convinces one that tools, vessels, appliances are almost always imported. Craftsmanship still persists in a few subsidiary items. America provides motors and derricks, while the native jeweller carves out his gold trinkets. Hardly a fair division! One has merely to glance into shop windows to realize what a flood of 'articles' and 'products' has poured over Arab society and indeed, to make a cruel pun, invested it.

At this stage, the productivity of the Arab world as regards objects is confined to the archaeological sphere. It tells of a past rich in marvels, but ruined. In the cities, the possessions of noble families are put up for auction. What could we not learn from them, if we could search their lists! The venerable treasures of harems and palaces are scattered to the four winds. A profitable trade has grown out of their exploitation, their shame. They end up in antique shops, in bazaars,[1] eventually in

[1] One could learn much from a history of Eastern bazaars, auctions, antique shops, or conversely of their big ready-made dress shops! In Egypt, the ruin

museums. Oriental objects, shut up in glass cases, cut off from all activity, all living purpose, have lost their energy for the time being. And the society that produced them, because it disdains or has been made to disdain a civilization based on things, is liable to become itself a mere thing to other societies.

It is fascinating to trace in each individual case the transformation which this new status imposes on the object itself. It has changed its rôle and its meaning, and so, very often, its matter and its form. An oil-press screw made of olive-wood becomes a lampstand. The carpet which is no longer a bed, but a hanging, is turned round, showing its pile. Stitches and colours are therefore altered. Low tables become covered with mother of pearl and incrustations. Pedlars hunt for old mosque lamps; these will not be used for prayer henceforward. Government departments set up to encourage native arts sought for a long time only to save craftsmanship by means of the *objet d'art.*[1] Having lost its function, the latter becomes more elaborate, pandering to the taste for a somewhat bogus orientalism: a monstrous denial of its use-value. And meanwhile Japanese sandals, Italian knitwear, ironmongery, trinkets and trash invade the solemn *qaiṣârîya-s.* Brides' trousseaux, the composition of which differs from place to place, from class to class, from period to period, would provide a useful historic documentation about the unequal balance maintained between native and imported goods; the conflict continues right into the heart of intimate family life.

This had been the case almost everywhere in the Arab world until well into the inter-war period. Integration into the world market, the growing uniformity of taste, the decadence of old manual trades make the phenomenon even more marked today. Meanwhile, however, the revolution of *homo faber* is taking place, or rather striving to take place, in the East. And at the same time the Arabs have rediscovered Nature, thanks to their émigré poets. But had they ever lost Nature? And when? Let us look once more at the *Lisân al-'Arab*. Whereas the words *physis*, 'nature', in Greek and *natura* in Latin from the days of the earliest philosophical speculation bore roughly the whole of the meanings which we give them today, our fourteenth-century lexicographer gives no

of the upper classes flooded the market, in '59, with such a quantity of untaxable materials that the State was forced to regulate or proscribe the immemorial auctions, bargain sales—indeed bargaining in general.

[1] This disastrous and hopeless trend coincides with the decadence of the colonial system in the Arab East and in the Maghrib, and is closely paralleled by an equally indefensible tendency towards autarchy.

such meanings for the word *ṭabî'a*. Let us analyse the term. *Physis, natura* refer etymologically to the act of 'birth', or 'begetting'.[1] On the contrary *ṭabî'a* is related to a root *ṭ.b.'*. 'to print', 'inform'. *Ṭabî'a* is the 'character' conferred by the divine Form-giver. We are far from the meaning which Rîḥânî gives to the word in his poetry, clothing it with a cosmic breadth that reminds one somewhat of Lucretius.

In the 'thirties of this century, another phase, far more concrete, began: that of manufacture. I should place its actual outset at the first measures in defence of the home market, decreed almost simultaneously by countries as different as Egypt, Lebanon and Syria.[2] From that moment, and increasingly thereafter, the East set out to be its own manufacturer. Of textiles, of course, in the first place. It is true that at Maḥalla al-Kubrâ as well as at Damascus industrial development was fulfilling an old tradition of craftsmanship. The technical and psychological transformations involved have unfortunately not been studied in detail, so far as I know. Our knowledge of the East has not reached this stage. However, we can distinguish the sequence of types. The Egyptians, in the inter-war period, had already begun to follow and assimilate the lessons of Italian experts in building and (more interesting to us) in furnishing. The two are obviously linked, moreover; and the typical object of the period is no longer the traditional carpet but the heavily gilded console from Fîshâwî, which modern taste has relegated to the Sudan, Kuwait and Saudi Arabia. The third type of development is that which starts from small-scale workshops; thus at Sinn al-Fîl, near Beirut, there is a lift factory which began as a small repair shop. Here, as elsewhere, the transition from craftsmanship to industrial enterprise is promisingly fertile. And finally, more radical and highly organized methods are now being used in Egypt for assembling cars and aircraft and even for manufacturing engines. All planners dream of large-scale metallurgical industry. If we compare today the list of products of the Egyptian Federation of Industry, published annually, with the pre-war customs lists, we perceive that imported and manufactured articles tend to balance one another. This is a special case; intention exceeds achievement, maybe, but the evolution is undeniable.

Furthermore, the auctions that take place in Cairo today (particularly since the confiscation of the royal possessions) attract a mainly local clientele. Wealthy Arab bourgeois are now interested not merely in furniture but in bibelots, in collectors' pieces. And in this field they

[1] Lalande, *Vocabulary*.

[2] Burhân al-Dajânî, *al-Iqtiṣâd al-'arabî*, Beirut, 1958, p. 116.

have long since left behind the Turkish taste in mirrors, glassware and clocks: that species of 'metaphysical furnishing' in which a subtle but old-fashioned taste delighted. Today's taste in furniture cannot dissociate its function from its aspect. Young couples insist on having their double bed, their dining-room suite, their radio set, their pictures on the wall. And the East has even begun to take pride in its bazaars! A fair number of these are to be found in the Muskî, in Cairo, an old-world district much frequented by tourists and hitherto parasitical. In this respect it could only prove an embarrassment to town-planners longing for a clean sweep, and to the civic ambition for self-sufficiency. But once the decision to demolish it had been taken, public opinion rebelled and had this decision revoked. What a contrast between so mature an attitude and the iconoclastic vandalism denounced, a generation ago, by the Committee for Historic Monuments in Cairo! Note that in the case of the Muskî, the reaction came not from a committee of aesthetes or professors but from humble people, who appreciated the benefits of the tourist trade, of course, but, equally, the charm of ancient things and buildings.[1]

As for present-day Arab artists, a delight in things has, for most of them, replaced abstract inspiration. They have moved to the opposite pole of aesthetic feeling.[2] Side by side with literary realism, there is a trend towards representation in painting—too much so, sometimes, for our taste. For the West has meanwhile tired of the representational, and veered towards abstraction, except in the case of surrealist 'objects'. Another equally characteristic thing: at Cairo, at Beirut, at Damascus ethnographical collections are being made. Research is already being actively undertaken: not merely on folklore—and the Arabs have always cherished their verbal heritage—but also concerning concrete objects, specimens. There is something quite unprecedented about the study being made by Sa'd al-Khâdim for instance, of the relations between art and social education, based on children's drawings and the spontaneous self-expression of the people. It is the latest sign, and a far-reaching one. . . .[3]

Things, then, have changed their meaning for the Arabs in the space of one or two generations. And this by the help of that increasingly

[1] Reports in the Egyptian weeklies.

[2] Cf. W. Worringer, 'Abstraction et co-naissance', *Le Musée de Poche*, nos. 1 and 2, 1959. I shall study this important aspect in greater detail presently.

[3] Sa'd al-Khâdim, *Dirâsât fî taṭawwur rusûm al-aṭfâl*, Cairo, 1953, and his other writings on popular culture, the artistic re-education of youth, manual experience and its educative effects, popular universities (1953 to 1959).

keen struggle between their initiative, their reconquest of self on the one hand and dependence, '*reification*', on the other. This has only been achieved at the cost of a tremendous expense of spirit. And this outpouring, in excess of any plan and sometimes even of efficiency, has modified the system that governed their attitudes, their concepts and their actions.

Number

For more than a century, quantity in its most rapacious form—silk manufacturers' investment in Lebanon, capitalist strategy around the Canal, the Ottoman debt, the Egyptian debt—had invaded the East. This aspect, which has become familiar ever since the end of the war through oil deals, discussions about I.B.R.D. loans, U.N.O. assessments etc., is increasingly resented. For several generations these countries have had quantity imposed upon them, instead of producing it, and imposed by a Western world in its rising phase of large-scale manufacture and market seizure.

Consider for instance the importance of the cotton crop in Egypt's history over the last sixty years, the almost total alteration it has caused to the physical and mental character of the country. For a long time, as if still under the rule of their Pharaohs, the Egyptians have dug canals, shifted earth, levelled the ground, turned the wheels of irrigatory machines for the benefit of distant factories. Suddenly they have had to renounce that trust in Nature that came to them from the beneficent annual flood. They were forced, so to speak, to reconvert themselves in terms of an economy that devoured labour so greedily that it seemed, round about 1910, that Egypt might run short of man-power. Today, on the contrary, her huge unemployment figures disturb the Eastern statesman and, consequently, the foreign economist. Quantity takes its paradoxical revenge. The Western sorcerer's-apprentice has called forth, from below him and in opposition to him, *Eastern quantity*.

In the first place this takes the shape of a demographic increase spurred on by the progress of hygiene. Egypt has 29 million inhabitants today. Whence a terrible degree of unemployment, of course. But how can we avoid seeing in it an answer of a certain type to the challenge of the foreigner? True, it does not take place at the level of economic conflict or technical competition; but at that of a sheer vitality that rejects any sort of control or forethought. Proudly, these countries glory in their new dimensions. Every census, every declaration, every newspaper article boasts of the increase. For instance, the fact that in

Cairo alone 744,000 ration cards have been issued, entitling their holders to over 2 million *oques* of sugar a month, if their means allow. The capital city consumes £E10,000,000 of tea and coffee per annum. Education, too, has developed a quantitative trend. And not only in primary schools, but at University level. Every year the Higher Inter-University Council decides that so many thousands of students will be admitted to the four universities. In 1960, the number of pupils attending primary schools was 2 million, secondary schools over 200,000; at university level (including teachers' training) and at that of 'higher education' the numbers were 105,000 and 5,000 respectively. This is not the moment to ask whether this impulse is lacking in depth. One feels that in the realm of culture, despite its past tradition of esotericism and coteries, the East has opted for quantity.[1] Provisionally, or so it thinks: time will do the rest. But may it not be falling into a trap? No matter; the break with tradition is so violent that we cannot underestimate its manifestations. The authorities are decidedly turning away from the egotistic man-of-letters confined within his coterie, *ahl al-khâṣṣa*, and the intellectual minority concerned with an exceptional type of culture, in favour of the masses. Hence so many congresses about the expansion of compulsory (*ilzâmî*) education, the abolition of illiteracy, etc.

In every sphere a similar passion for enumeration is displayed. It gives the Arabs an intoxicating sense of modernity. Statistics are the orison of the contemporary world. . . .

Here are some characteristic examples. The United Nations had proposed to the Egyptian administration to take a census of the population in 1957. This could not be done, for various reasons; for one thing because the operation would require the collaboration of 30,000 agents or experts. But a sum of £E2,500,000 was spent on spreading amongst the public 'an awareness of statistics',[2] to borrow a remarkable expression from one of their newspapers. Institutes and journals of statistics flourish everywhere. Beirut alone boasts two or three of them. It would require a detailed study, which we lack, to explain how the Arab student, in spite of his old ethical prejudice against probability, which implies risk, has taken up this branch of learning. Doubtless from the angle of mathematical abstraction: here he feels at home. Compu-

[1] At which Georges Ḥinain protests in a shrewd but paradoxical editorial of the *Bourse égyptienne*, July 1958.

[2] *Bourse égyptienne*, 17 July 1958; various congresses of Arab statisticians, or with a view to creating Arab statistics, notably in Cairo in 1943, 1955 etc.

tation, the calculation of averages, represent one way of exorcizing chance, of rediscovering the *logos*.

The time is long past when, describing Damascus, a commentator on the Koran, Shaikh al-Qâsimî, depicted dozens of corporations, each with its individual character and doubtless, too, with its religious qualification![1] The time is long past when Kurd 'Alî, again at Damascus, industriously strove to interpret the teaching of places, people and customs according to the old style of the *Khiṭaṭ*. Today we find Shafîq Akhras describing, with the aid of graphs, the market at Damascus: price fluctuations, according to the harvest in the Ghûṭa and the international exchange, movement of funds, development of plans. Indeed, there is a fruitful comparison to be made between the successive aspects of the Damascus market as shown in the widely divergent studies of al-Qâsimî, Kurd 'Alî and Shafîq Akhras. Is it the same reality, seen in turn by a traditional shaikh, a nationalistic scholar and a Western-trained economist? Or has the reality itself changed?

About 1900, in spite of the growing menace of impending events, and in spite of the Arabs' subjection (indirect and disguised, indeed) to foreign industry, it was still possible to study life in Damascus in terms of the old oppositions—between morality and trade, between faith and worldliness—the whole thing being resolved and redeemed by a sense of glorious citizenship. In the 'thirties this all formed part of the twofold conflict between traditionalism and modernity, emancipation and dependence. Today, the figures that express and control quantity act as a brake on national passions and, at the same time, provide the stake for which they play. The Arab countries expect these figures to supply direction and compensation, as well as expression, for the outburst of feeling, the expansive surge of heart and speech that is now agitating them. They find, or seek to find, in growth—economic if possible, and meanwhile demographic—a concrete moral code whose requirements are superadded or opposed, with varying degrees of opportuneness, to those of sentiment.

A census is no small thing in Arab countries.[2] It is undertaken seriously, as a task, and yet lightheartedly, like a game; it combines an exercise of new capacities with the smiling humility of old days. Iraq has devoted a whole volume[3] to its 1957 census: a highly instructive document for us!

[1] *Qâmûs al-Ṣanâ'i'* published in 2 vols., Paris, 1961.
[2] Cf. Aḥmad Ajdar, *Statistiques économiques et sociales*, 1961.
[3] *'Amalîya al-Tasjîl al-'âmm li-sanati 1957*, Baghdad, 1958.

The census starts one fine day at four in the morning in all urban centres. Here and there we note characteristic incidents. Students and teachers, the new lettered class, go hither and thither knocking at doors. 'What is your profession?' 'Journalist: *ṣaḥâfî*'—herald of new types of information and enthusiasm. Then, next door, the old tanner, *dabbâgh*, the *fallâḥ*, dating from Sumerian days, and his neighbour the plumber or radio engineer, or the 'town-planning engineer', *muhandis ma'mârî*.

A knock at the door: 'What is your profession?' 'Census-taker.' 'What is a census-taker?' 'Somebody who knocks at people's doors at four in the morning.' 'And what is his professional status?' 'A salaried official without a salary.' Another anecdote: 'How many rooms have you got in your house?' 'Wait a minute while I go up and count them!' Or again: 'How old are you?' 'Sixty.' 'And your wife?' 'Forty.' 'How many years have you been married?' 'Forty.' Or else: 'What is your profession?' '*Khabîr bi'l-biṭâla*, an expert in unemployment.' 'Your wife's profession?' 'An expert in extravagance.' 'Your mother-in-law's?' 'An expert at mischief-making.'[1]

The census-taker finds it hard to refuse hospitality in the houses he visits; he must accept a few eggs, at least! And what a problem learning all the names! Those of the older generation tend to be forgotten; they can always be replaced by imams' names. Many Kâẓims and Ḥusains of course. But in the latest generation, a good many Nassers. . . .

As a conclusion to the census, the Minister of the time, Arkân al-'Abbâdî, draws a lesson.[2] He points out the importance of such an operation in such a society: its didactic aspect, its moral and ethical aspect. Society is learning to know itself, to reconsider itself: thereby scandalizing many by its break with the old Semitic tradition which held it sinful to count a flock, and *a fortiori* human beings. And finally there is the delight, not only in accomplishing a task but in going forward, and, as the Director of Statistics has said, providing a concrete foundation (*asâsan kunkritîyan*) for the future enterprises of the State. Note the neologism; the undertaking itself was surely without precedent!

In any case, this new-found zeal with which the Arabs count, measure, and consider things in terms of quantity, betrays a somewhat superficial rationalism, the attraction of what is borrowed from abroad. But we must recognize something else in it. Number has its metaphysical aspect. To establish, or re-establish, a hold over things and beings, means renewing contact with certain old logical and theological attitudes,

[1] Ibid., p. 304. [2] Ibid., p. 338.

which contain the secret of a fruitful optimism. True, the Eastern world has not yet sought to reinstate Reason at the heart of the Universe through the progress of experimental science and reliance on practical methods. But it is directly involved in these ambitions, which are those of the more highly developed countries. This was inevitable. And one cannot wonder at the zeal with which, in its effort to restore its own self-mastery, it counts and measures itself, which is really another way of playing with figures and creating a universe out of them, as arithmetical speculation once strove to do.

Hence certain instructive excesses.

The arid abstraction of numbers has now dared to attack the Arabic language itself. A Syrian professor of my acquaintance has devoted a thick volume to reckoning the frequency indices of words, not in the spoken language, which would have been useful, nor in the Classical language, which would have been precious, but in the language of the handbooks used in five Eastern countries. What boundless energy![1] We recognize it, too, in many pedagogical experiments. When we glance through one of those educational journals which are so numerous and so meticulous, when we study some of these first attempts at an Arab sociology written by Arabs, we are struck by this exaggerated tendency to consider everything in terms of quantity. Study implies a questionnaire, and a question means a calculation. This is the result of an ill-digested 'economism', too readily satisfied with formulae, too enamoured of statistics in the name of realism and accuracy. We can trace a tendency to the old casuistic cult of abstractions in this passion for numbers, in so far as it is justified neither by the requirements of its subject-matter nor the reliability of its information.

Herein there lies an undoubted danger. The cult of numbers may be a disastrous sequel to the self-examination of these countries. It can lead at the very least to 'unauthenticity', loss of personality. This obsession with quantity, which some dread, is denounced by others as leading to '*reification*'; to this may contribute forces from without and from within. From without, whatever under one form or another tends to perpetuate the colonial era; from within, an over-hasty zeal assimilating only the *methods* of others. A paradoxical accumulation of evils, against which the Arabs, in their striving towards a future, must arm themselves by analysis and by action.

[1] Discussed, with horror and admiration, by R. Blachère, *Arabica*, 1954, p. 238.

A General View

Let us briefly gather together, despite the uncertainties of such a synthesis, the elements successively considered in this chapter. Broadly, they sketch the evolution of basic attitudes. The Arab world, seeking emancipation, strives to create an economy, both because it sees that this is crucial for independence and because it hopes by this means to reach the level of its former overlords. To do this it must disturb much of its old stability. The relations between the individual, society and nature cannot remain what they were at the traditional stage, nor what religion would have them be. Henceforward the attempt is made to master the laws that govern industrial phenomena. In the second place, the element of risk and hazard must be accepted, for it is the common ground of the capitalist game, of enterprise and of statistics. Meanwhile, mastery over things is sought, through the intermediary of manufacture, and over the world of number. All this more or less successfully achieved, more or less effective, more or less clearly conceived according to the group and the individual, but everywhere discernible, a conscious aim, a living force.

But the whole thing, of course, could not take place without meeting resistance from old-established attitudes, nor without the active persistence of inherited tendencies under the new dress. There is open controversy between the past and the present, but even more frequently there are subtle transactions and compromises, disclosing or concealing a complex game; none the less, the whole thing results in a tremendous alteration. An Egyptian critic, perhaps the most philosophical of them all, wrote in his recent book on the problems of modern art: 'The old distinction we were taught between style and substance has disappeared, for our generation has witnessed something amazing—essence has intermingled with object: *ikhtalaṭat al-dhât bi'l-mauḍû'*.'[1] It is more than the interaction of subject and object; another interaction is taking place between the essence and its concrete manifestations, between ideal and action, between the wish to be and the wish to make. The West, in this conflict, plays the dual rôle of model and foil.

But let us not anticipate the developments which are to follow. For the moment we are back at the initial antitheses suggested to me by the markets of Baghdad, and which much of the physical or moral scene of the contemporary Arab world recalls. Symbol or reality? Analysis, after this preliminary approach, may perhaps be able to follow more closely their many-sided exchange.

[1] Muḥammad Mandûr, *Qaḍâyâ jadîda fî'l-adab al-ḥadîth*, Beirut, n.d., p. 8.

3. Will the veil be worn for many years more? Women in the *sûqs*. Iraq.

4. Beirut: news with a new look.

5. Villagers cheering agrarian reform. El Minya region, Egypt.

6. Young people with political views: a procession in Iraq.

CHAPTER IV

The Problem of Finance

As the Colonial phase of Arab history draws to an end, it becomes obvious that the road travelled together by dependent and dominant partners has not led to the same issue for both. They had been moving at a widely different pace. The Arabs had been dependent because the rhythm of their life, mechanically accelerated in some respects—a hackneyed theme today in studies on the 'social implications' of technical progress—had on the whole slowed down, grown sluggish. The ruthless companionship which had begun in the days of the steam engine is ending, for the former colonist, in the period of the atomic pile. The former colony, however, has only advanced from the stage of human or animal motor power to that of imported machinery. Egypt, which has taken the lead in this sphere, has barely begun to make use of its own foundries, factories and installations.[1] Emancipation, we must repeat, came to the Arabs through the play of non-economic forces. Up to the present their linguistic and demographic revolution has provided their principal weapons.

True, many of them now reject these ambiguous forces. Above all, the people of these newly liberated countries find language and emotion of little help when they are faced with the oppressive power of money and the urgent need for money. Thought and poetry cannot be converted into capital. In Arab lands, capital is weak and artificial, and remains so

[1] The fear of a widening gap between developed countries and ex-dependent countries has given rise to a great deal of political, economic and sociological writing ever since the summer of 1959; this has been abundantly quoted by newspapers and in speeches on international occasions. Is this a well planned campaign, or a pause in the tension between the two blocs? We need not only a sociological study of 'orientalism', but also one of the world attitudes towards the East, and of the East itself in relation to these attitudes and towards itself....

as long as demographic luxuriance hinders the growth of individual income.[1] And as in systems where social inequality is gross any talk of averages is a euphemism, the national reformer, who is aware of this, is the more distressed by it. And just because the Arab East adheres to classic economic theories, its more lucid minds are liable to despair at the immensity of the effort required.

Promises and Threats

Investment must be considered as the modern form of fate. A country such as Egypt ought to increase its resources to the same extent as the most highly developed countries, merely in order to maintain its humble standard of living: that is to say, it should invest far more of its national income than the 10 per cent proposed by France, for instance, and should also allot other available funds in order to liquidate illiteracy, develop social hygiene, etc. Egypt is endeavouring to do this, after a fashion. Between 1952 and 1957 the savings made available rose to £E460 million or £E115 million per year out of a national revenue of c. £E900 million. The Government plans to raise it, by 1978, to £E3,264m., namely an individual promotion of £E40–60[2] and possibly even more. Iraq is equally ambitious. The official brochure published in 1961 on the occasion of the third year of revolutionary power, announced that the Plan, proposing a total annual growth of 7 to 9 per cent, would reach an investment level of 22 per cent, including, it is true, oil dues. At the end of this five-year period the total invested would be not less than 550 million dinars.[3]

Despite these optimistic views, it must be admitted that apart from oil rights and the anticipated profits from the Canal, part of the rôle traditionally ascribed to savings is played in these countries by foreign finance. This involves colossal risks. Now, at the end of the colonial phase, the former dependants are themselves seeking some of those centrifugal investments which had been thought of as the ultimate form of capitalism. This paradoxical return may cause justifiable anxiety, while necessitating a revision of theory. Of course international organizations like the I.B.R.D. to which we owe some good preliminary studies

[1] Dr. Nazîh Aḥmad Ḍaif stresses the natural connection between economic planning and calculations of national and individual income. His dissertation on planning is entirely taken up with an exposé of the method of 'keeping the nation's accounts'; *Rasâ'il* of the Egyptian Planning Committee, no. 7, p. 1.

[2] Shafîq Akhras, 'The doubling of the national revenue of the U.A.R. in 10, 15 or 20 years?' *E.F.S.P.A.*, 2nd year, no. 18.

[3] *Thaura 14 Tammûz*, Baghdad, 1962, p. 39.

on Iraq, Jordan and Syria,[1] do not expose their clients to the same political risks as did the Ottoman debt or the Suez Canal Company, 'universal' though the latter called itself. But a new country needs a good deal of idealism to believe that credits can be so disinterested as not to involve undesirable short- or long-term influences. Point Four, disdaining even the cloak of internationalism, has been subject to a campaign of bitter opposition. French and British banks and firms in Egypt have paid dearly for the connection which the people of the Arab world, with considerable justification, assume to exist between all foreign activity, even when it is disinterested (scientific research) and still more when it is lucrative, and the colonialism, the *isti'mâr* which they detest. . . .

Considered squarely, the need for capital, in the present phase of these countries, may well result from constructive designs and not, as formerly, from financial dilapidation. It represents none the less the same position of inferiority. And this involves strategic dependence today, as once it involved colonial dependence.

The susceptibility of a country like Egypt can be understood when we gauge how deeply foreign credit had penetrated into rural life.[2] Here, the agrarian context is all-important. It entirely dominates the active economy of the country. Now for a long time the fellahs were encumbered with debts to foreign banks. So much so that in 1907, landed estates valued at 120 million guineas owed 20 million, namely one-sixth of their value. Since then the situation has grown healthier. But in spite of all efforts made, the fellahs have never really become solvent. The substitution of a capitalism with Egyptian majority has not brought about the creative results that might have been expected, but has favoured speculation. For instance, an agricultural branch founded by the National Bank of Egypt in 1902 was liquidated in 1932. It was then seen that every £5 share had made a profit of £8. Foreign customs have been adopted. . . .

Indeed, the excessive cost of rent is perhaps, in the traditional context, the only factor capable of mobilizing capital, short of the drastic methods used by the Egyptian Revolution since 1952. As we know, this endeavoured to release the capital which was entirely sunk in land, so that the peasant's field was more of a symbol than a reality. The rent of a *feddan* of land rose, in 1953, to £E50 per annum, almost the entire revenue from that same *feddan*. Why did the fellah cling to it?

[1] Published at Johns Hopkins, Baltimore, U.S.A., in 1952, 1955 and 1957 respectively.

[2] Ibrâhîm 'Âmir, *al-Arḍ wa'l-fallâḥ*, Cairo, 1957, pp. 70 ff.

Not to live, in the economic sense of the word; merely to exist! An admirable symbol, but a terrifying economic state.

I have already mentioned the theses of M. Teilhac,[1] which are echoed in M. Gannagé's book.[2] According to Gannagé's researches, the economy of the Middle East suffers from deep-seated vices. It is inhuman, through the disproportion between the growth of resources and that of the population, and through the relative inferiority of its social equipment. Moreover it is patently crippled and disintegrated by its dependence, to a large extent, on foreign finance: oil concessions in the South East, speculation and three-cornered deals on the Mediterranean seaboard, the bondage of single-crop agriculture in Egypt, and so on.

Recourse to the Unknown Factor of the East.

What, then, is the Arab world to do? It must recover its own individuality. Gannagé's theses have encountered significant opposition. They have been criticized by a Syrian economist not so much for their matter as for their point of view.[3] This, it is said, does not ascribe sufficient importance to Arabism. It is superimposed on, rather than integrated with, the reality described, which at the present time is in a state of upheaval through moral, as well as material, conflict. This emotional tone pervades all Arab interpretations. But under the vehemence of the controversialist we should recognize a sure sense of this X, the unknown factor in Eastern life.[4]

As long as ten years ago, the U.N.O. assessed at 1,300 million dollars the total amount required to raise the economy of the Middle East by 2 per cent per annum. Using somewhat formidable methods, U.N.O. reckoned the existing reserves at 540 million: whence a deficit of 760 million.[5] Now, since these calculations, a good many things have happened in these countries, apart from political revolution: official statements boast of important developments, social as well as material, accumulating figures and proclaiming triumphs at an ever-increasing

[1] 'Le Moyen-Orient', *Cahiers de l'I.S.E.A.*, Paris, 1957, and unpublished lectures.

[2] E. Gannagé, *Croissance économique et structure au Moyen-Orient*, Paris, 1958. A later book by E. Teilhac is *Economie politique pour les Arabes*, 1960.

[3] Dr. Hishâm Mutawallî, 'A propos d'un livre récent', *E.S.P.S.A.*, March 1959, pp. 68 ff.

[4] H. A. R. Gibb has used the expression *Factor X* in a different sense: cf. *The Middle East in Transition*, W. Laqueur ed., 1958.

[5] Gannagé, op. cit. pp. 47 ff.

rate. Optimism grows rapturous over the Iraqi Development Weeks,[1] and in the speeches, folders and brochures issued by the Production Council and the Services Council, referring to the progress of planning in the two provinces of the U.A.R.[2] If outside credit is refused, strange upheavals are provoked in international law, and a crisis in political relations; this was evident in 1956. On every plane, none the less, projects are being realized: hydraulic, industrial, cultural. Bankers note with surprise that finances do not collapse, nor does the dynamic impulse slacken.[3] I need not point out here what restrictions and what tensions are the price paid for this achievement.

These nations, according to all the laws of common sense, should—except for oil landlords such as Kuwait and Saudi Arabia—be struggling against appalling difficulties due both to their lack of technical preparation and their rate of population increase. However, they are tackling these difficulties with an almost ostentatious confidence. How is the anomaly to be explained? By our underestimation of local resources or the extent of foreign aid? Rather by our failure to recognize factors which are not strictly economic ones, and which at this phase of development and in this political context undoubtedly deserve more attention than they are usually granted by orthodox observers. My approach, which is not that of an economist, will find no difficulty in admitting this sort of puzzle as a fundamental factor. We may recall the surprise of an international expert invited to make a study of finance in Lebanon who, finding prosperity where strict analysis would have expected destitution or discomfiture, advised this subtle Mediterranean people to go on doing what they had done hitherto. But what? On this, the expert's special knowledge was able to shed no light.

I do not wish to imply that the irrational or the inexpressible should be erected into a system. On the contrary, the well-being of these

[1] Which published illustrated reports in Arabic, English and French.

[2] This literature includes, naturally, propaganda pamphlets, but also popular informative booklets (cf. *Taṭawwur al-intâj al-ṣinâ'î wa'l-zirâ'î fî 'ashr sanawât*); theses such as those published by the Planning Committee, which I have been kindly allowed to see; a few detailed studies such as that of Dr. Marei on agrarian reform and an anonymous one on industrialization: finally the *Kitâb al-Sanawî* on Egypt.

[3] Cf. for instance the report on 'The Situation in Egypt' in the *Revue économique trimestrielle* of the Belgian and International Bank in Egypt, Oct. 1958. Useful historical study of former stages of investment in Egypt in *Ec. Bull.*, 1956, ix, 310. Ḥusain Khallâf, 'Financing Development in Egypt' and Henry Tadros, 'Recent Developments of Egypt's Balance of Payments', vols. 1955 and 1957 respectively of *Middle East Economic Papers*, Beirut. More recently, statements in the press by Dr. al-Qaisûnî and in the *Kitâb al-Sanawî*.

countries depends in many respects on logical reconstruction. But the analysis of present difficulties should lead not to the use of cure-all remedies drawn from a store of international experience and economic doctrine, but to the quest for an individual way of life. In this matter as in every other category of life in the Arab East, the primordial duty is to 'know oneself'. This was impressed on his Egyptian listeners by A. Piatier in two lectures given in 1956.[1] He showed that in spite of classical theories they must be hopeful and enterprising and reject the notion of *homo economicus*; this notion inevitably shocks the sociologist by its excessive arbitrariness, its neglect of geographical, historical and psychological elements which play a decisive rôle. 'The psychological tone of a nation is its most precious possession.' What distinguishes the 'developed' from the 'underdeveloped' nation is its capacity to 'respond'.

Now this capacity, derived both from the splendours of their past history and the fresh energy of today, is one that the Arabs possess to a high degree. Their economic impetus, according to such a view, would merely be the transposed continuation of the impetus by which, in frequently surprising ways, they have been recovering their national personality. Only, the secret of failure or success lies in the accuracy of the transposition. Many of their potentialities, which may serve either for creation or for evasion, must now be turned in a direction which ten years ago could not have been foreseen. Hence the vital necessity, for them, of analysis and revision. This is indeed a sort of revolution.

Creation of Capital in the Arab World

On a question of such prime importance in professional eyes as that of the creation of capital, numerically precise data are lacking. There is no really substantial study.[2] We are still at the stage of enquiries based on 'outward signs' and on interviews, which are too apt to interpret interpretations! However, the risk is not prohibitive for a study which is chiefly attentive to evolutions, movements and attitudes.

Such a study will observe a torrential flow of currency from Iraq, Saudi Arabia and the emirates of the Persian Gulf to Lebanon in the shape of real-estate investments or ostentatious consumption: to Cairo,

[1] A Piatier, '*Inégalités économiques et politiques du développement à l'échelon régional et à l'échelle mondiale*', S.I.P. (Société Indigène de Prévoyance) Press, Cairo, 1956.

[2] In spite of valuable scientific efforts, such as those of economists at the American University at Beirut. Meanwhile there is much to be got from the specialist press. A remarkable historical account of Egyptian finance has been given by Dr. Hishâm Mutawallî.

in that of buildings on the left bank of the Nile: and more or less everywhere, as salaries, gifts and influences. Correspondingly the oil concessions, whence the flow issues, provide the Arab world with ready money and financial power. One should trace the course of the latter and its repercussions, sometimes unforeseen, sometimes only too well foreseen. . . . A partial resumption of the I.P.C.[1] concessions, a revision of percentages on the product, an appeal for wider competition involving the inventive M. Mattei and Japanese initiative, have enabled the Arabs to derive greater profit from these resources, providentially emanating from the depths of their soil. Foreign aid and, henceforward, the income from the Canal, provide two other sources of currency.

A second phenomenon, less closely linked to geography, concerns the transference of wealth from the land and is related to the fate of a class of great land-owners, as a result of agrarian reforms in Egypt (1952), in Syria (1958) and in Iraq (1958). The object of these reforms was twofold: to exploit potentialities which had lain dormant for ages owing to routine methods of agriculture, and to liberate the peasant. This second aspect, although the more radical, will not concern us for the moment. As regards the mobilization of land-capital, it appears, in the country which first embarked on this course, Egypt, that the effective restriction of estates and the equally decisive restriction of rents have begun to attract a proportion of investments to industry. The participation of private capital is thus anticipated to a considerable extent by the Egyptian programme, and it has formed the theme of official declarations tending to encourage it, if not to provoke it.[2] It is too soon to see whether in Syria and Iraq the same evolution is taking place. In the latter country a certain section of the landed patriciate had already undertaken reconversion. In 1958, in the Baghdad market, eight or ten millionaires were quoted, some of whom bore ancient names: Damirjî, Qudairî, Shabîbî. In Egypt, too, these transferences from the country to the towns had taken place so markedly that the Government recently expressed anxiety about the same ruinous tendency to camouflage investment in rentable buildings, which is rife in Lebanon.

[1] Iraq Petroleum Company.

[2] Declaration by Nasser at the opening of textile mills at Ḥaush Blass in Syria, March 24, 1959; a regular rehabilitation of private capital combined with an appeal for 'co-operative socialism'. Another conciliatory venture: the conference of the M.I.D.E.C. held in Cairo, 15–17 Nov. 1959. Note, too, the relative moderation of Arab delegates to the Oil Congress held in Alexandria (1961). And meanwhile Egypt's official attitude was stiffening.

A third sort of assets goes back to the occupation of the Allied Armies. The considerable sums they spent provided a store of wealth that proved a godsend to speculators. In the same context one must consider the part played by middlemen, forwarding agencies, brokers and factors, mercantilism in general, where old commercial habits, rooted in the tradition of the city, are competing with ever less efficiency against the new trends (Aleppo, Damascus, etc.), and where active foreign deals form the king-post of the nation's economy, and as it were the financial counterpart to a sentimental cult of the West (Lebanon).

How are these different contributions interrelated? This is where we need figures. Now according to a recent publication of the Arab League, the present possibilities of documentation leave much to be desired. Burhân al-Dajânî, grouping the data collected on the occasion of a Congress of Chambers of Commerce, complains of the unreliability of these statistics.[1] On this point there is considerable inequality between various countries. In some, immaturity of method is accompanied by excessive propaganda. In others, on the contrary, a serious information service is developing.

Let us glance at the booklet by Dr. Fénelon on Iraq's national revenue.[2] The author is one of those experts who formerly inspired the Development Board. The latter, almost extra-territorial to the country, had been conceived of as a machine to transform into equipment part of the income from the oil wells. A *de facto* divorce between material equipment and its human aspects seems to have been one of the deeper causes of the Iraqi revolution. None the less an important piece of work was achieved. With great firmness, the report examines first certain economic and social indices: for instance the consumption of electricity. If the export of petroleum rose, in Iraq, from 6 million tons in 1950 to 29 millions in 1956, with all the refunds ensuing therefrom, the total of other exports only rose to 13 million dinars at the same date. This is a more or less constant feature in these countries: the relative weakness of imports and exports in relation to the national revenue. In Iraq, this revenue was estimated in 1956 at 303 million Iraqi dinars. Note that in 1956 the Development Board alone invested 45 million dinars, and this quite apart from all administrative and private investments, in relation to a total revenue reckoned at 303 million: a huge percentage.

No one is at present in a position to check these figures, to which we may be allowed to prefer the following disillusioned observation,

[1] Burhân al-Dajânî, op. cit., introduction.

[2] One of the most reliable of the published works at our disposal.

taken from the report of other authorities in another country. 'The proportion of savings in this country is very scanty on account of the feeble percentage of the annual revenue. . . .' 'Most of the development projects are shunned by individuals either because they involve many risks and few benefits, from the point of view of exploitation, or because they require the mobilization of a great deal of capital for a long term.'[1]

This simple phrase implies two or three noteworthy facts. First, the old dislike of risk: this is deeply rooted in Arab ethics. How it can be combined, in these merchants' mentality, with a love of gambling, only a subtle historical analysis would allow one to discern. Then the mistrust felt for long-term tying-up of capital. For instance, a tradesman of Aleppo,[2] such as could still be found between the two wars, would keep part of his fortune invested in land, thus bordering on the landlord class. He would multiply the rest through exchange, at a rate that grew intenser in proportion to his prosperity. He operated somewhat like the nimble needle of an embroideress on the canvas of city life. His success was related to the density of his relationships. This type of activity no longer corresponds to modern times. But the same mentality persists. That is why, according to a Syrian economist, the State must supplement the insufficiency of individuals. State action is necessary here, not from deliberate theoretic choice, but to make up for the deficiencies of the inherited structure of society.

In a recent publication by the Miṣr Bank a significant article is devoted to the difficult problem of creating industrial capital.[3] The author begins by stating the orthodox view that the basis of investment must be sought in savings. Now there are two forms of saving: free

[1] *E.F.S.P.A.* The official report of the *Majlis al-dâ'im li-tanmîyat al-intâj al-qaumî* for 1955 analyses, with equal frankness, the unsound direction of revenue and savings, pp. 11 ff.

[2] On this point I am grateful to Maître Edmond Rabbath, son of a great merchant of Aleppo, for his precious childhood recollections. Aleppo, with its underground *sûqs* above which Abraham's Citadel towers, a traditional meeting-point between Europe and the Near, Middle and Far East, provides an impressive series of historic 'tests'. How the twofold relationship between East and West on the one hand, and between manufacture and raw material on the other, are organized there, and how this organization has varied and even changed its direction in the course of ages, would provide a theme for research of capital importance. But what research is being done about the Near and Middle East?

[3] *Al-Nashra al-iqtiṣâdîya, Miṣr Bank,* Sept. 1957, pp. 18 ff., article on the financing of economic growth. Cf. particularly the pamphlet by Muḥammad Sâmî on the rôle of the monetary factor (*Rasâ'il* of the Planning Committee, no. 2). Numerous articles on the desirable development of habits of saving and investment, e.g. *A.S.*, 15 Dec. 1961.

savings and forced savings (taxation or other forms of State intervention). He favours the first sort. He recommends that spontaneous accumulation should lead to the formation of a supply of capital, *ilâ takwîn ra's al-mâl.* Only this creation is hindered by *sû' al-tanẓîm*, 'structural vices'. And so, in spite of his professed liberalism, he is forced to the view that the set-up ought to be changed from top to bottom if economic laws are to function properly there. Its very foundations, *usus*, are pernicious, particularly its psychological foundations, its mistrust of investment, its fear of stocks and shares, certain disastrous financial habits; all of which leads the author to desire a correspondence between savings and certain limited projects of increase. 'Poles of development' will have to be created, which will stimulate saving. This would be a sort of compromise between State control and liberalism. But investment would also have to be controlled, although only through the medium of banks and other monetary institutions. There would be no direct interference or control by the State. Still, there is a great difference between such an attitude and that which, a few years before, had inspired the chairman of the National Bank of Egypt, M. 'Alî Shamsî.[1]

In his 1953 report this financier, a member of the upper bourgeoisie, had deplored a tendency to hold back from investment, a torpor which, in his opinion, grew out of the twofold dread of 'spasmodic' State interference and of unsound national finances. What would he have said since then? He expressed the point of view of an orthodox financier, indeed of an international capitalist. And it was in this fashion that he reacted to the earliest Republican initiatives. The collected reports of the National Bank[2] in previous years had shown similar criticisms. The same complaint is uttered throughout: available funds are swallowed up in land, in building, in luxury consumption—traditional assets, representing an unwholesome compromise between the townsman's commercialism and the aristocratic moral code of the Bedouin.

Through some deep instinct Islamic society has always sought for syntheses between the City and the desert, differently stressed according to the milieu and the time. But the characteristic compromises of the previous age, which was that of bourgeois nationalism, could no longer

[1] Report by 'Alî Shamsî in 1953. The same regrets are expressed in the 1950 report of the National Bank of Egypt, and periodically, up till 1952, in documents of this sort. Similar laments from private capital are heard in Syria after the break-up of the U.A.R.

[2] Or of other Banks, particularly the *Crédit Foncier Egyptien* and the *Crédit Lyonnais*, which have kindly provided me with relevant documents of great interest. Thanks are due to MM. Escarra, Vincenot, Roger Machard.

satisfy present-day requirements. State control, which we are apt to ascribe somewhat hastily to foreign influence, appears as a logical reply to this anomaly. But logic triumphs only after strenuous tussles with internal and external difficulties. These are not lacking in the U.A.R., which faces them resolutely. The deficit in the balance of payments has not yet been mastered; a vigorous employment policy has so far failed to cope with the challenge of demography. But the foreign observer, in whose eyes such difficulties are quite normal, will note as a symptom of maturity the fact that they have been published in an official publication: *Ec. Bull.*, 1963, XVI, nos. 1 and 2, pp. 14 and 134.

Rise of the Banks

But no concepts are entirely pure. Action by rulers and action by businessmen are mingled throughout, in varying degrees, until our own day. They give evidence of an equally variable keenness to gain control of foreign capital. This double conflict can be traced in the history of Arab banks. The National Bank of Egypt,[1] founded in 1890, was not granted the privilege of issuing bank notes until later. In 1920, the Miṣr Bank was founded: a great date in the history of business enterprises in the Middle East. In 1951 came the creation of the Industrial Bank, which inaugurated a policy of specialized credit. This development came later in Iraq, for up till 1921 Iraq formed part of the Indian currency zone; and this was not pure coincidence. Only in 1947 was the National Bank of Iraq[2] established; it did not begin to function until 1949 and only in 1956 did it become a Central Bank with a capital of 50 million dinars, the right of issuing notes and also of control and co-ordination.

Since then there has been considerable development, with increased specialization, almost everywhere in these countries. They all have a Central Bank except Lebanon—a heritage of the Mandate. But from now on we see functional banks trying, not very successfully, to create poles of credit. And finally, some ten or twelve Arab business banks have appeared: for instance, the Arab Bank, with Iraqi and Lebanese capital—among the Lebanese capitalists we note the financier the late

[1] A useful historical study of Egyptian banks in *Ec. Bull.*, 1948, II, 63 and same year, IV, 176. Cf. also the study by Dr. Muḥammad Zakî Shâfi'î, *Rasâ'il* of the Planning Committee, no. 49, pp. 29 ff. Here the historical study is usefully made against a background of international evidence concerning monetary organization in under-developed countries.

[2] *Ec. Bull.*, 1949, III, 138 traces the history of this evolution. Cf. also ibid., 1956, IX, 271.

Emile Bustânî, and among the Iraqis some of the leading notabilities of the old regime. The balance sheet of 1957[1] gives an impression of growth which may be true or misleading, for naturally I cannot make use of technical criteria here. But we may note that the revenue has risen from 2,400,000 dinars in 1956 to 2,700,000 dinars in 1957. And the net product has doubled, from 300,000 dinars to 620,000, of which almost 400,000 dinars have been distributed.[2] I note, in passing, the importance of these allotments: necessary, apparently, to attract capital. Another feature of nascent Arab capitalism: it will only assume risk in the hope of lavish redemption.

Although progressive in intention, the action of these banks reflects certain local characteristics which Dr. Fû'âd Mursî formerly criticized: the disproportionate effect of the fluctuations and shifts of the stock of currency on banking operations and on the economy in general; the weakness of deposits and the corresponding importance of money-lending practices; the incoherence and dispersal of credit; the inadequacies, *ta'akhkhur*, of the central establishment itself.[3] All this as regards Egypt in 1955. And according to the same author, even in 1958 the situation was no better in Lebanon and Syria where, until the creation of the Central Bank, the preponderance of foreign establishments, the relative weakness and non-specialization of Arab banks (including the Miṣr Bank) were so marked that the latter's principal merit seems to lie in having survived in spite of competition. This situation, as we know, is altering daily, according to the country in question, either in the direction of ever-greater State control, or in that of an increasing number of private enterprises. Foreign bankers justifiably denounce the extravagant practices of some of the latter. They are obviously controlled by an interesting alliance between certain men whose abilities are of international calibre and others who cling to an outworn type of frantic speculation palliated by good manners and a respect for the *istikhâra*, the Koranic system of augury.

Of course, in such cases we need not accept the evidence of competitors who have more or less been dispossessed. But are Arab business men

[1] The *Twenty-eighth Annual Report*, Arab Bank Ltd., Baghdad, 1957. The booklet is copiously illustrated with photographs and coloured graphs. On the cover, a photograph of the Tripoli Branch (Libya).

[2] The balance for 1961 is even more favourable. Cf. *Âdâb*, no. 4, 1962, pp. 8–9. The report ends with the *ḥamdallâh*!

[3] Dr. Fû'âd Mursî, *al-Nuqûd wa'l-bunûk fî'l-bilâd al-'arabîya*, Egypt and Sudan, Cairo, 1955, Syria and Lebanon, Cairo, 1957. These reports form part of the useful documentation published by the Arabological Institute of the Arab League. I am grateful to Dr. Shafîq Ghurbâl for letting me see them.

themselves kinder in their comments? One of them, whom I have consulted, writes to me: 'The real truth is that speculation and commerce are intimately linked. There is no speculation without commerce and no commerce without speculation.' As for hoarding, the extreme mobility of the Lebanese economy has caused this to decrease; it is less marked in Lebanon than it formerly was, or than it may still be in a country like Syria. And yet Beirut is still the great traditional gold market. But is gold, or in broader terms is a solid reserve of available assets, still at the base of big business transactions? As the same correspondent tells me, 'in our country there reigns a capitalism without capital'. Arab banks, foreign banks, Lebanese banks use their prestige as cash, sooner than involve their reserves. Between them a frenzied competition rages, which is evident in the display of luxury cars in front of showy shop-fronts. And in the centre of Beirut, where land is so dear, a score of powerful establishments jostle one another—French, Belgian, British banks, the aforesaid Arab Bank, the Iraqi Râfidain, the Cairo Bank, the Saudi Bank of Commerce, the Beirut-Riyadh Bank, the Ḥimṣî Bank, the Intra Bank, and so on. During the last few years Lebanon has absorbed, like a sponge, the capital that has fled from other countries: from Egypt after its nationalizations, from Iraq after its revolution, from Kuwait at the time of its tension with Iraq, from Saudi Arabia, whose finances are no longer prosperous. But this unhealthy influx has begun to arouse anxiety.[1]

Against this picture of liberal competitiveness we must set, as though symmetrically, that of the great State establishments which, in this modern phase, enjoy vigorous expansion and play the part of moral critic. A recent report of the Central Bank of Syria subjects its picturesque and stubborn rivals to a censorious enquiry, which may be the modern equivalent of the old-time *ḥisba*—police control of market morals.

Customs, Morals and Things

Changing attitudes involve a change in speech. No further proof is needed than the business language, exactly the same as that used in European or American circles, employed in Stock Exchange reports in Cairo, Alexandria and Damascus, and in specialist journals. Indeed, the multiplication of economic periodicals is a significant feature: Kisrawân Labakî's *Levantine Trade* in Beirut, the Alexandrian *Journal*

[1] On this flight of capital, so profitable to Lebanon, see *Jarîda*, 5 July 1961, *Ḥawâdîth*, 7 July 1961.

of Commerce and Shipping, and 'Âdil Thâbit's *Egyptian Economic and Political Review*. Or booklets published by the banks, in French, English and Arabic, in Cairo and in Beirut. The collection of those from the National Bank of Egypt constitutes a most important source of documentation. The leading Egyptian daily paper, *al-Ahrâm*,[1] has begun to publish an economic fortnightly. In one of its latest numbers we find articles by financiers, some of whom are international specialists, closely analogous to those found in our own specialized publications. Their preoccupations are identical: studies of the market, statistics, financial anxieties, comments on the Stock Exchange. A few pages further on we note repressed or overt threats of interventionism, with reference to that stock market, *sûq al-aurâq al-mâlîya*, which is fairly active in Cairo as well as in Alexandria, despite frequent State taxation, or in Beirut[2] despite excessive involvement with foreign securities. And finally, careful if sporadic reports on the gold market in the old Muskî.

For the Muskî still exists, and the old Arab world—the brokers of Lebanon, the contrabandists of Kuwait, and many more all over the place—still takes an interest in gold.

These picturesque activities, indeed, are often lucrative. Lebanese holdings abroad are valued at 200 million dollars. A popular anecdote tells of two pedlars, one called Mârûn, the other Kâẓim, which suggests their creed and origin. In a remote African jungle they are captured by savages and tied to the stake while the water starts to boil in the great pot. Mârûn appeals to Our Lady of Bikfaya while Kâẓim prays to Our Lord Ḥusain. Meanwhile the cannibal chieftain, who has been listening to them attentively, speaks to them in Lebanese dialect; he is himself an emigrant from Dair al-Qamar!

Lebanon remains head of the great combines which make use of everything, as we have seen, even of the most intimate factors, such as family influence. Just as the great banks of the market-place raise money on their prestige, so do the great Lebanese families. Their cosmopolitan ramifications serve them as support and backing. Everything is done by means of transoceanic telephone calls. Dialect is used as a code, to prevent outsiders from understanding. Thus the sale of Egyptian cotton from Czechoslovakia to France, or the transfer of Uruguayan securities to Portugal, may be settled in Beirut. The decision, taken

[1] *Al-Ahrâm al-iqtiṣâdî*, no. 71, 1 Jan. 1959.

[2] On the securities market in Egypt see *Ec. Bull.*, 1950, III, 22. For Beirut, R. Pringuey, *Le Marché des Valeurs mobilières à Beirut*, thesis, Beirut. My thanks are due to the author and to Prof. B. Ducros.

recently, to ensure secrecy in banking operations has won much foreign support for these agile transactions. . . .

A Tolstoyan socialist such as Janbulâṭ is severely critical of such behaviour, which indeed is not wholly representative of the 'Lebanese spirit'.[1] For even wealthy émigrés display an admirable stubbornness in maintaining their connections with the land. At great cost they invest in cultivated terraces and mountain villas. Apple growing has become as symbolic of Lebanon as mulberry growing was in old days. And they aim at an Arab market, equipped with services by the former Phoenicia which thus, so to speak, becomes reintegrated in its geographical home.

These developments, together with these enduring factors, prove that any study of social types in the East should distinguish between various periods and settings. The open liberalism preferred, up till our own time, in Lebanon constitutes merely one zone, which has been challenged from outside and even from within.[2] Elsewhere a glance cast, in June 1958 or thereabouts, at the economic situation of the Middle East would have discovered a zone of aggressive technocracy, Iraq, and a zone of voluntary centralism, Egypt. The pattern has altered since then, on account of the Iraqi revolution. It will alter still further. In any case, any reduction of it to neat compartments is bound to be artificial. The three types intermingle in varying degrees in the same group, even in the same course of action.

Liberalism is deeply rooted in the urban life of the Arab East. Technocracy—whether that of the Pharaohs, of Lord Cromer or of the Development Board—enjoys keener opportunities in countries confronted with the sudden mutations of technique. And State control, as I have said, acts as a traditional counterpoise to the excesses and deficiencies of mercantilism.

The common need to build, moreover, covers many diversities and tends to impose a uniform rhythm on life. In Lebanon, the power of trade is meeting its first adversaries. In Iraq, the Revolution has not hitherto cancelled its contracts with the I.P.C.[3] The 'Egyptian Economic Organization' reports £E57,000,000 invested in 1957, 38,000,000

[1] Kamâl Janbulât, *Ḥaqîqat al-thaura al-lubnânîya*, Beirut, 1959, p. 10, on the mercantile factor—*markantîlî* or *tijrlî*—which he would like to see abolished in the country.

[2] Controversies echoed complaisantly by the U.A.R. press since the summer of 1958 and since revived at Damascus, this time from the opposite point of view.

[3] The account by Jamîl Sa'îd, *al-'Irâq al-jadîd*, 1958, the first book to appear after the Iraqi revolution, contained no attack against the Development Board. Since then the Board's budget has lost its autonomy and the organization has been absorbed under State control.

of this in industry alone (65 per cent). And simultaneously we read in the Stock Exchange report of a Cairo journal that 'Egyptian capital is becoming increasingly interested in the Stock Exchange; its investments have begun to count; its efforts are being increasingly directed towards industry, for which it foresees a brilliant future'. Or else: 'The engineer Aḥmad 'Abbûd,[1] who has been granted a loan in dollars by the Import-Export, is about to extend his chemical fertilizer factory and to increase its production.' But such observations grow rarer as State control grows stronger, although they still offer provisional opportunities to capital. The same is true of the Stock Exchange. Government bonds are inevitably at a premium. Those of the steel works of Helwan, in particular, foster bull and then bear speculation. A new social stratum, more or less devoted to the regime, competes for the new 'financial papers', *aurâq mâlîya*, in the wholly traditional hope of fruitfully increased values. The anticipated boom did not occur and uncertainty increased.[2] At the end of 1961 the State provisionally closed down both Stock Exchanges. When it reopened these it undertook revaluation itself. Meanwhile, private enterprise had almost disappeared.

Syria, in September 1961, applied the opposite political conclusion to these conflicts. This was one reaction, among many, of its traditional commercial capitalism. The polemic which then arose between the two countries emphasized the opposition between their systems, and even more between their ways of life. It is still too soon to make any objective assessment of the value of the arguments exchanged. We will only draw a general conclusion from them.

Local traditions, psychological tendencies, although inspired by a will to recovery and emancipation, must in effect come to terms with the political regime, and at the same time take their place in an international setting and give proof of convincing experience. The efficiency of an undertaking, in any case, will depend on its rightness, its adaptation to local conditions. Any such action must satisfy the requirements of its historic milieu and follow as closely as possible the inflexions imposed upon the economic process by the influence of a variable factor, that Eastern Factor X which is so readily felt, so hard to define.

Mistrust of Self

But although he can only base valid experiments on faithful fulfilment of his own needs, the Arab innovator means to follow up the lessons he

[1] He died recently in exile.
[2] *Egyptian Stock Exchange*, 12 July 1958.

has learnt: to balance exchanges, to take his right place in a market, to avoid inflation and a deficit in his budget, scrupulously. His unconcern, at least in theory, for the unusualness of his behaviour is equalled only by the incapacity of his foreign partner to understand it. Our theoreticians who, at home, no longer consider investment as an obligatory consequence of saving, still apply these punctilious rules to Eastern countries. A concern for budgetary orthodoxy was apparently among the reasons which, in 1956, caused the I.B.R.D. to refuse the loan requested for the Dam. The effects were infinitely greater than the cause. Eastern and European economists, or the majority of them, need urgently to revise their systems of analysis.

To convince oneself of this it is sufficient to examine the behaviour of Arab countries, rather than their own interpretation of it.[1] They are drifting in quest of themselves. Their bargainings, their State control, are aspects of this quest. Egypt's monetary policy has described the most disconcerting zigzags: and this is, paradoxically, out of respect for orthodox solutions. The phases of violence which shock the West may be considered as part of their attempt at readjustment; so perhaps may their habit of seizing what they consider their rights, or their lawful prize (the nationalization of Suez and all that ensued therefrom). And this is more logical than it may appear; for such actions constitute a sort of reversal of the colonial phase. Domination is met with *de-domination*, at the cost of an excess of incident and emotion, and of dangers. . . .

The Arabs thus display to others and to themselves their skill in the business of living. And they need the conviction of this evidence, just as much as the excitement of an existence in revolt against a hostile world. Seen from this angle, their agility in speculation or their rigid State control appear as two methods, concurrent or competitive, of going beyond mere utility, of gaining acceptance for their utilitarian demands or palliating the defects of these. Hence their charm, so disconcerting for their adversary, and their excesses, so disturbing to their friends. Hence their skill in persuading others, from the weakest to the strongest —basing their arguments respectively on their own strength or weakness. Hence, too, the cunning with which they make use of the policy of

[1] We must welcome with interest attempts such as that of Dr. Yusrî 'Alî Muṣṭafâ to assess how far different methods of national accountancy can be applied to Egypt's actual economic situation (*Rasâ'il al-takhṭîṭ al-qaumî*, no. 51, pp. 35 ff.). I cannot undertake here a more detailed study of the evolution of economic thought and financial technique in the Arab East, despite the immense interest of these psycho-social questions.

economic aid which developed after the war, so as to make it a moral obligation for the aiding nation, denouncing any lapse as an outrage; and concurrently, the mediocrity of the aid thus secured!

The Arabs' economic attitude[1] is thus, for the time being, truer than their systems. Underneath the contrasting, but in each case characteristic, behaviour of their leading businessmen and their leading statesmen, we can trace an instinctive aspiration towards something that will breathe life into the prosaic lessons of the outside world. In this way, the Arabs, surrounded by the brutal and underhand competition of which they are the stake even more than the actors, hope by self-reliance to save their zest for life and their hopes, undermined by appalling delays. In this way they hope, sooner or later, to escape from a way of life imposed by others. We can only hope with them in this attempt. For its success would mean, for them and for ourselves, that man had eventually become master of his own symbols, amidst the appalling disturbances of the industrial age.

[1] Cf. J. Berque, 'Les Arabes et l'expression économique', *Studia islamica*, 1952, XVI, pp. 95 ff.

CHAPTER V

The Acquisition of Technique

We can find other examples of discord or harmony in a site of classic grandeur, now fallen upon evil days: the neighbourhood of Bâb Zuwaila, in Cairo.

You reach it through the crowded street of Taḥt al-Rab‘. The name refers to the huge many-storied tenement houses in which, since medieval times, whole family clans have led their busy lives. Few of these dwellings now harbour romantic ladies such as ‘Â’isha al-Taimûrîya, nor even the frustrated bourgeoise depicted, in the inter-war period, in the novels of Najîb Maḥfûẓ. High society has fled towards the newer districts, leaving to plebeians the mingled squalor and charm of old loyalties.

Here are stalls displaying ironwork—toy horses for children, traditional measuring-vessels. We witness everywhere the skill and industry with which waste products are turned to good account—sheltering in the niches[1] of the monumental doorway, or in the corners of ramparts, or amidst the solemn decrepitude of the old ‘*okelles*’. Sandals are being made instead of the babouches of the Maghrib. Here again, in a corner of the old wall, a cabinet-maker boasts of his ‘masterpieces’: a wooden model of a mosque, put together in Alexandria, a door in delicate marquetry. Ancient skills, rejected by modern life, seem still to subsist in these poor districts: the glass-blower's, the monumental mason's, the cabinet-maker's.[2] The carder wields his paradoxical harp-shaped tool like a Greek bard. Still further down, a semi-parasitical throng is

[1] These wall niches of Bâb Zuwaila are called *fajwa*, a symbolic term to which I shall return later: cf. Chapter XIII, p. 277.

[2] Al-Ḥâjj Muḥammad Marzûq is ninety-five years old. Since the age of ten he has been weaving rugs for the Ka‘ba. Cf. report in *al-Jîl*, 13 March 1961.

busily scavenging and salvaging. A stone's throw from the al-Mu'ayyad mosque, or the Byzantine majesty of Bâb Zuwaila, leaden pipes trail across peeling house-fronts—the city refuse, which confronts the Municipality with a problem hitherto unsolved, is thus used to heat a Moorish bath and also to cook *mdemmes*, gruel, for the enjoyment of plebeian gourmets. Caterers' carts start out before dawn from these august and sordid precincts where, within a narrow circle, you may meet a popular doctor, expert at curing all ills, a professor from the Azhar who lodges in a corner of the ramparts, a thousand dealers and hucksters, the importunate custodians of a merchant's palace,[1] and the crowd of people who pass through uninterruptedly by day and by night.

Words and Men

These poor, ingenious folk, sheltering in the porches of the past, display a vitality and natural verve which the modern novel has sensitively perceived. They are by no means certainly 'doomed to perish'.[2] For in spite of the background of majestic ruin and the many symptoms of decay, this section of humanity is saved by its constancy and its fecundity. It carries on the thread of Middle Eastern history. But what a contrast it presents with the types fostered by the technical revolution, those children of the machine whose aggressive bitterness has been portrayed by Muḥammad Ṣidqî![3] Consider the effect of electrification on the village of Maḥmaiya, in the Delta. Does this bring light to it figuratively as well as literally? Shops stay open late into the night; people sit up later; three radio sets a day are bought, as compared with two a month in the old days. The pious fellah, who had hitherto neglected his after-dinner prayer, now has time to say it. He has achieved the perfect circuit: he has preserved the traditional symbol thanks to the new-found object.[4] More frequently, different circuits are formed—that, for instance, of working-class life, which becomes the more conscious the more it is repressed, and which State syndicalism will not always be able to canalize. It is undoubtedly a problem for the Governments of these countries to determine the proper relations between the mass of workers of modern type and that larger mass in which the past still survives. Is this survival merely residual, or does it give promise of

[1] The house of Jamâl al-Dîn Abû Dhahab (seventeenth century). Cf. Pauty, *Palais et maisons d'époque musulmane au Caire*, p. 56.

[2] Cf. Cossery's sordid and distressing story.

[3] *Al-Anfâr*, 1956; *al-Aidî al-khashina*, 1958.

[4] Reported in the *Muṣawwar*, 8 Sep. 1961.

powers yet unfulfilled? Which of the two masses is more representative, or rather more significant of the collective impetus, here and now? For if an industrial future is as inevitable for this society as for our own, its stages, its inflexions, its possible deviations, the validity of the human types involved, must all be judged in terms of the particular milieu. Whence the difficult reckonings and dangerous choices incumbent on the statesman, and the sociologist's hesitations in front of such scantily explored material. From the point of view of history and psychology, one ought to know how such a peasant and craftsman stock has been able to engender industrial attitudes, wherever a continuity of time and place, perhaps even of group life, can be discerned. Such a problem has not been elucidated as regards nineteenth-century Europe. But what has happened in Egypt, in Syria, for the old manual skill in weaving to give place to the cotton industry? Is it a case of substitution or of transformation? We cannot tell, unfortunately.[1] Sociology in the Middle East has not yet reached the stage of detailed research. But this may happen, perhaps, within the next few years.[2] 'Coincidences' between the craftsmen of the past and the factory workers of the present are in any case not unusual. And it is not without interest that a plan of industrialization like that of Syria seems to be deliberately seeking them.

In any case the transition to machine techniques constitutes for these societies an abrupt leap, almost an essential change. The mathematical speculation of old days, the shrewdness of tradesman and money-lender differed from modern capitalism only by their mistrust for probability. Whereas craftsmanship, which is akin to art, is cut off from industrial production by technical innovation. And the distance is increased still further by the historical conditions under which European manufacture has been thrust on the East: more or less those of a colonial pact. Industry in the Arab East has grown up on a subsiding soil.

The language expresses this phenomenon.[3] Arabic is ill fitted to render technical matters. It has recourse to neologisms drawn from

[1] We may mention the researches of Ḥasan al-Sa'âtî concerning industry. But in Egypt, at all events, the enquiry is bound to be a historical one, for the process began a long time ago. The *Khiṭaṭ* of 'Alî pasha Mubârak enables one to understand the transition between traditional craftsmanship and an elementary industrialization, developing steam engines (*wâbûr*), workshops (*warsha*) rotary apparatus (*dûllâb*).

[2] Particularly if proper collaboration can be established between local and foreign scientific organizations. Sociologists, for instance, should be enabled to take advantage of the invaluable investigations made by State organizations in Egypt during the past few years.

[3] On *fann* and *âla*, see *Lisân al-'Arab*.

European languages. In the local publications which I frequently consult, there recur words as harsh to a classically trained ear as: *tiknîkî, tiknî, mikânîkî*. . . .

The old idiom, it is true, had a term that is sometimes used today in the sense of 'technique', but more readily in that of 'art'. The ambiguity is instructive. The distinction between craftsmanship, art and industry is blurred. In fact, the word *fann* originally meant 'sort', 'modality'. A *rajul bi-fann* means an adept, particularly in the use of speech; which in certain respects, for a race as enamoured of the Word as this, authorizes the shift of meaning to technique: such a man is adept in his technique, which is language. Hence the expression of wonder, *fannan*! And perhaps we should go back to a more concrete etymology: *fann* in the sense of branch, bough. Is this image at the base of the word's derivations? Does the spreading branch convey the meaning of diversity, of virtuosity? We cannot tell.

Another word is used today to signify 'instrument': *âla*. It goes back to a root whose meanings and harmonic implications are almost infinite. *Âla*: the first material sense we can trace is that of 'tent-pole', whence the transition is easy to 'tool' and eventually to 'machine'. The epithet *âlî* is used today to condemn something mechanical, drably material or even materialistic, by contrast with *waẓîfî* which means 'functional' and *'udwî* which means 'organic'. We must note however that almost regularly in these writings, which themselves display extreme virtuosity, since even reports on industrial standards are produced in Arabic at congresses, terms taken from Western languages are used. It is a case of substitution and addition rather than of transposition.

Discontinuity in speech reflects discontinuity in things. There is nothing surprising about this. The products of modern industry had been imposed upon the Arab world long before its appearance there as an active productive force. One might even say that the evolution is far from complete, and in some parts has not yet begun. Here, too, the history of the Arab East seems just the reverse of contemporary Western history. The latter, in fact, begins by a technical revolution and then, by degrees, establishes a national entity and economic entities, then proceeds to plan social reform, moving always from the concrete to the ideal, from strength to justice. The reverse is true of the Arab world. It starts from an ideal, or at least for a demand for justice. One might almost say of its history what Marx said of Hegel's philosophy: it must be turned upside down, for it is standing on its head. Some of these countries are attempting such an operation. Thus the Middle

Eastern man does not proceed from technique; he strives towards technique, he acquires technique. But basically he seems to us, in contrast with Western man who is so essentially *homo faber*, to belong to another set of values. He is, or was, *homo non faber*. And European employers have freely criticized and condemned him for this. True, the 'mechanical' strength of the Egyptian worker has long been valued; but, it was said, he loses all faculty of initiative at adolescence![1] We know how such comments, due to a prejudice itself founded on sociological misunderstanding, have served to justify discriminatory measures in the Middle East and elsewhere, up till our own times. . . .

In any case, in Cromer's day, when the dislocation of the old craft system was pointed out in official reports,[2] skilled workmen were fetched from abroad: Maltese, Greeks (still ubiquitous today), and, even more, Italians. The rôle of the latter, which belongs to a definite period in history, deserves a moment's attention. During the early years of this century, in Egypt, the Italian workman joined forces, so to speak, with the artisan tradition of the country. Italians built modern Cairo, and adorned it with a yellowish plaster reminiscent of Genoa or Turin. They created quite a school. Many a small-scale manufacturer, middle-aged today, can boast of having learnt his trade with a *mu'allim* from overseas. Italianate taste in furniture, building and glassware lasted until the second world war. On another level, and over a more extended period, there was the influence of the managers. Discreet British advisers, French engineers and wits, all wearing the tarboosh, moving in fashionable society, on good terms with the local bourgeoisie, well paid, entertaining well, enjoying the moral support of the ruling nations' prestige, of banks *in situ*, of navies near by, of the Canal and all its promises. . . . This world, which was practically dead by 1940, lost its last stronghold on the occasion of nationalization in 1956. Meanwhile the era of the expert had begun. Egypt sent its functionaries into sister countries, and imported the foreign *khabîr* (expert). The latter had scarcely any link with local society, which indeed had greatly altered. His human experience of the country was limited in general to professional relations with the Eastern experts, his colleagues. The government which employed him seemed reluctant to extend it further. A country like Egypt, in spite of its traditional friendliness, tends

[1] Abbate pasha, 'Prééminence des facultés mécaniques dans la race égyptienne', *Bulletin de l'Institut d'Egypte*, 3rd series, no. 2, p. 205 ff. At the opposite end of the Mediterranean world, Mgr. Lavigerie is quoted to the same effect!

[2] Lord Cromer's *Report for the Year 1904*, Cairo, 1905, contains prophetic views on this subject.

increasingly to isolate, as though prophylactically, the technicians it imports, who now may be Czech, Russian or German: to integrate them into a sort of press-button machinery—for any particular requirement you push a button, and the expert does the job which he is paid to do. Thus the country can import all the technical skill, all the technical men it requires, without contributing too much of its own. It does contribute, however, and spares no effort to produce its own *fannîyîn.*

If you question these Arab experts you will notice that they are seldom self-satisfied. They consider their countries as having entered on a transitional phase—with a consequent uneasiness of which they often speak in pessimistic terms. I remember hearing an Iraqi industrialist deplore the reluctance of his country's youth to become interested in technical things. For a long time, he told me, the splendid *Kullîyat al-hindasa*, the engineering school, attracted nobody but orphans! In any agnatic system, indeed, orphans and illegitimate children are often expected to take up professions that other people despise. Or consider the comments of a Lebanese engineer on the deplorable use made of the young men graduating each year from the school of engineering at Beirut. They satisfied their aims to some extent: noting that in a country that was short of architects many houses were being built without architectural advice, with consequent danger to the families inhabiting them, these graduates claimed and secured for themselves as architects the monopoly of building contracts. But at this point inequality came into play again; some of them were much more in request than others. An annual quota of buildings was therefore allotted to each. Unfortunately some of the more popular began making money out of their signatures. . . .

Technical development and corporative demands, on the one hand, against the resistances and wiles specific to the milieu: we have here a live example of one of the conflicts in the Arab world today. The engineer, as we have seen, feels ill at ease in that world; perhaps precisely because his training and his ideal separate him from his own society, so that in certain extreme cases he no longer recognizes it. And it no longer recognizes him. A painful Iraqi novel, *Hand, Water and Earth*[1] depicted the desperate attempts made, shortly after the treaty of Portsmouth, by certain young intellectuals seeking to reform their country, and their eventual defeat. Here and there you will be told of the lamentable failure to make use of highly qualified graduates from foreign schools. I can think of one of these, who studied at the

[1] By Dhû'l-Nûn Ayyûb, who has come back to his country after a long exile.

École Polytechnique; he became a Minister, indeed, but he was unable to create in his own country anything worthy of his training. And if it can be said, in one sense, that the military revolution represents, in Egypt particularly, the advent of a class whose rôle is analogous both to that of the bourgeois and that of the technician, nowhere has the *muhandis*, the engineer, yet triumphed. . . . It is highly significant that active politics and real power choose other paths, and the technician only enjoys the support of banking interests and the military junta.

Equipment and Landscapes

The cover of a recent book displays, in contrast, a donkey-driver and a derrick. On the booklet published in honour of the Helwan steel-works, factory chimneys soar up triumphantly. The documents produced for the Iraqi 'Development Weeks', the propaganda brochures of Aramco[1] abound in such images. The antithesis between the Bedouin draped in his head-veil and the complex machinery of a factory has become a classic one. It is one of the emblematic themes of Arab societies and Arab minds. The world of curves and decorations is contrasted with that of metal tubes and utilitarian drawings: angles, screws, precision and mystery combined. The machine versus the arabesque. Industrial civilization has created a new *kufic* in the Arab East today!

It does not merely imprint its signature, provide a way of speech. Of course it brings things too. And it is primarily in this concrete form that the Arabs take possession of it; for one thing, because this was how it was first imposed on them from abroad, in the days of European expansion; but furthermore because it has stirred up in them a longing for solid assets, so to speak, the more violent because it has been long frustrated.

That 'corporateness' which is never absent from Islam and which may indeed govern even its theory of contracts, can be recognized in the contemporary love of exhibitions. I am thinking of the fair at Damascus, or the incessant displays now being organized in the Gezireh park at Cairo. These exhibitions are set out like zoos in which the objects of the industrial world are exhibited, tamed. When the doors close, however, the exhibitor seldom takes his bear away with him. The more elaborate, complicated and exciting an article appears, the more keenly the local industrialist yearns to acquire it. So he will collect costly plant which sometimes serves no immediate purpose: electronic statistical

[1] Arabian American Oil Company.

devices for instance, or spectrographs. The U.S.S.R. recently offered the U.A.R. a research reactor. One of the attractions with which it endeavours to supplant the U.S.A., or with which Japan hopes to win its way into an Afro-Asian common market, is a return to barter: machines for cotton. Less money in circulation, less 'monetary tokens'. Or, in a deeper sense, the machine has now become a token.

Reciprocally, the Arab countries have also begun to exhibit abroad. At Brussels in the summer of 1958 for instance, where their combined pavilions occupied 1,500 square metres, as much as Mexico's. Of the 52 items in their list, Egypt provided 23, Syria 13, Iraq 9 and Jordan 7. And if the tobacco manufacturers' display was particularly prominent, the stands of such enterprises as industrial tannery, textiles, metallurgy, and chemical industry exhibited their latest progress with justifiable pride.[1]

The fact that in their enthusiasm these countries immediately aspire to the highest technical peaks may disquiet the economist, but it will not surprise the historian. On the contrary, it is doubtless in their interest to transform their methods without letting themselves be restrained by what may have succeeded elsewhere—peasant prudence or petty-bourgeois deliberateness. But I am even more concerned with the psychological symptom revealed by this impetus towards the concrete aspect of the machine, and its fate.

For many forms of technical equipment have a compulsive power. By their very presence they set in motion around them waves of industrial creation. They have their own educative and stimulating value. They create new sequences of cause and effect in the life of the country. Hence any study of such techniques should begin with an inventory of the equipment which they involve, including military stock. Such an inventory would take into account not only the apparatus but also the spare parts. For these are highly important; machinery ceases to be of value if after a certain length of time such and such a detail of it cannot be renewed. Long after the 1956 break with the West, Western equipment maintained its value because it had its store of parts; there were on the market nothing but parts of Western origin (French, British or American). The import of other machinery was thereby slowed down. In this case, Western economy was defending itself on the Cairo market by its 'viscosity'.[2]

[1] Documents of the International Fair.

[2] This term, unpleasant in itself, is further burdened with the meanings imposed on it by Sartrian philosophy. But 'viscosity' is a powerful economic factor; many applications of it in the cultural field might be found. . . .

In the long run, the landscape is transformed by the invasion of industrial objects, which have their own power of initiative. Naturally the towns are affected first. Cairo, Alexandria, Damascus, Beirut, Aleppo develop industrial suburbs, while their town-planners aim at the last word in technical achievement.

The Gezireh, at Cairo, now has its Eiffel Tower: a tall concrete campanile, proud and mysterious in its purpose: asserting, at all events, technical ambition, just as the French Eiffel Tower proclaimed the metallurgical skill of the late nineteenth century. Lower down the Nile a tremendous fountain spurts up from the river: the 'Fontana', copied from Geneva. At Damascus, factory chimneys rise among the apricot trees of the Ghûṭa. And when you enter the town, after the orchards of Baradâ, a proud avenue greets you, laid out by Ecochard, and an enormous exhibition park forestalls the mosque of Sultan Salîm.

Baghdad is equally transformed. This town, which for so long seemed to be at the end of the earth, has become a great airport. Every fifty yards along Rashîd Street some aviation company's offices ensnare you with offers of escape, the Maya of the modern world. Their windows alternate with those of the great stores. The smartest of these display dresses of Parisian cut. Close by, the dazzle of cinema posters. The banks raise proud façades; one of them, the Râfidain, is entirely built honeycomb-wise to protect the interior from the sunlight. Of course this latest visual stratum does not conceal older strata: in the distance an earlier attempt at town-planning, that of the Turks; near by, a horrible Colonial style, part English, part Indian, part inspired by Munich; and finally—to simplify the picture—the deposit of our own post-war age, here still restrained by the past but elsewhere, beyond Bâb Sharqî, spreading triumphantly towards the Tigris in a flood of neon-lighted streets, luxury hotels and magnificent esplanades decorated with bas-reliefs and mosaics; here town-planning seeks to become popular culture.

It is not only through outer appearances that the modern world claims its victory. It affects dress, medicaments, and even cookery. It increases the proportion of foodstuffs imported from afar, 'processed', as they say. Round about 1930 Egypt began to produce its own canned goods, and many economists were disturbed at this. In a country which yields so many green vegetables, where the earth breaks out, so to speak, in cellulose twice a year and the very camels look bloated, what a paradox, they said, to start canning food! Now the consumption of canned goods is rising—some imported from Morocco (sardines), some from Australia, and so on. A curious investigation made at a provincial grocer's shop at Shibîn al-Kûm revealed that 91 sorts of canned goods, representing 26 per cent of the tradesman's capital, were displayed there.[1]

Thus, from within as from without, the new man takes over from the old. If we discount the various categories of good wishes for the year 1962 addressed to its readers by one Cairo newspaper,[2] we find in it almost nothing of the old Arab spirituality, the *rûḥ* so dear to the hearts of Orientalists, but the announcement of dozens of industrial 'projects'. Can the 'project', *mashrû'*, have become (by an impious pun!) the 'law', *sharî'a*, of modern times?

Towards a Civilization Based on Industrial Objects

A remarkable feature of the Arab press, particularly in Egypt but also in Beirut, is the amount of space devoted to technical promotions: the visit of some mission to Europe or the United States, or to Czechoslovakia, in order to acquire qualifications; the arrival in Cairo of the first Viscount aircraft piloted by an Egyptian (summer, 1958); the inauguration of a factory, or better still of several, by the head of the Government. One is aware of a deliberate will to stimulate the process by celebrating it, which is sound psychology.

We ought, of course, to examine what underlies this movement of opinion. But such means as we have of assessing this drive towards technique belong to the sphere of specialized research, and a study which is concerned chiefly with social attitudes can scarcely make use of them. We should have to examine internal evidence, which is moreover hard to come by. Nevertheless a certain number of criteria can be grasped: the growing attendance at science faculties and engineering schools, the frequently substantial participation of Arab delegates in scientific colloquia concerning such difficult subjects as cybernetics or atomic science,[3] the grants made towards research in these subjects, relatively huge in a country such as Egypt. This is a wholly admirable development.

[1] Reported at the fifth Congress of Engineers at Cairo.

[2] *Akhbâr*, 30 Dec. 1961.

[3] At the second Congress on atomic energy, held in Geneva in 1958, Arab countries made an important contribution. Some of their opinions influenced the position taken up by the President, F. Perrin. At Geneva again, in 1963, the Congress on technical assistance organized by U.N.E.S.C.O., at which a considerable number of Egyptians read papers, gave proof of the growing maturity of Arab attitudes, which now pay due attention to theory, research and application. Such progress is most encouraging.

The more advanced of the Arab nations are now moving in a direction which was by no means inevitable. It takes a certain maturity of outlook to realize the necessity of research, to distinguish, even in material progress, between what is deliberately assumed and what is gratuitously acquired (even if at considerable cost). Such a conception, which shows increasing sagacity in the way it reconstructs reality, takes the form of planning in economics, of research in science. These two correlative aspects are clearly set forth in the opening article of that excellent review, *al-Majalla.*[1] The author of this important study was careful to repudiate a point of view too closely concerned with practice at the expense of theory; and this is indeed a tendency to be combated in Eastern countries, where utilitarianism too often constitutes a counter-type to the old fatalistic attitudes, *qadarîya* or *ṣabr*. And on the day when this clear-sighted attitude is strengthened by a deeper study of facts, when research in the exact sciences goes hand in hand with perspicacious research into human behaviour, a decisive step will have been taken. . . .[2]

Meanwhile, as far as exact science is concerned, the progress of research has varied in different countries and with different subjects. U.N.E.S.C.O. publishes periodically an analytical résumé of such endeavours, and I have classified them for my own amusement. In a single past year, 1955, we find the tidy figure of 692 papers published in the Arab countries on scientific and technical subjects; general science 13, astronomy and geophysics 11, applied physics 10, chemistry 47, geology 38, biology 64, medical science 355 (a traditional profession in these parts), agriculture and veterinary science 139.[3] The investigation might be completed by seeing whether patents have been taken out by local researchers. I made enquiries on the spot, and was told that there were scarcely any. In Lebanon, where they are versed in law and always twist the argument in their own favour, most of the patents are taken out by foreigners. But there are also a few local inventions: for instance, a process for closing whisky bottles; this is not to be sneered at, for

[1] Ibrâhîm Ḥilmî 'Abd al-Raḥmân, *Al-thaura al-'ilmîya al-kubrâ wa-mauqifunâ min-hâ*, pp. 53 ff. I am indebted to this scholar, who is now at the head of the Egyptian Planning Committee, for allowing me to study the *Rasâ'il* he edits, and for a most interesting interview.

[2] Many of these countries have founded or developed Institutes of Social Science with the help of U.N.E.S.C.O. The interest taken in the social sciences is a decisive index of development.

[3] *Abstracts of scientific and technical papers*, U.N.E.S.C.O., 1955. The bureau of scientific documentation at Duqqî, formerly 'bilateral', is now purely Egyptian.

after all technique has everything to gain by starting from humble beginnings. Another inventor has patented the pattern of a postcard for pilgrims to Mecca; on all the great occasions of life, people send one another greetings, and this cunning Lebanese had discovered a formula which doubtless brought him considerable profits. Moreover, in the Shî'ite village of Nabatiye, there may be seen the mausoleum of a member of the Ṣabbâḥ family[1] who emigrated to the U.S.A. and won distinction there by taking out a number of industrial patents. We should mention here the fruitful career in Egypt of the engineer Musharrafa, recent inventions there such as the base-heated furnace, and that industrial 'masterpiece', the famous *burg* of Gezireh, made entirely of concrete, without metal, so it is said, and conceived and executed by local technicians.

However, these are still only the first fruits, *bawâdir*, of future development. Public opinion in certain of these countries is concerned, quite rightly, with the social obstacles which such creation still encounters. In the polemical campaign waged against the Azhar by Fikrî Abâẓa, the chief reproach he brought against traditional education was its sterilizing effect on young people who might well have won fame abroad in the scientific domain, among others; and he cited a number of Egyptian technicians who had made their mark in the outside world. This suggests a line of research which, for the moment, we cannot pursue: a comparison, by way of tests and other methods of investigation—biographical for instance—between the attitude towards technique of those young Arabs who stay at home and those who are transplanted.[2] No doubt such an essay in comparative psychology would reveal a number of difficulties inherent in the local background. We are ill equipped to deal with these delicate matters, and shall remain so as long as we lack basic studies and while, for the time being, the bulk of these phenomena are hidden behind a thick veil of prejudice and passion.

Three Cases of Self-criticism

Failing the detailed research which has not yet been undertaken, or which has not come my way, I shall refer to three sets of documents whose spontaneity is adequately guaranteed: examples of that self-searching which is practised periodically at Arab congresses. The

[1] The glory of the little town. His family has published a documentary booklet about him. He left an unpublished correspondence with the greatest scientists of his time, including Einstein.

[2] Such as Dr. Medawar, of Lebanese origin, who won a Nobel prize for Britain.

thing is extremely instructive for us, since in these congresses, particularly if they are not international but exclusively inter-Arab, the participants shed all complexes and relate their experience with sincerity. My examples are already ancient history, where everything happens so fast; this will serve to show all the better how the sequel was to confirm their intentions.

Here, for instance, is a Congress for technical instruction, held in Cairo in December 1957,[1] at which the various Arab countries were represented. Among the distinguished figures present was an Egyptian educational expert, now assistant director of the I.L.O. in Geneva: Dr. 'Abbâs Muṣṭafâ 'Ammâr. His speech contains the most judicious advice. He appeals to his colleagues not to confine themselves to mere verbal elegance, *ṣiyâgha*, to rhetorical exhortation, but to pass on to the stage of practice and performance. The viewpoint of an experienced and responsible man. Almost always you find in these congresses advice of the same sort, criticism of empty talk and a summons to realization. Unfortunately they frequently remain unfulfilled. On this particular day each of the Arab countries had contributed a report. Several of these documents contained historical and statistical analyses. That of Iraq for instance, and Egypt's. Here the author distinguished no less than six periods of development, starting with the creation of a practical school at Bulâq; this was a nursery of technicians or semi-technicians, who played an important part in the development of the region. Finally the author, after sharp criticism of the efforts of the monarchy, came to the sixth period: from 1956 to our own day. Regulation 22 of 1956 provided a charter for technical education in Egypt; first, preparatory schools, free for all, which would produce workers of ordinary (*'âdî*) level; then secondary technical schools, open only to boys who had won their primary certificate; these would take a three-year course, followed by an examination qualifying for entrance into the engineering schools. Besides offering valuable opportunities for working-class candidates, this scheme provided a training school for industrial teachers and a general extension of practical studies; for the defect of technical education in every country is a tendency to remain abstract and only rarely to stimulate action.

In any case, here are the results, not of the reforms, which have not yet borne fruit, but of the long history of technical teaching in Egypt. For the year 1956–7, the technical secondary schools had 9,800 pupils;

[1] Its report (duplicated) provides valuable information from a historical, statistical and educational point of view.

it was hoped to raise this figure to 12,000 by 1960–1. The relative figures for the preparatory course were 13,000 and 17,000. At first sight one might wonder why the disproportion is not greater; there are relatively too many 'secondary' scholars as compared with the 'primary' ones. Criticism was not spared on this head; for technical achievement implies not only the higher reaches but the intermediary stages too, and the foundations were too often neglected. The final selection, indeed, was very stiff: 1,244 successful candidates out of 9,800 students. But what was to become of those who failed?

In Syria, roughly the same problems arise; they are those that confront technical education in all countries. Numbers remain deplorably low; for the year 1956–7, only 483 students, 33 graduates. We can well imagine the recommendations of the congress: wider efforts, a greater emphasis on practice, etc. Similar resolutions are passed at almost every congress on technical education, all over the world. But here, beneath the historical and statistical exposés in these various reports, we can discern original traits of social psychology.

A Congress of engineers was held in Cairo in 1954.[1] It provides us with some fifty papers on specific subjects: a source of documentation about these countries without parallel at that time. The contributors were specialists, some of whom have become ministers since then while others are in prison. Despite the inequality of their fate, and that precariousness which seems to threaten the intelligentsia in all Arab countries, we feel in all of them the same striving towards objectivity. Dr. Rashâd al-Barâwî denounces the grave handicaps that hinder the progress of industry, arising from unfavourable social and pyschological conditions: reluctance to take risks, fear of responsibility, the lack of a real bourgeoisie. Another contribution, which is almost Saint-Simonian, advocates 'social harmony on the basis of technique'. Critics deplore the casual nature of many projects, the lack of preparation in town-planning schemes among others, the shortcomings of engineering schools, etc. There are interesting comments on the immaturity of the workers, their physical deficiencies due to undernourishment, and on the responsibility of the employers, who have proved as incapable as the Government of selecting from the mass of workers those whose professional aptitudes might be developed by apprenticeship.

[1] Besides its general report, it published a series of brochures from which much of the preceding information has been obtained. Cf. particularly statements by Manṣûr Khalîl, Ḥifnî Sayyid Fahmî, Rashâd al-Barâwî, and Sa'd Lûqâ among others. I am indebted to M. Yûsuf Najjâr for these.

But if many contributors incline towards pessimism, the high quality of most of their papers is a hopeful sign. Many seem to attain a very high scientific level: for instance that concerned with the Institute for the study of soil dynamics, a paper on the lighting of Cairo which is both historical and technical, and so on. They also show an admirably practical spirit. A national industry, if it is to be really independent, must adhere as closely as possible to local production, consumption and habits. Whence the considerable interest for these countries of processing industries: these have a primary emotional appeal.[1] Iron metallurgy is impressive and exciting; but the preservation of vegetables and fruits is closely linked with the habits of the peasantry, themselves often consolidated into ritual. The apricot pulp of the Ghûṭa near Damascus plays a part in Ramaḍân. And it is significant that the drying industry, in Egypt, merely carries on that of a small town, among others, in the canton of Mît Ghamr devoted, from time immemorial, to the preservation of the *bâmya*. . . .

Thus the 'new industrial world' these technicians hope for is served not only by the serious scientific training of its promoters but also by their keen social conscience. Engineers do not minimize their responsibilities. But they are sharply aware, with typically Eastern alternations of pessimism and optimism, of the ambiguous rôle incumbent on them: agents of material progress, but with gloomy forebodings about progress in the broader sense; disillusioned intellectuals, but a powerful social motive force. . . .

And here is the third example of self-criticism. It is the account of a congress on standardization held in May 1958 at Beirut.[2] Necessities of mass production and commercialization impose upon industrial articles forms, standards and scales which gradually become international. They permit of large-scale exchange of goods, and allow one to hope that harmony will eventually be reached between the various countries as regards production, consumption and mental attitudes. It is highly significant that the Arab East has consented to show its mettle in this sphere, and that this Congress should have been held in Beirut. At its opening the Lebanese Minister pointed out with pride that Lebanon was, after Egypt, the second country to set up a centre for

[1] Significantly, the *Rasâ'il* of the Planning Committee (1958–9) devote the same attention to consumption. Cf. brochures 25, on soil products; 39, on metallic products; 41, on the food industry; 46, on consumption policy (by Dr. Kamâl Ramzî Stinio).

[2] Reported in a special number of *Courrier de la normalisation*, May–June 1958; cf. also *Economie libanaise et arabe*, June 1958.

standardization. There is in fact a centre of industrial research at Beirut already. One of its members, Dr. Kamâl Sa'd, shows how harmful the lack of standards can prove. Hitherto Lebanon has exported well-made valves and taps; a fraudulent manufacturer makes some which of course are not up to standard, since there is no standard, and the whole market is lost for Lebanon. There is still no standard in the organizations concerned with the export of fruit and vegetables, so closely bound up with the country's essential efforts: and so this industry loses value. It fails to reach the level of commercial prestige at which it should aim, through lack of measuring instruments, etc.

Regrets are not lacking, as we see. In actual fact standardization has hitherto been practised in only one of the Arab countries: Egypt. Dr. Maḥmûd Ṭal'at has traced the progress of this quiet victory. The idea of setting up standards only occurred to Egyptian engineers in 1939. The request for such a step to be taken was put forward in 1947 by their Association. In 1949 committees were formed for that purpose. It is interesting to note that a skilled linguist was attached to these, for the inherent difficulties of standardization throughout the world are accompanied in Arab countries by a difficulty in terminology, which was a particular source of anxiety. This did not impede their efforts in more concrete spheres. The Association of Egyptian Engineers sent a delegate to standardization committees in Great Britain and France. Finally in January 1957 a Government decree established an Egyptian standard. This was a decisive step. An Eastern country had come into line with great productive and industrial countries. It had gained access to a civilization based on material objects. And this necessitated such measures as the establishment of a legal authority for the unification of weights and measures, the elaboration of standards for materials and products, the search for ways and methods of making these materials and products conform to standard classifications, the supply of spare parts to manufacturers, etc.

The most important response was Egypt's adhesion to the metrical system. As a matter of fact this was not easily achieved; in 1951 the decision was taken, but in 1957 the step was postponed for another five years so as to allow a greater margin for adaptation. As late as July 1958 a notice in the press announced that the Weights and Measures authority would cease stamping non-metrical units at the following dates: measures of grain, January 1959; petrol pumps, June 1959; non-metrical scales, January 1960.

This tremendous revolution took place, let us notice, during the

Suez crisis. It passed unnoticed. And yet the historian might have drawn instructive conclusions from this coincidence; at the very moment when the Arab countries, led by Egypt, were displaying aggressive nationalism, they were meticulously and indeed meekly operating their transition to industrial standardization and to the metrical system. This evolution has now been completed. The Arab League has taken the decision on behalf of all its members. And the historian who is accustomed to discern the negative and positive aspects of any social action will note that the more the Arab world shakes off the yoke of the industrial West, the more resolutely it intends to adopt its cultural content. . . .

And meanwhile, what of its feelings?

Fû'âd Shâ'ib tells a revealing anecdote.[1] A peasant wanted to sell his mule in order to acquire a car like that of a rich man in his village. He left the city in spite of his wife's entreaties. But on his way, by chance or by God's will, he came across the car, broken down; the mule drew it back to the village. A humiliating return journey for the machine, but a cheerful one for the worthy beast, which had thus triumphed over the car and no doubt over a good many other things. This sort of story or fable does not belong solely to the old peasant civilization. In *Riḥla ilâ'l-ghad*, Taufîq al-Ḥakîm uses science fiction to relate the interplanetary journey of two men, both condemned to death but as dissimilar as possible: an idealist and a materialist. His sympathies are naturally with the former; he takes him to an unknown world and makes him marry a dark woman, who represents spiritual values, the past, the East. This choice is hotly criticized by Maḥmûd al-'Âlim,[2] who in a fine passage of pro-scientific optimism praises *âla*, the machine.[3]

Attitudes, then, are divided. This is the case even in the Western world, where those who long nostalgically for a lost Golden Age are at odds with Utopian enthusiasts; and we know how even in the realm of literature Marxism exalts the hopes of industrial man. But in the Arab world this conflict is accompanied by another, a specifically Arab conflict. The Arab is torn in his feelings about technique, towards which he is moving so swiftly; it had hitherto appeared to him as the

[1] Cf. passage translated by V. Monteil, *L'Orient*, Beirut, 6 Sep. 1958.

[2] Maḥmûd al-Âlim, *Falsafat al-masraḥ 'inda Taufîq al-Ḥakîm*, *al-Shahr*, Nov. 1958. One of the most important theoretical works of Arab Marxists, together with Anwar 'Abd al-Mâlik's article on history in his preface to his translation of Gordon Childe; cf. also, from a different viewpoint, 'Abd al-Jalîl Hasan, 'Ma'nâ al-insân wa'l-âla', *Âdâb*, *tishrîn*, 1958.

[3] This pro-scientific optimism is not new in the Middle East; at the beginning of this century it inspired the *Muqtaṭaf*, echoed today in the work of Dr. Fû'âd Ṣarrûf. Cf. his recent work on scientific positivism.

prerogative of foreigners, of the West.[1] He wants to acquire it, but meanwhile to reject the foreigner's ethic, which is so closely bound up with his technique. Can such a thing be done?

[1] Dr. Shukrî 'Ayyâd, discussing this book in a friendly article in *Ahrâm*, 24 April 1961, disputes my analysis on this point. In his view, the ethics of industrialism are not the special characteristic of the West, since in the Middle Ages the Arab world anticipated the West in this direction. I believe, however, that just as a certain rationality was 'Arab' in the twelfth century, so the industrial revolution is marked today by the contemporary historical characteristics which make of it a discovery, and a weapon, of the West. Nevertheless the Arab countries may well find through a return to their classicism an authentic impulse towards modernity.

CHAPTER VI

The Reluctant Entrepreneur

Enterprise is a dynamic union between capital and technique on the one hand and personal initiative on the other. An individual strives to grasp forces which are too great for him and to combine them in an ever-closer hold over nature. And the entrepreneur has been hitherto, as much as the inventor, the agent *par excellence* of economic history, as described by Western authors. His rôle, already glimpsed by Cantillon, and defined by J. B. Say, has been acclaimed by Schumpeter.[1] According to this distinguished Viennese writer, the entrepreneur is not to be confused with the financier, the director or even the technician. He combines something of all these. He unites and utilizes all their activities to his own ends, which are to create and to innovate. And this is why different stages of history involve also a sequence of types: from the trading manufacturer of the early stages of the Industrial Revolution to the captains of industry of the first half of the nineteenth century, leading eventually to those characteristic figures of the twentieth, directors, managers, founders of industry, who are increasing all over the face of the globe: agents and products at once of industrial civilization.

Application of Theory in the Middle East

Arabic has no word to express this concept. *Mu'assasa* means rather 'institution', as does *munaẓẓama*. *Muqâwil* refers to a jobbing workman, one who subcontracts a piece of work. And neither *muhandis*, the engineer, nor *muta'ahhid*, the contractor, conveys the idea of concrete

[1] J. Schumpeter, *Capitalism, Socialism and Democracy*, 1961, and the criticism of certain of his views by F. Perroux, *L'Economie au XXe siècle*, 1961. On the Arab East, see the article by Ch. Issawi, 'The Entrepreneurs' Class', in *Social forces in the Middle East*, Fisher, 1955, pp. 116 ff.

initiative and of technological and economic solidity suggested by the word enterprise. In fact the type, in Arab countries, is split into a number of others, which hitherto have never been combined. The engineer, the big business man and the big bureaucrat assume the functions of the entrepreneur, in different capacities but always incompletely. These functions do not yet appear, therefore, to be clearly outlined. Their uncertainty is due to other features of the formation of capital and of technical evolution in these countries. And it is not surprising that the language, as well as any typology that might be based on the evidence of press reports and photographs, confirms such correlations. This uncertainty implies backwardness, or promise: a choice must be made between the two.

The American University of Beirut has studied the problem. One of its professors, Yûsuf Ṣâyigh, devoted to it a thesis as yet unpublished, but accepted at Johns Hopkins.[1] The Department of Economic Sciences last year launched a project of investigation, the results of which are unknown to me, but whose programme reveals its direction.[2] The chief question was whether the distinctive features of the entrepreneur, as revealed by Western experience and technical methods, are or are not to be found in the Arab East. Now this deductive method inevitably leads to an impasse. And we had been aware of this from the beginning. In Ṣâyigh's view the Arab environment acts as a restrictive and even as a repressive influence on the type. Although potential entrepreneurs are highly susceptible to the profit motive, it influences them less than it does those of Western countries. The Iraqi entrepreneur, for instance, turns for preference to trade, for he dreads the risk involved in industrial ventures. He is discouraged, too, by the slenderness of his original capital, he feels helpless through his ignorance of organizational processes. This is why those individuals that reach the entrepreneur level are usually foreigners or members of national minorities. Those nationals who do attain it become outsiders, says Ṣâyigh, in relation to their own country; they take on a social and mental colouring that jars with their original background. In the end their homeland no longer recognizes them.

[1] Yûsuf A. Ṣâyigh, unpublished thesis (1953) and reprint of an article in *Entrepreneurial History* (Research Centre in Entrepreneurial History), Harvard, 1958, pp. 123 ff.

[2] Under the direction of Professor Yûsuf Ṣâyigh, 'The conceptual framework and phasing of the study of entrepreneurship in relation to development in Lebanon', A.U.B., Beirut, 1 Aug. 1958. Cf. Arthur E. Mills, *Private Enterprise in Lebanon* (A.U.B., n.d., 1959?)

Equally pessimistic is a dissertation by the American professor, Morroe Berger, whose forecast for Egypt's future is a negative one.[1] He does not believe that the Arab world can hope for progress from enterprise nor from any development of enterprise, but chiefly from conjunctions and combinations of various sorts between local and foreign capital, whether public or private. It is likely to attain its industrial development by bringing into contact, flinging together, capital (irrespective of its source) and groups of workers, rather than by following that specific course of action known as enterprise in Western countries. In short, the economic process would issue from the pragmatic interaction between a monetary flow and a labour force.

As a sociologist, Morroe Berger insists on the 'differential' factor, and we shall follow him on this point. But, basing his observations, quite correctly, on interviews, he has perhaps been too easily impressed by an attitude frequent in Eastern countries, and exemplified by Yûsuf Ṣâyigh: the ambiguous reaction of all Arab researchers towards their own background. This leads them alternately to dispute anything that differentiates their countries from more highly developed ones, whether a nuance of character, an accident of condition or a phase of growth, and then to deplore that nothing happens to them as it does elsewhere. According to such a point of view, economic doctrines hold good for the Arab world and yet, at the same time, make its deficiencies exaggeratedly apparent. But these judgements, rather than expressing reality, reveal the uprootedness of the Arab thinker. We shall be on surer ground if we consider many of these 'singularities' from a historical angle.

Islam, as we have seen, advocates immediacy in transaction, almost simultaneous exchange. As soon as there is delay in fulfilment, as in forward deals or limited partnerships, the Arab hesitates. He grows strongly suspicious of the very formulae to which world economy owes its growth. It is founded on a study of probabilities, whereas Islamic dogma proscribes the taking of risk. However, the obstacle is only a theoretic one. It no longer causes moral conflict, in most cases. Our enquiry should be directed on contemporary attitudes: not that these have completely shaken off the doctrinal background, but because history transforms situations. Our business is not to denounce, on the ground of certain Western postulates, the supposed inefficiency of Arab bourgeois or young people as entrepreneurs, but to try to distinguish in this matter the part played by continuity or discontinuity.

[1] Morroe Berger, 'The Middle Class in the Arab World', *Princeton University Conferences*.

Concretely, such a study should distinguish between various psychological levels, geographical zones and evolutionary phases. The latter may even be observed with the clarity of an experiment. For the different Arab milieux reveal successive stages and varied types of modernization. The fact is that in spite of theory, the Arabs are becoming entrepreneurs; and they are doing so, as is only natural, by means of enterprise.

Historic Characteristics of Egyptian Enterprise

Before 1930 we note nothing but hesitant beginnings. The starting-point of industrialization coincides with the early stages of protectionism. At this period the activities of the Miṣr group were already developing. Loans were being systematically granted to industrial establishments. In 1945 it was generally admitted that Egypt, to consider that country alone, provided for its own needs in the following proportions: sugar 100 per cent, alcohol 100 per cent, cigarettes 100 per cent, salt 100 per cent, flour 99 per cent, cotton goods 96 per cent, footwear 90 per cent, cement 90 per cent, soap 90 per cent, furniture 80 per cent, matches, beer 75 per cent, vegetable oils 60 per cent.[1] The progress of investment follows the same rhythm. From £E86 million for the single year 1939, it rose to 91·4 million in 1945, 114 million in 1947. By the end of 1950 it was nearly £E140 million, being a total increase of 50 per cent and an increase of 170 per cent for industrial capital.[2]

It is instructive to compare these figures, taken from the Bulletin of the National Bank, with those given at a much later date by the Arab Chamber of Commerce for the period 1950–53, reproduced in a recent work. Egypt at this time was supplying its own needs to the amount of 95 per cent: cotton goods and industrial cotton 47 per cent, sugar 64 per cent, chemical industries only 15 per cent, fertilizers 69 per cent, small-scale production, small iron and steel articles, 40 per cent.[3] These figures show, although certain percentages have dropped, a progress in the realm of self-sufficiency, at all events in that of raw material production, and especially in systematization and conception, one might even say in sincerity. Added to which Egypt enters henceforward on a phase of active growth. The production index (taken from a statistical report of December 1958), considering the basic index as 100 for the year 1952, is made up as follows: electrical energy 260 per cent,

[1] *Ec. Bull.*, 1948, III, 113 (1945 census); 1951, IV, 249 (post-war progress); 1954, VII, 10 (review of Egyptian industries for 1953); 1952, V, 124 (on the Industrial Bank).

[2] *Ec. Bull.*, 1957, X, 338 (progress 1945–54).

[3] Burhân al-Dajânî, op. cit., p. 136.

petroleum 141 per cent, fertilizers 363 per cent, cement 154 per cent, iron 190 per cent, iron ore 154 per cent.

Naturally, we have no means of checking how far such encouraging figures are due to governmental optimism; in any case they imply considerable dynamic power. This is the best reply to the objections of academic critics. The historian cannot, however, rest satisfied with so crude an index, and dares not assert that a mentality of industrial type is exclusively dominant in Egypt's economic life. As late as 1948 most businesses were being run directly by the owner; there was little dissociation between the position of the owner, still close to that of landlord from which it was originally derived, and the function of director or technical expert. There were still, at this period, many foreigners in managerial positions, and very few among the workers. And in particular the classification of private enterprises according to the number of their employees yielded the following curious result: 13,957 businesses with a staff of less than 5; 4,917 with a staff of 5 to 9. Obviously, these are still at the stage of craftsmanship, in technical methods if not in volume of production. Everywhere, small-scale businesses linger on.[1] This makes it difficult, in many respects, to interpret the statistics of the Arab countries. For if in Egypt, for some time past, only firms employing more than 10 workmen have been considered as industrial undertakings, the corresponding figure for Lebanon is only 5, for Iraq only 1![2] And as for Syria, an author who had just been attending the Congress of Chambers of Commerce admitted that he did not know the answer. For a long time, preliminary definitions were discrepant or lacking.

However, it is impossible to deny a certain progress, which the banks' documents make palpable. See for instance the figures for 1948; in textiles (we should imagine that textiles would create an immediate demand for great masses of workmen, great numbers of machines, hence for large-scale investment) for 9,644 businesses there were 12,595 owners! More owners than businesses! On the other hand, if these 9,000 businesses employ a total of over 100,000 workers, that is to say an average of 12 workers each, the 58 firms concerned with mineral extraction belong to 39 owners and employ a total of nearly 7,000 workers; here, technique has brought about the rule of economic concentration.[3]

[1] *Ec. Bull.*, 1948, III, 113 (historic study of the cotton industry); 1949, II, 70 and 1951, IV, 95 ff.; sugar: 1950, III, 13; cement: 1950, III, 242.

[2] Burhân al-Dajânî, op. cit., in the preface.

[3] *Ec. Bull.*, 1948, III, 120–21 (charts).

In the Annual Report of the Federation of Egyptian Industries for 1951 we still find strong reservations made as to the industrial faculties of the country. The authors criticize the customs regulations, as flagrantly inconsistent from an administrative and legal point of view.[1] Nevertheless, a great step has been taken since 1930; producers are no longer satisfied with a timid protectionist policy, but aspire to total self-sufficiency. Only they complain of the country's indifference to the problems of production, of the absence of any general policy, of the fact that their action is alternately sacrificed to the demands of provisioning and disturbed by social upheavals or the requirements of the treasury. In short, they want the impossible: namely total protectionism without State control or insistent taxation. They denounce the almost clandestine attitude adopted by many entrepreneurs. 'Each week they avoid declaring their production, and fake their accounts, their profits, the number of their workers.'

Let us not be so severe. Surely the small producer, lurking in his dusty workshop in the slums and far removed from the mentality of the great factory or *warsha* (the word is akin to 'workshop') is the same that we saw in the Bâb Zuwaila district? Through him can be brought about the union between modern manufacture and old craftsman's skills: the sort of thing that happened in the old Faubourg Saint-Antoine in Paris. And much that is modern and acquired can be combined, through him, with what is traditional and instinctive. A theme for the Utopian to dream about, and for others too. . . .

Regulations and Life

Let us pass quickly from this pre-Revolutionary period to our own. We recognize today the same general characteristics. No doubt they are less easily distinguished in such a troubled context. To trace them too assiduously would smack of tendentiousness, or at least of journalistic methods which this study hopes to avoid. I will confine myself to recognizing these constant factors in an official report which attacks them: the Egyptian Law 26, reorganizing joint-stock companies.[2] It endeavours to extend the number of shareholders so as to counteract family group concentrations and trusts. It raises the ceiling of reserve funds and limits the maximum of dividends to 10 per cent. It must be understood that capital is only invested, as a rule, if it can be renewed in three or four years; also that too often the point of view remains that

[1] According to *Ec. Bull.*, 1951, IV, 247.
[2] Commentary in *E.F.S.P.A.*, 1959, p. 86.

of a tradesman, rather than an industrialist's, even if the investment is in small-scale knitwear factories such as we see in Cairo today. Building concerns are preferred to anything else, because the money thus invested is multiplied within a few years, and also because of their impressive and monumental character. Sometimes a block built in 1930, and still sound, is pulled down to make room for a new building: rent restrictions are thus avoided. And that is why in every corner of Cairo you hear the sound of hammers knocking pile foundations into the clay subsoil. And the makeshift buildings crumble, as was recently seen in Alexandria. The law is directed against such behaviour. And it quite rightly mistrusts the sumptuous allotment of dividends which, too often, so it is said, were possible only by dint of faking the real results. Big city blocks, elevators of gleaming metal that suggest a futurist metropolis, glossy Cadillacs, costly chalets at al-'Ajamî or 'The Desert', wealth flaunted at the Pyramids Inn, all meant to reassure shareholders and encourage endorsement, are henceforward viewed unfavourably. And by a correlation which cannot surprise the sociologist, their retreat means also that of a certain social class, a political attitude, almost a certain physical type, and a way of speaking. We shall not here go into the aesthetic changes, the cultural hazards, the individual odysseys involved by such measures. The fact remains that they have been speeded up in Egypt since the so-called socialization laws of July 1961; accentuation of agrarian reforms, dispossession of a whole number of businesses, radical increase of taxation. Meanwhile, as though in a sort of structural alternation with Egypt, Iraq, has been striving, after two years of restriction, to encourage foreign and private investment once again. The 'climate' is none the less, even in easy-going Lebanon, one of State control—of control, at any rate.

Of course the dead do not willingly submit to burial. Supporters of the old tradition of free trade and of its extreme form, speculation, resent such measures. Geneva becomes the centre of a group of Arab émigrés—bourgeois, capitalist and working class.[1] The reaction, subdued or violent, varies at different times and in different countries. It takes place moreover in a wider context than that of the Arab world, one in which the mutual antagonism of two economic concepts are at odds, each with its own champion: U.S.A. or U.S.S.R. Moreover, local conditions incline men's hopes in different directions: the rival claims of trade and manufacture affect the initiative of individuals and groups. Thus at Beirut, where simultaneously a solemn petition of

[1] *Usbû' 'arabî*, 21 Aug. 1961.

tradesfolk demanded a return to unbridled *laissez-faire*, while industrialists put forth protectionist plans.[1] The latter are concerned with structure, as it were, the former with contingencies. In any case, the two are at strife, involving a number of other factors and concealing many more.

Lebanese Ingenuity

While these new regimes seek to maintain between the hostile orthodoxies of East and West on the one hand and, on the other, the specific character of the Arab world, that sort of astute experimental balance at which Arab statesmen are so adept, let us observe the wholly pragmatic progress made during the past generation by the manufacturers of Beirut.[2]

Some twenty-five years ago a young man emerged from his back-street school. He had always enjoyed handling tools; and for a long time he worked as a handyman, repairing, adjusting, taking things to pieces and putting them together again. At last he began to make things himself; he set up his own little workshop. He was asked to make a lift-cabin. He copied an imported model, but his customers were satisfied. Seized with ambition, he installed a small factory at Furn al-Shibbâk, then a larger one at Sinn al-Fîl, which covered 3,000 square metres and employed 120 workmen. His evolution had followed that of the household equipment of his country. And that is what is interesting about his experiment. He first manufactured some of those oil-burning stoves which have come into common use in Lebanon, as the Primus has in Egypt, and which are a sign of the gradual lightening of women's tasks, and of the growing scarcity of the natural fuel. Towards 1950 luxurious elevators came into use in the Middle East; this was also the era of concrete buildings, speculation on rents and urban investment. And today a third development is taking place: that of middle-class domestic accessories, including washing-machines; all of which implies an upheaval in household economy, of which our man, without analysing it, takes advantage. One of his fellows, in 1956, began to specialize in refrigerators. Refusal to accept the limitations of one's surroundings is one aspect of contemporary civilization. A certain Arab king, when he goes hunting, takes a refrigerated cabinet along with him, which would have astonished the poets of the pre-Islamic era. Our manufacturer does not waste time over such nostalgic comparisons. He produces a

[1] Cf. for instance *Jarîda*, 16 Nov. 1959 and *Orient*, 23 Nov. 1959.

[2] Investigation reported by Lucien Georges in *Orient*, summer 1957.

great number of refrigerators and sends them as far afield as Kuwait and Saudi Arabia.

We can see how important a part is played by the more luxurious, if not the more natural, forms of consumption. These promise the biggest profits. Hence, too, the interest taken by entrepreneurs in the brilliant nightly illumination of the wealthier districts. Neon lighting made its first timid appearance in Beirut in 1943, the change in the city's aspect coinciding, curiously, with political change. A Lebanese engineer, duly provided with European diplomas, devoted himself to this development. His art made good progress and invaded the whole field of electric lighting. He produced the first national light bulb in 1951. By 1956 he was making half a million lamps a year.

But these rapid changes are not only noticeable in the background to good living. They affect food, too, as we have seen; and thus they reach more extensive layers of society. Wine, indeed, is too heavily discredited by the doctrinal ban; beer far less, fortunately. And mineral drinks not at all; whence all the noisy attempts to push various brands. In the case of one famous make, the controversy caused the importers some anxiety for a time. Punctilious lawyers had smelt danger: was the dreaded imputation of *ḥarâm*, taboo, going to make sales drop? They soared, however, for the public relations officer was able, by means of whispered propaganda, to spread the fame of the beverage's aphrodisiac virtues. And now the blood-red bottle-crate and its resounding slogan—in Arabesque writing, of course—have become a familiar feature of the rural or urban landscape. Meanwhile hierarchies and fashions persist in consumption habits: the choice of wine or beer, whisky, champagne or Coca-Cola, characterize ways of life, social levels and one might almost say, psychological or even political trends.

In Lebanon, which makes passable wines, an industrialist set up a brewery, in competition with a French firm. Patriotically and profitably, he got the better of it. He did so through a rustic habit of concentration of labour; whereas his competitor was ruining himself through excessive costs, he did everything himself with the help of cousins come down from the mountains, as sober as they were stalwart. Meanwhile another competitor appeared, a compatriot unfortunately. And then there began a war between the two brands of beer, the 'two sisters' war' as it has been called. Today the export stage has been reached, together with some anxiety about the home market. For other breweries have been set up in Syria; and our industrialists are now dreaming of protective tariffs. . . .

Such initiatory efforts are not confined to articles of current consumption. By tradition, they are applied to the building industry. To build, you need cement. And this time, innovation, Schumpeter's favourite theme, was to be strengthened by spiritual prestige: a bishop founded the first factory, in co-operation with some Frenchmen. Another remarkable historic coincidence. . . . But the business did rather badly, and a Swiss group had to refloat it. In any case the initial inspiration had been correct: the result is the important factory of Shikka, on the Tripoli road.

Weaving started in a picturesque fashion in Lebanon even before the rise of Maḥalla al-Kubrâ. The brothers 'Arîḍa, who came from a great family in the north of the country, began the experiment. In 1937 one of them made his fortune in Mexico. This émigré did not remain there with the *Mahjar* poets. He returned home a capitalist. He settled in the back streets of Tripoli, in Bahsa, an unsavoury district which, like Rausha in Beirut today, had a reputation for suicides and criminal assaults. The younger of the two brothers believed in the future: he ventured boldly into the unknown, risking his whole fortune. It was during the days of the Mandate. He had to wage a lively war against officialdom, he tells us. The development of industry in these countries has always met with opposition from Colonial authorities; this has given it an extra spur, and that moral character which always appeals to the Arabs. In general, foreign authorities do not favour industrialization, and they are moreover bureaucratic. Eventually, exasperated by these officials and all the problems of duties and currency, 'Arîḍa decided to give up speaking French! On the eve of the war he was even considering going to Iraq, a country which was still new, still coloured by Feisal's adventure. There is much to be said for being an efficient Westernized industrialist in a romantic and primitive country; such a contrast may yield considerable profits for a limited period. Eventually the affair was taken to the League of Nations, and a French arbiter, M. de Caix, was sent to investigate; he persuaded 'Arîḍa to stay at home, in consideration of a customs protection of 20 per cent. Today the factory produces annually 12 million metres of stuff.

The Miṣr Group and its Rivals

A glance at one of the Annual Reports published by the Federation of Egyptian Industries shows that a considerable number of articles are now made locally. Some of them are rather odd, for instance those Basque berets which the writer Taufîq al-Ḥakîm was, for a long time, as far as I know, the only civilian to wear. On the other hand, the manufacture of concrete in all its forms was inevitable: cellular concrete, pre-compressed concrete, pre-cast concrete, etc. . . . Other items, such as pharmaceutical products, recall the stubborn conflict between foreign importers and local trusts. The list of entrepreneurs includes a great majority of Egyptian names, mostly Muslim, but including certain traces of the immigration from Syria and Lebanon at the beginning of the century. We should not, however, have received the same statistical impression from consulting an Annual Report of only ten years back. In the interval, Egyptian economy has picked up. Where cosmopolitan participation still asserts its claims is in the section discreetly headed: 'Principal purveyors of Egyptian industry.' These, by their origins and especially by their contacts, display a piquant eclecticism. One of them represents at the same time Danish, Bulgarian, French and American firms. And social psychology will find a scrutiny of this commercial heraldry rewarding—this picturesque display of labels, slogans, telegraphic addresses, often eulogistic in tone and auspicious-sounding, such as the address of M. X: 'Admiration, Cairo.' Or revealing ethnic odysseys, like that leather merchant whose sign, 'Cueros', suggests Salonika, with Spain in the background.[1]

We might discourse at length about these slogans, these *shi'âr-s*. Meanwhile the economist would assess the success or failure of the undertaking, the psychologist would seek to collect biographies and catalogue attitudes. Here unfortunately we are faced with the need for thorough investigations, including personal details. This presents an additional difficulty to the foreign enquirer, who must not overstep the bounds of discretion. The only method within his reach is the interview, and that is an uncertain one. None the less it would bring out some obvious differences in character and in degree of development. The picture of Lebanese experiment, from which I have quoted a few examples, is chiefly one of individual efforts and aptitudes, stimulated by keen demand from the consumer. Elsewhere, of course, conditions are more primitive. At Baghdad, for instance, the type does not seem to have emerged so clearly. It is perhaps only in small transport businesses, themselves bound up with the increased circulation of men and merchandise, that the local entrepreneur comes into view. Wealthy landed proprietors, in certain privileged cases, turn towards banking activities

[1] *Annual of the Egyptian Federation of Industry* and *Foreign Trade of Egypt*, for 1954–55. The secretary of this organization, the noted historian Ṣubḥî Waḥîda, died recently and has been replaced by Dr. Aḥmad Rif'at.

and, more rarely, towards manufacture. Thus the Damirjî family, who owned almost the whole of the Bâb Sharqî district in Baghdad, launched out into industrial tannery. Parallel to the rôle of landlord families, evident here as in Damascus (the 'Aẓm-s for instance) we must set the still distinctive part played by national minorities. The latter, however, is subject to variations. It has dwindled markedly in Egypt during the last few years. And a certain form of economic symbiosis between the European manager and the Coptic assistant, or the Syrian underwriter, is passing more and more into the realm of the past.

National feeling and the instinctive desire of local bourgeois to regain their own from foreign business men cannot in fact be dissociated from such developments. The most distinctive of these, old-established but new in its ideas, its resources and its general aims, is the Miṣr group.

Its founder, Ṭal'at Ḥarb,[1] was as conservative in his way of living as he was enterprising in business affairs. He took his stand against Qâsim Amîn who advocated the unveiling of women. He is said never to have collected the interest on his investments. Hostile to all forms of gambling, he forced one of his most important directors to sell his racing stable. He was a Licentiate in Law and a great connoisseur of French novels, and a man of letters of traditional type. Death overtook him while he was re-editing, with a preface, the collected verse of his friend Ḥifnî Nâṣif. He was greatly attached to his library. He combined the character of a business man with that of a scholar, *adîb*, and a Muslim moralist. His rigorism reminds one, *mutatis mutandis*, of other conjunctions between the economic and the spiritual, about which one might discourse endlessly: the rôle of Protestantism in the rise of industrial capitalism, or Puritanism in the early days of the United States, etc. . . . Be that as it may, this man was equipped with a sound experience of management acquired, notably, at Kom Ombo and on the Council of the Egyptian Co-operative Society. As early as 1910 he had envisaged founding a bank. His ideas, as set forth in his book *'Ilâj Miṣr al-iqtiṣâdî*, had to conquer much sceptical criticism before he eventually succeeded, on May 27th 1920, in founding the group. The registration of shareholders was made compulsory, so that the group should remain entirely national. Arabic was used in all its operations, for any revolution here must have its linguistic side. From the start the group's programme included the promotion of economic

[1] This now legendary figure has been the subject of many portraits, biographies and press articles.

projects, participation in financial and industrial firms, the foundation of Chambers of Commerce, the spread of a spirit of action, solidarity and organization among the youth of the country and the laying of sound foundations for its economic education.

Thus there grew up a huge cluster of enterprises, more than twenty today. The logic of this development is instructive. Things start at the highest level; the very first thing to be set up was a printing press. In a photograph taken on the day of the group's inauguration, Ṭal'at appears significantly flanked by the shaikhs al-Taftazânî and al-Najjâr (1922). The starting-point of these enterprises is not coal mining or the invention of the spinning-jenny, it is a cultural affirmation. The symbol comes first; what we call material reality will follow. But we may note also that this implies a far less risky beginning, secures easy and reliable sales and avoids foreign competition. In 1925 there was formed the Society for Stage and Cinema: a fine example of foresight of the social force—on the whole a constructive one—that these 'superstructures' were to exert over the whole Arab world.

Of course, a third of the Miṣr companies are connected, more or less closely, with textiles. It could not be otherwise. The insolent appropriation by the factories of Lancashire of Egypt's land and peasantry, and eventually of the State itself, was bound to awaken a desire for revenge or at least for emulation. And so we see Miṣr companies for cotton spinning and weaving, for cotton seed, for silk weaving, for cotton export, for fine cotton spinning and weaving. And in 1946 for artificial silk. Seven textile firms. And a miscellaneous group of others: companies for fluvial navigation for instance, for insurance (here we recognize the notion of risk, the core of modern capitalist development), for the preparation of pharmaceutical products, for the production of reinforced concrete, for the commercialization of oils, etc. . . . All of them enterprises of some weight which have not always been very successful, it seems, and which may sometimes have been affected by the corruption which the latest Egyptian law attacks. But from 1930 onwards, under the leadership of Ḥâfiẓ 'Afîfî, the trust revived and showed greater vitality and enterprise. Especially since the war, it has benefited, like so many others, from the flow of currency introduced into the whole region from Morocco to Iraq, owing to the upkeep of the Allied armies, which served to finance the leadership of the local bourgeoisie in the various struggles for independence. Recently (1955) the directors of Muḥammad Rushdî could boast, for the Miṣr Bank, of a capital of £E2 million, with reserves amounting at the same date to £E5,798,283 and net profits of over £E750,000.[1]

At the Industrial Fair at Gezireh[2] in 1959 the Miṣr group occupied the major part of the section allotted to private enterprise, in the central hall. Their cotton, silk and woollen goods showed that here they could compete on the international plane: a fine achievement for this old fellow-traveller of Egyptian emancipation! However, if the Miṣr group can rightly claim seniority for its venture, it no longer stands alone in the Arab world. In Egypt itself other figures deserve our attention: a metallurgist such as Henri Ribbâth, men like François Tâghir, the Sibâḥî-s, Shurbâjî-s, etc. . . . We should in particular stress the significance of a career such as that of the engineer 'Abbûd. Of Palestinian origin, he became interested towards 1930 in the industries of the Aswan region: fertilizers, for instance, and sugars. Then in the famous Alexandrian corniche road, so much discussed subsequently in the press. Then in the Kom Ombo affair, in Cairo buses, and in all sorts of undertakings which were being carried on as best they could be under the existing regime.[3] Yet it was apparently too late, in Egypt, for such a career to run its full course. Following certain misfortunes, 'Abbûd, like so many other business men, had to leave the country.

The regime, as is well known, was hostile to certain other great capitalists, more or less involved with the Wafdist movement, Maḥmûd 'Abd al-Fattâḥ for instance. Actually, the active-minded bureaucrat is the entrepreneur of today. For example an engineer like Muḥammad Yûnis, the skilful director of the organization which succeeded the Suez Company;[4] or those financiers, some of them highly distinguished men, whose realistic and courteous behaviour did so much at Geneva and at Cairo to mend things after 1956. These were Egyptians who could hold their own in the sphere of international intercourse. But do such men exist, are they being trained, in sufficient numbers to take over right away from private capital? This is the grave problem which has faced Egypt ever since its latest nationalizations, which have

[1] Since nationalization, Miṣr still controls a huge group of enterprises now State-owned. See the special number of *Muṣawwar*, Aug. 1961, *A.S.*, several articles, 1 Aug. 1961.

[2] *Economic and Political Review*, Jan. 1959, p. 31.

[3] A good study of modern enterprise in Egypt, already somewhat outdated by the country's accelerated development, is to be found in 'La Société moderne égyptienne', *Tiers-Monde*, April–June 1961, pp. 194 ff. by a group from the S.E.D.E.S. (Société d'Étude et de Développement Économique et Social).

[4] *Economic and Political Review*, 'Suez Canal under Egyptian Management'. April–May 1959.

spared neither the National Bank nor the Miṣr group, now a State holding.

Meanwhile, however, in our capricious wandering from country to country, in a study of types which disregards territorial limits, we are led to discover a sort of counter-type to these State-official-managers in the jovial person of the Director of the C.A.T.M. The late Emile Bustânî was a Maronite from the mountains, who turned Protestant and acquired English culture, a formidable accumulation of potentialities. . . . His *Doubts and Dynamite*[1] is an analysis of the Middle East by a business man who has undergone Western influence, but whose business undertakings, uniting Westernism with a keen appreciation of local needs, offer a synthesis which should satisfy both sides. It seems to have met with scant success at the latest meeting of Arab oil firms, from which indeed one great shareholder was absent, namely Iraq. This time, the Arabs' emotionalism conflicted with their practical opportunities: a just return for all the occasions when, on the contrary, it forwarded them. In any case Emile Bustânî, with the skill and willingness which he exerted in difficult negotiations—polygonal rather than merely triangular—represented, in a Middle East inclining towards State control, the extreme case of a virtuoso of the liberal type, or of the liberal era.

[1] E. Bustânî, *Doubts and Dynamite. The Middle East Today*, London, 1958. Cf. an interview in *Âkhir Sâ'a*, 25 Oct. 1961.

CHAPTER VII

A Contemporary Imamate

At the end of July 1958, the Egyptian Minister of Industry inaugurated a number of new factories: one for black sand in Alexandria, a cannery somewhere else, and finally the famous iron and steel works set up at Helwan by the firm of Demag. Not to mention a power station for South Cairo, a railway-coach factory at Helwan, a factory making batteries and another making medicaments.[1] A year later, the Rameses motor-car was on the market.[2] Every newspaper devoted its third page to reporting industrial activity. You could pick up there at random, any day, scores of small facts as eloquent of struggle and victory as of the difficulties encountered. For instance: a credit of £E5½ million granted for the purchase of medicaments from abroad. For on this point the national trust has to reckon with the prejudice of certain customers. 'Locally manufactured medicaments have been taken into account. However, a small quantity of certain products similar to these will be imported', admits the paper. And the resistance of a certain category of consumers may be guessed from this paragraph. A credit of a million and a half granted for workers' homes: this work has been going on at Duqqî and elsewhere with varying success from an aesthetic and social point of view, but with striking determination. We are told of the visit of Soviet experts concerned with zinc and coke; an ominous sign from the Western point of view, an encouraging one, within strict limits, for local socialism. As if by chance the paper announces a few lines lower down the arrival of British goods at Alexandria, and exchanges made with Sweden. Again, under other headings: the establishment of complex production units in Syria, in

[1] *Egyptian Stock Exchange*, 23 July 1958.
[2] July 1959.

Sinai; a prospective clothing factory, anticipating a typical garment for students, 'obvious customers'.[1]

The newspaper speaks volumes. . . . Under the misleading simplicity of its information we glimpse, simultaneously, the power of the central authority, the desire to control economy on all sides at once, and the stubborn resistance of realities.

The Suez affair and the Egyptianizing laws have merely speeded up a trend towards national recovery which had begun in Egypt a long time before. Nevertheless the speed, and above all the systematization, have increased. Two important offices were set up, concentrating production, *Intâj*, and social equipment, *Khadamât*. Following the incidents of 1956, the management of the nation's business was taken over by the 'Economic Institution', the *Mu'assasa*. And the Planning Committee, *Takhṭîṭ*,[2] exercised similar functions. It is not my purpose to examine the mutual relations or the respective power of these various organizations. Only their common trend need concern us. Thus the *Mu'assasa*,[3] closely connected with the President of the Republic, is responsible for developing the economy by all sorts of industrial, agricultural, financial and even commercial operations. Secondly, for exercising direct control over private enterprise. Whence the formation of commercial, financial and industrial companies, in which the State is an important shareholder. And it is decreed in Article 6 that this body can form companies directly, on its own responsibility, without assistance from any other founders. The members of the organizing bureau must be Egyptian by birth, and must have no interest in the companies with which the bureau works: a measure of considerable social importance, for it aimed at changing the agents of power.

Since then this trend has grown more marked. At the beginning of 1962 Egypt had 361 State enterprises grouped in 39 directions, and themselves connected with 19 Ministries. The latter are controlled by a Higher Council of Public Bodies, itself governed by the Supreme Planning Council. The public sector, thus divided into economic branches, *taqsîm*, has encroached on the private sector or rather has absorbed it, so much so that the State Budget today exceeds in amount Egypt's total revenue for the year preceding the Revolution.[4]

[1] *Egyptian Stock Exchange*, 13 July 1958.

[2] See *Industry after the Revolution and the Five Year Plan*, Cairo, July 1957 *Ec. Bull.*, 1957, X, 40, etc.

[3] *Ec. Bull.*, 1957, X, 37.

[4] *Economic and Political Review*, Dec. 1961–Jan. 1962, p. 25.

Characteristics of Middle Eastern 'Étatisme'

Is not the term *mu'assasa*, which I have translated as 'institution' and which is known to Europeans as 'economic body', in actual fact the equivalent of 'enterprise'? I have already replied in the negative. But it might be said that Egypt, where this trend is carried very far, has found in State initiative its own original type of enterprise. This type, at a first glance, seems a counterpart to the 'big businesses' of the era of free enterprise, such as may be found at Beirut for instance.

Yet we must beware of over-simplified contrasts. There is a kinship between all Arab undertakings, even when their aims and principles are in rivalry. This gives rise to conflicts and interactions which often disconcert the foreigner. It is true that events help to clarify definitions, and that the political situation has simplified things. The Egyptian *Mu'assasa* has to a great extent taken over and liquidated the Franco-British undertakings, of which the most illustrious was the Suez Canal Company. It has set itself up as a counter-type to the universal Company which is characteristic of all capitalist enterprise. This antithesis governs all its actions. In the Middle East today, two economic forces are in opposition: on the one hand the great foreign companies, on the other State-controlled undertakings. The *Mu'assasa* stands in opposition not to such enterprises as those of Emile Bustânî or 'Abbûd, or that of the famous Company of Five, the Khumâsîya of Damascus, but to the former Suez Canal Company, that of the Port of Beirut, the Tapline, Aramco. This contrast can be confirmed in detail. Aramco, I.P.C., etc., with their advanced technique, their world-scale strategy, their greed for monopoly, constitute an extreme form of the old expansive capitalism: far more 'colonial' in fact than many of the things that are stigmatized today as *isti'mâr*. Reciprocally, the State control practised in the Arab world is primarily directed towards resistance and recovery. Hampered by local conditions, by inexperience, by its financial precariousness, it has the advantage of being attuned to popular feelings, which call forth the deep-rooted and hitherto unexpressed will of these countries. Hence the singularity of many of its undertakings, the enthusiasm which these arouse and the individual character which, despite analogies which have been over-stressed, differentiate them from the actions of other nations under other systems. We are surely not ascribing undue importance to the special nature of this approach and of this milieu when we discern substantial differences between the nationalization of Suez and that of the Renault works, between the programmes of the *Mu'assasa* and those of the Soviet planners![1]

This is so true that analysis cannot dissociate these Middle Eastern experiments from the tumultuous support enjoyed by the leader, the *za'îm*. Indeed his rôle is partly, and from certain aspects, that played elsewhere by the economic innovator. He proceeds from that Muslim, or more broadly that Eastern tradition, many of whose guardians—devout, conformist or pharisaical—had been tainted by compromise in the Colonial era. So long as he enjoys unanimous support, he can awaken a profoundly sympathetic response. His speech gives momentary life to the *umma*, the Islamic nation. We see now why the authority he wields, the order he establishes, the colleagues he delegates often appear as the only ones capable of tackling the tasks of modernization. In this field, he must inevitably supplant the business man and dominate the engineer, not only because their weapons—capital or technique—are far less powerful than in our own countries, but chiefly because he contends victoriously with them for their functions.

In the Arab state of former days the merchant and the man of law counterbalanced one another. Dependence on the foreigner has, at the present period, upset this equilibrium. Merchant and man of law both came to terms with dependence, even if they opposed it. Their participation in the bourgeois nationalism of the inter-war period (Syrian *kutla*, Egyptian *wafd* for instance) did not ensure the survival of their type nor fit it to undertake fresh tasks. Whether they benefited by the former regime or opposed it, they too often settled down within its framework, and today they are suffering from its fall. In the new Arab world which has suddenly acquired the responsibilities of independence, and which no protective power, even in self-interest or complicity, safeguards from world competition, it is no longer to the merchant, the lawyer or the king that the masses appeal to assume powers of resistance and revival. It is to the *za'îm*, whose rôle is to recover or at least to reassert their rights, to polarize the forces of a system that had formerly been alienated or centreless.

On the authority of a popular impulse towards justice and reason, he promises to restore the long obliterated harmony with an ethical code

[1] Maḥmûd Muḥammad Ibrâhîm, in his lecture on Egyptian and Indian planning, begins by stressing that any Egyptian plan 'must be derived from a national source; its methods must be based on the positive reality of our needs, *min wâqi'i iḥtiyâjâti-nâ*, and the economic, social, political and cultural circumstances, *ẓurûf*, surrounding us.' *Rasâ'il* of the Egyptian Planning Committee, no. 6, p. 1.

to which these countries, even throughout their liberal phase (which paradoxically coincided with their colonial phase) have instinctively clung. Whereas the canonic reform movement, carried to intolerable extremes by the Muslim Brotherhood, fell into disrepute through its reactionary attitude even more than through its bewildering excesses, the economic initiative of the *za'îm* reconciles the modern world to the ethic of Islam in a tangible context of realization. On this point too it proves itself more authentic than its rivals and adversaries, and more respectful of the old symbols.

For, even in their most astute adaptations to the industrial world, the Arabs of the Middle East find it hard to shed their suspicious attitude towards interest on capital and speculative risks. This explains the uneasiness still shown by Arab statesmen regarding financial affairs. If they profess a virtuous horror of inflation, it is not merely because their advisers have studied under orthodox teachers. It is chiefly because of their reaction against the point of view of the money-changer, whose vain subtleties they instinctively dread. And the Islamic ethical code that inspires them, with all the vigour of an upsurge of majority feeling hitherto unsatisfied, expressed traditionally, through its prohibition of usury and its repudiation of gambling, its preference for a different sort of symbol—the word. This attitude has remained consistent up to our own day. Today, indeed, verbal and numerical signs alike are threatened by the victories of *things*. But these can satisfy another Islamic tendency. The old propensity of Arab society to the immediate and the tangible is favoured by the growth of industrial objects. Islam, by a change of front so to speak, may achieve new harmonies. In this field too the *za'îm* outclasses the business man, and promises more and better things to his compatriots.

Moreover the Middle Eastern merchant has hitherto been notable for shrewdness in speculation rather than for readiness to take risks. Hence his fondness for bargaining, his reluctance to invest, his easy-going elegance and a certain unreliability.[1] On the other hand, the new centralism of the Middle East is acclaimed by some as betokening the advent of modernity, by others as a return to tradition. By its very defects, bureaucracy, so apt to evade responsibility, so dependent on the leader for the least decision to be taken, edifies and reassures its victims. It fits into a pyramidal system which was exactly that of the canonic magistracy. Its inadequacies are more acceptable than the pleasant but

[1] Cf. Dalton Potter, 'The Bazaar Merchant', in *Social Forces in the Middle East*', 2nd ed., pp. 99 ff.

disorderly methods of the Arab business man. Or rather its failings and merits are assessed by contrast with his. It is national, where he is more or less involved with the foreigner: dependable, where he finesses: ruthless, where he is slippery. A closer study shows how it benefits at every turn from the reaction against the colonial period, whose entrepreneurs were men like Willcocks[1] or Paul Bourde, builders of bridges and planters of trees, rather than any colonist, whether manufacturer or tax-farmer. Such men represented a movement of innovation which sought to go beyond what was strictly lucrative, and a power which, while dominating, still strove to convince. And surely it is from the same innovatory trend, reinforced now by a patriotic effort towards *de-domination*, that economic initiative in our own day gets its validity in this part of the world.[2]

And when such validity is wedded to a continuous authoritarian tradition, such as is deeply rooted in the Egyptian people, not only will it command unanimity, which in itself would mean little, but it will gain efficiency. The unexpected promotion of the Egyptian pilots of the Canal after 1956 confirms the close connection of all these phenomena and the effect of collective dynamism in a field which liberal theoreticians assigned to experts and specialists. But let us not anticipate too rashly. For it is easier to comment after the event on the success or failure of such ventures than to forecast them scientifically. But how dare we neglect the contribution of such a 'lesson'?

Egyptian Activism

I have already examined some historical aspects of industrialization in Egypt as regards enterprise. From the angle of Governmental efforts it goes back to the granting of State funds as security for the credits offered by the Miṣr group as early as 1923.[3] In 1947 the Industrial Bank was founded. Since 1956 a planning policy has been under way, in which stress has rightly been laid on study. A set programme controls the various projects, which are organized under various heads: manufactures,

[1] To whom the Egyptian press has been very fair. Another irrigator, Scott-Moncrieff, is, if I am not mistaken, the only Englishman to have a street named after him in Cairo.

[2] An interesting study by E. Terry Prothro and Levon Melikian, *Public Opinion Quarterly*, vol. 17, no. 3, based on tests made in the American University of Beirut, confirms the validity of the F. scale ('Californian'), 'but do not show a positive correlation between authoritarianism and politico-economic conservation'. It is not only the style which is revolutionary, but the function, which is that of the classical *tajdīd*!

[3] *Ec. Bull.*, 1948, III, 133.

mines, petroleum, and productivity combined with professional education. Each project is to be studied from ten points of view, neither more nor less. For example, the incidence anticipated on the national revenue; the amount required for financing; the amount required in foreign bills; the profit anticipated; the possibilities of eventual capital formation; the effect on production, on consumption; finally the strategic consequences, which aspect, though listed last, is in certain respects, and from the angle of self-sufficiency, perhaps paramount to all the rest.

Nevertheless there is no attempt to discourage private capital. Public investment shows the way. Private funds are expected to increase their margin of profit after five years.[1] Thus in 1960 private investment was to rise to some £E50 million as contrasted with 23 million of public investment. It is true that manufacturing industries are of direct interest to private capitalism. In other sectors the proportion is reversed. At the same time, all sorts of measures confirm and strengthen the economic power of the State: the Bank of issue[2] acquires the lion's share of functions, control of credit and control of other banks, from which it can claim a deposit according to a ratio fixed by itself. It further decides the amount of ready money available to these banks, it may even create commercial departments in direct competition. An Egyptian economist[3] has protested against this latter provision as savouring too much of direct intervention. The same trend is seen in the law on joint-stock companies, destined to make the running of these more democratic. Such measures, in conjunction with the Egyptianizing of personnel in enterprise, are aimed at reducing the excessive part played in economic matters by notables and by foreigners, the bey and the *khawâjâ*, traditional and picturesque figures; they seek to enlarge the participation of the small saver, they are carried out by a whole host of bureaucrats, they bring about, sooner or later, a redistribution of functions and of funds; they clearly tend to promote a petty and middle bourgeois class of which the army will, to some extent, have been the spearhead.[4]

Such designs, of course, cannot be carried out without causing repercussions and involving mistakes, some of them regrettable. They incur criticism from the opponents or victims of State control. Complaints of inefficiency seem more serious. These refer, with varying

[1] *Industry after the Revolution*, pp. 104 ff.

[2] Egyptian Law 163, of 1957. But this Bank was to be nationalized too.

[3] *Egypte contemporaine*, no. 292, 1958.

[4] Its rôle has been correctly assessed by Clovis Maqṣûd, *Azmat al-yasâr al-'arabî*, Beirut, 1960, pp. 31 ff.; Morroe Berger, *Military Elite and Social Change*, Princeton, 1960; and *The Arab World Today*, New York, ch. x, 1962.

degrees of justification, to disorder and excessive haste. An oven has burst, we hear, because the coke did not come in time; a German underwriter cannot understand the inadequately formulated criticisms levelled at his paper-pulp factory; what with this and the heat, he nearly goes off his head, and rants to himself in Sulaimân Pasha Street. Elsewhere we hear of a case of costly over-equipment to be discreetly liquidated, or the failure of Taḥrîr province, the only one apparently to be openly admitted. To the general difficulties inseparable from State management are added those arising from a host of defects and deficiencies due to an oppressive past, that 'burden of history' denounced in an extremely clear-sighted book by the late Ṣubḥî Waḥîda. And this burden is so great that efforts to lift it are sometimes inadequate and sometimes excessive.

The investment of private capital had always shown itself extremely timid in these countries. It has perhaps remained so. For a long time it took the form of landlordism. When rents were lowered at the agrarian revolution it moved over into city property. It had to be dislodged with a rent restriction act applying to new as well as to old buildings. Thus harried, capitalists started hoarding, deposited in banks, or gambled on the Stock Exchange. Capital thus took advantage in its own fashion of the economic boom created by autarchic measures. But it can hardly be said to have begun investing creatively, on its own initiative. I need not go into the difficulties resulting from the inadequate training of personnel. These petty bureaucrats are often timorous, incompetent and irresponsible, unable to take the most trivial decisions without recourse to the leader or his military representatives. The law itself in many cases requires its administrators to refer for all questions of principle to the Council of State. Now every specific question involves a question of principle. And decisions are not speedily got from the Council of State, a slow-functioning organ. All enterprises have to apply to the highest authority before paying salaries over £E15, or again before dealing with foreigners. Certain defects of bureaucracy, common to all countries, are here aggravated by defects inherent in the milieu and by the uneasiness of the newly promoted social strata: afraid of initiative, baffled by action. The State displays an increasingly isolationist ascendancy. Exit visas for purposes of travel are obtainable only after long and tedious negotiations.

It is perhaps this severance from the outside world that is most keenly resented, at any rate by the wealthy bourgeoisie, but also, more dangerously, by intellectuals. Of course it is intended as a means of economizing currency and escaping foreign influence, at least on manners and ideas. Such aims are quite legitimate; but they involve the risk of an insularity which is hardly conceivable in the modern world, and to which the urge to self-sufficiency inevitably brings a stimulus more disastrous than failure would have been. The attitude towards the foreign expert illustrates, as I have already noted, these new tendencies. Once imported, this foreigner is considered merely as a purveyor of equipment or technique, and his contribution must be duly disinfected beforehand. The whole policy of visas, preliminary permits, screening committees, labour restrictions, expurgated translations and censorship is intended to strain and purify what comes from abroad, be it merchandise, services or ideas. Thus it is hoped to make use of foreign science, or rather foreign technique, once it has been passed through this autoclave and detached from any ethical or spiritual context. Such a position, though understandable, is nevertheless disturbing. It might lead eventually to a 'deculturation' such as many scholars already anticipate with dread.

There are undoubted risks, excesses or weaknesses which are often corrected by the sympathetic good nature of the Egyptian people, the generous welcome they afford—Egyptian intellectuals in particular—to any expression of sincere feeling from a foreigner, even if it be critical. Comparative studies should reassure them on this point. During such a phase of development, mistakes or frequent failures are less surprising than occasional successes. Good observers such as, quite recently, André Philip, have noted substantial progress in the preparation of the latest Egyptian plan as compared to that of 1956. Other observers have been more severe. The social historian is not disturbed by failures or deficiencies. But he would like more criticism and more information. What strikes him about the year-books periodically published by the U.A.R. is not the increase in figures, which he has no means of checking—and in any case this could not be the aim of the present work—but their scale, together with the orderly survey of facts and the continuity of efforts unparalleled in the rest of the Arab world (e.g., *al-Kitâb al-sanâwi* for 1962, with its lucid reports on planning (p. 77) and on economic policy (p. 25). These statements show a definite improvement on those of previous years). And he welcomes the advance of an idea[1] which is of greater interest to the U.A.R. than material success or

[1] I should like to quote here the lecture of Dr. Ibrâhîm Ḥilmî 'Abd al-Raḥmân, 'An equilibrium consideration of progress, social organization and freedom in a transforming society', at the Congress of Rhodes (Oct. 1958).

the lack of it. An Egyptian sociologist, Ḥâmid 'Ammâr, defines the twentieth century as 'the century of planning'; this, broadly conceived, consists of a 'global figuration', social as well as economic, of what has to be achieved within a given period. This perception of 'globality', of wholeness, is the ultimate key to the Arab countries' potentialities of improvement, and their chances of development, which it can reconcile with what is universal.

A Panorama of Middle Eastern Planning

Industrial objects, as I have said, first invaded the Arab world in the shape of consumer goods, then of tools. At a second stage the Middle East takes over the machine: witness the exhibitions, the imports, the systematic and often ostentatious equipment of the present day. A final stage, which is just coming into evidence, is that of manufacture. Industrialization in the Middle East has a symbolic as well as a historic and psychological interest. The conditions of the milieu being what they are, the greatest degree of success can be anticipated from the launching of vast programmes and extensive projects. These are State projects, if only by their hugeness, and they offer moreover the advantage of providing employment for the masses of workers made available by the breakup of the peasantry, and of transposing naturally into economic authoritarianism old hierarchic concepts which still form part of the national way of life.

The system goes in for pyramid-building. Or rather it feels, in a new context, the centuries-old need to build new pyramids. An economic need, undoubtedly. But almost equally an intellectual and moral need. For such an endeavour asserts and fosters an impulse which is in no way foreign to the country, which does not come to it from outside, as in the case of colonial exploitation, but rises from its own subsoil. Correlatively, too, this explains the interest, often excessive in the eyes of the economist pure and simple, that these countries take in fundamental production, of which steel is a typical example. For steel, *ṣulb*, is essentially 'hard stuff'. When on the occasion of a fair, a figure representing steel was set up in the Place Sulaimân Pasha instead of the romantic statue of the old warrior, a change of symbols was involved, which inevitably had its painful aspect.

There was traditionally a small iron industry in Egypt.[1] It made use

[1] Brochure presented at the 5th Congress of Engineers; *Industry after the Revolution*; brochure on the Iron and Steel Egyptian Co.; *Ec. Bull.*, 1954, 110, on the initial agreement between the Industrial Bank, the Miṣr Bank, the Miṣr Textile Company, the Miṣr Insurance Co. and the German Demag Co.

of scrap iron, *gharda*, which it recast, recovering about 30,000 tons a year. One good result of the war was to bring a great deal of scrap iron into the country; about 200,000 tons. The idea of organizing a metallurgical industry then took shape. Missions were sent to Sweden and Germany. Fuel was a pressing problem: there was a shortage of local fuel, at least in a usable state. Could substitutes be employed, such as bitumen or sugar-cane stalks? These yielded poor results. Finally a daring step was taken. A report was asked for from the German Demag Company. On its advice, plans were drawn up for the Egyptian Iron and Steel Company of Helwan, which began to function in 1958. A metallurgical industry of this sort, where practically everything had to be brought in from outside, flung a real challenge to its surroundings. The difficulties were enormous, but so was the moral reward!

The same is true of the High Dam,[1] of which we have heard so much; it seemed a sort of counterblast to the Suez Canal, being national rather than cosmopolitan, an integral part rather than something imposed from without. The aura of emotion surrounding this project is highly revealing. Egypt expects this sensational achievement to provide her with a source from which everything will flow: water, fertility, food, electricity, little by little a whole new Egypt. But also, and above all, a sort of geographical and logical fulfilment, combined with an amazing revival of her old history. Remember the Egypt of the Pharaohs, the unitary character of the valley, the tremendous power enjoyed by the controller of the water, the ruler of the Nile. There was certainly something of this sort in the High Dam project, as well as economic calculation. And the same thing may perhaps be true of that project for irrigating the desert from oasis to oasis along the *darb al-arba'în*, the 'Street of the Forty': forty days or perhaps forty saints. It runs from Kharga to Siwa and then on to Sollum. It is the old Darfur caravan road. Camels' feet have trodden such deep ruts in it that the path looks like a long harrow stretching out before you to infinity.

If these two projects are realized, Egypt will be reborn on the scale of the Pharaohs. From this angle, Egyptian planning seems less a result of the Soviet example or the advice of the I.B.R.D. than a transposition of its ancestral heritage, an attempt to restore its own authenticity; the very thing towards which the whole of this society is now tending, in its values as well as in its material activities, and with varying degrees of success.

[1] Brochure of the engineer Yûsuf Simaika on the utilization of the Nile Waters. *Rasa'il* of the Planning Committee, no. 33.

Whence the popular enthusiasm now strengthening a *za'im* like Nasser in his ventures. We must not seek the sole explanation in the prestige of the popular leader or the emotionalism of the Arab people. True, he has known how to arouse those ecstasies of feeling, that verbal delirium, as well as those swirling mass movements in which I have already recognized archaic forms of exchange. But underneath, and beyond this, lie the basic constituents which this study aims at discovering under the complexity of men, events and things.

All the Arab countries are not following the same route. In the early days of the Union, Syria seemed to opt rather for industries processing raw material.[1] In its national revenue the position occupied by agriculture was still preponderant in 1957; £S1,059,000,000 as against only 257 million for industry and 388 for commerce (for the country is sparing in the practise of its commercial vocation). The whole added up to £S2,085 million, of which agriculture absorbed 45 per cent, nearly half. Processing industries, therefore, formed a necessary part of the Plan. To which, naturally, other factors were added in consequence of fresh political combinations. This gave rise to controversies which only broke out openly later on.

In former days Syria was dominated by a traditional alliance between three sorts of activity, three types of men, three tendencies: around Damascus the groves of the Ghûṭa, with their olive trees, poplars and apricots; within the city the *sûq* and its traders; finally a very old tradition of literary thought, represented formerly by the Academy of Damascus. These three activities, these three types of men were bound by a common system of civilization. It gave them the exquisite and irascible sensibility which the foreigner has often encountered to his cost. Such a type of humanity remained closely linked to natural phenomena and to the beauty of the setting. This was its poetic, as well as profitable, way of propagating the pre-Islamic tradition through loyalty to Islam. Thus culture and nature were welded together in a whole whose powers of resistance were often experienced by foreign powers, Ottoman or European. Is it far-fetched to recognize today, under the columns of figures and the austere pages of financial documents, the same persistent alliance?

In a recent report of the Central Bank of Syria, references to agricultural life and even to the course of the seasons recur constantly. In 1956–7 came the Suez crisis, and a consequent fall in the price of

[1] *Annual Report of the Central Bank of Syria,* discussed in *E.F.S.P.A.,* Nov. 1958. This review is naturally a mine of information about the Syrian economy.

these foodstuffs, which the author of this report ascribes not to the international upheaval but to an abundant harvest of cereals and fruit. Such a pastoral note amidst the clash of nations brings to our eyes the leafy groves of the Ghûṭa. In 1958 and early 1959 the bankers note with regret a contraction of fiduciary currency and hence a slowing down of commercial activity. But they ascribe this to the bad harvest of 1958. Inversely they anticipate, on the strength of a promising future harvest, an end to the banking recession. These hopes were not fulfilled, as is known. And this had its effect on political developments. Similarly in Egypt the drop in the output of cotton, whatever its origin—an invasion by the parasite known as 'red spider', the failure of the product used to save the plant—had enormous and unforeseen consequences in the latest campaign. In any case, the Syrian Five Year Plan had a long way to go to adjust itself to local realities. For this plan was originally based on theories and pre-established schedules. The Egyptian method, as we have seen, laid down ten criteria of priority. Now out of these ten, in Syria as in Egypt, those related to the nature of things came only in the sixth and eighth places respectively. And yet for all that, the special characteristics of the country are clearly evident. True, the Syrian plan only envisaged, as regards metallurgy, a single factory, at Aleppo, forging chains from Egyptian wire, and metal frames, vessels, chassis and tanks from Egyptian sheet metal. The planners' attention is concentrated on consumer goods. On a total of credits reckoned at £S500 million, processing occupies the second place, immediately after the oil industry (which is of greater strategic than economic importance: £S216 million) and metallurgy only £S2,730,000, about one-tenth. Consumer goods are what matter, and also processing, which turns natural objects into consumer goods in visible and active fashion. The plan therefore takes a close interest in salt, canning, milk, packing, oils, and naturally, too, cotton in spinning and weaving. We note an interesting effort towards decentralization. Homs becomes the capital of weaving; Damascus of the knitting industry; Aleppo will make carpets and blankets. And the five large towns will share the production of 6,000 square metres of *kilîm*, rugs.

And then there is intellectual consumption; this has always played an important part in the Arab world, and it has grown even more important. From the forests of the Syrian republic, from the groves of poplar and willow that surround Damascus, paper is being made for the press. The need is immense and unbridled. The U.A.R. consumes annually 17,000 tons of newspaper. Moreover 25,000 radio sets are being produced; here again, we notice, unexpectedly, the claims of the Word.

There would certainly be much to say about this plan and the differences between its orientation and that of the Egyptian plan. The integration of the two countries as a result of the Arab Union involved a distribution of labour which it is not for me to praise or criticize; public opinion was to fulfil that task and future events to give the casting vote. But although it is invidious for a foreigner to intervene in family quarrels,[1] we may note that the Syrian plan paid more attention to psychological and local factors. Perhaps it thus displayed a sort of compensatory zeal. This seems to be a permanent characteristic of the somewhat irregular evolution of Syrian economic policy. In October 1962 a request from Damascus to Dr Timberghen for expert help resulted in the recommendation of a specifically local approach.[2]

Even Lebanon, the citadel of free enterprise, now aspires to planning in its turn, aiming systematically if not at nationalization, at least at industrialization; some £L600,000,000 are invested under this head. Here is something even more characteristic. Saudi Arabia, as is well known, offers a paradoxical example of what one might call economic and political narcissism, since everything there depends on the king, his family, his allies, his 'brothers' (*Ikhwân*). Everything, even the name of the State. This name, which goes back to 1932, coincides curiously enough with the granting of the first permit of exploitation. In 1944 this was taken over by Aramco. And then began a phase of financial ease, and political prestige unaffected by any constitutional scruples. The first budget dates from 1954–5. And this took the form of a commercial document. But the riyal collapsed. The royalties were devoured as soon as they were received, and even spent in advance. In 1958 this precocious squandering of wealth had risen to 300 million dollars. At this point Prince Feisal's reforms introduced an equalization of dividends to which the new middle class—a sparse but already challenging group—aspired as their minimum. It is true that this provoked a considerable flight of capital. In any case, even here, the economic point of view grew stronger. In 1960 there was formed a Ministry of Petroleum with the wily *shaikh* al-Tarîkî at its head. And even a High

[1] The Egyptians stress the important refloating loans granted by them to Syria; the Syrians, the evil effect of inflation, disproportionate public expenditure and the hindering of private initiative.

[2] *E.F.S.P.A.*, October 1963, p. 7.

Council of Money and Economy. This centralism will no doubt survive when theocracy has disappeared.

Iraq, unlike the U.A.R., has enormous sources of currency. In 1958 it levied by way of oil dues no less than 113,000 million francs[1] for 32 million tons of petroleum. Normally 70 per cent of this was diverted to the Development Office, which was partly managed by international experts. Only five years ago, we should have had to quote as an example of planning and Government effort those Development Weeks which were held in Baghdad every spring. That of 1958 displayed impressive results. And we recognize there that concern with hydraulic engineering which is as characteristic of Egypt and Iraq as of Syria, Lebanon and even Saudi Arabia, and which is not only a hereditary attribute and a sign of perspicacious choice, but an example of close adaptation of Arab societies to the conditions of their milieu.

We are not familiar enough with the course of events in Iraq since 1958 to be able to assess how far these economic plans have taken new directions. In the first book published in Baghdad after the revolution Ḥusain Jamîl, in spite of passionate diatribes against the old regime, made no mention of the Development Board, either favourable or unfavourable; no doubt because he considered it only as an instrument, and ascribed its faults and failings to the influence of the Government. The Board has been subjected to Western criticism inspired by the new requirements self-imposed by economic science, in the analytical studies of 'retarded development' undertaken under the direction of F. Perroux.[2] In order to prove itself capable of economic progress, a milieu must fulfil three conditions: it must have the capacity for economic creation, the latter must be able to spread there, and must have a certain significance.[3] Unfortunately the meritorious achievements of the Board took place within a system where the two latter possibilities were lacking. This was doubtless what caused its failure. But it has been replaced by a Ministry of Planning (1960).

[1] 'Old francs.'

[2] G. Blardone, *Cahiers de l'I.S.E.A.*, Dec. 1958, p. 98.

[3] R. Stransz-Hupe attributes the 'lesson' of July 1958 to 'the indifference or hostility of Iraqi society towards the exact discipline of Western technology' (preface to Fahim Qubayn, *The Reconstruction of Iraq*, 1958). It is surely unreasonable to blame those concerned for the non-significance of the 'progress' imposed on them . . . Cf. also M. N. Quint, 'The Idea of Progress in an Iraqi village', *The Middle East Journal*, autumn 1958, pp. 369 ff.

From Fundamentalism to the Choice of Sudden Progress[1]

Seen from this angle, the Iraqi revolution was, like all revolutions, merely a violent attempt to readjust the meanings of a society. In the world of today this implies, primarily, a transformation of the economic structure. And it is on such a transformation that the future of the Arab countries depends. Although liable to variations according to the material and moral conditions prevalent at different times and in different countries, all experiments in planning in these countries show common characteristics. It is not by chance that the most advanced of them from the economic point of view, Egypt, has had recourse to a sort of fundamentalism which has led it to create a heavy industry almost without possessing any of the natural means for this.

This fundamentalism—and I have deliberately used the term which describes the *uṣûlî* reformist—if it postulates a radical reconsideration of the past, also involves, paradoxically, the deliberate choice of swift progress. Economists argue about the relative merits of slow transformation and sudden mutation. The merits of both are referred, in the last resort, to an indispensable criterion and agent: a change of mentality. So long as this change is lacking, all gains are neutralized, and the cumulative effect is lost. It is no doubt through not having secured this powerful mainspring that many colonial policies have failed, if not to develop their country, at least to integrate this development into the country's life. Most of the partisans of slow progress insist therefore on a psychological factor of adaptation or adhesion which, they rightly consider, can alone stand surety for the rest. But they fail, no doubt, by their dependence on individualist psychology, to grasp the totality of the motivations they invoke. For these cannot be equated with the continuity of mental attitudes. On the contrary, progress, which has got to be total progress if it is to be anything, appears as a point of convergence towards which all the streams of an integral life would flow. Necessarily radical in the inflexion it imposes on each of them, it conciliates them only in its project. In so far as it expresses an impulse towards the future, it inevitably contradicts the continuation of the past. The effort and the resistance it incurs—I almost said that it calls forth—are psychologically characteristic of such situations and postulate a definite type of action and of men of action.

[1] This paragraph owes much to the discussions at the Colloquium on the subject held in May 1959 at the VIth Section of the École des Hautes Études, and in which Charles Bettelheim took part.

This is the case with planning in the Middle East. In order to achieve concrete results, that is to say on pain of failure, it must not only solve difficult problems of finance and technique, but also master whatever in the traditional mentality of these nations resists such aims or even the tensions they involve. Hence the choice is for total change, even if this is not as yet consciously made. For it has only been expressed, hitherto, in the field of economic and social equipment and in that of education in the broadest sense. And a complete overhaul of human attitudes and conditions would involve even wider fields than these; and it would meet with opposition from other forces, still formidably powerful, which the reformers might not be able or even anxious to brave. It is no doubt this greater or less degree of radicalism that distinguishes the various regimes, tendencies or countries. And it is here that the internal conflict of the Middle East becomes part of the world conflict, on an ideological as well as a strategic plane.

The foreigner, even though he may have special knowledge, generally envisages Middle Eastern problems as forming part of the general world conflict for hegemony. Possibly certain Middle Eastern statesmen take the same view. Now it is always misleading to explain internal by external phenomena. On the contrary, at every step in my research I am struck by the distinctive character both of internal conditions here and of the interaction between the internal and the external. If the Arab countries are more and more coming into line with the outside world, if they borrow from others their economic theory, their pedagogic method and all the rest, the pattern into which they organize it all is their own. No doubt they do not always admit to themselves the need for total commitment and personal invention which is essential to their success. No doubt their newborn 'economism' must take account of stubborn facts, of established values, of the world habits in a word, which they pride themselves on acquiring. They have not hitherto put forth any doctrine clearly their own.

But they make up for this instinctively by their collective attitudes. Popular enthusiasm, strenuous assertion of rights, loyalty to the *za'îm* counterbalance the drabness of their situations, the timidity of their analyses. Thus they regain as a whole what they had only conceived or performed in part. Thus, too, by unexpected ways, they recover a certain exactitude. The fact remains that the procedure is instinctive rather than deliberate, and that it may be jeopardized by the irrationality of the methods or the archaic character of the elements involved. The risk is a grave one. It is the price paid for unquestionable successes.

This ambivalence provides, with good reason, one of the most serious subjects of meditation for the historian of the Arab world today, and of preoccupation for its citizens.[1]

[1] This is no doubt why recent Arab publications vie with one another in stressing the notion of 'consciousness', *wa'î*. Hence the florescence of a whole set of neologisms: 'saving consciousness' *idhkhârî*, 'consumer consciousness' *istihlâkî*, 'fiscal' *ḍarîbî*, and 'planning consciousness' *takhṭîṭî*, etc.

CHAPTER VIII

Ascent to the Basic[1]

Reason, trying to fashion reality in its own image and establish logic and justice therein, comes up against the stubborn grain of facts. Amongst these, many, deriving from a closed chapter of the past, are as such repudiated. Others on the contrary remain valid because they constitute both the substance and the object of reason's initiative. The Arab world does not enjoy the privilege of this experience, common to all legislators and men of action. But it faces it the more dramatically, because difficulties that are graver here than elsewhere spring from its internal and external context, and tend to paralyse reform. And also because the distance seems wider here between the possible and the real, between the ideal and the concrete. Whence the vehemence, torn between enthusiasm and suspicion, of attempts to reach 'the basic', one of which is known, almost everywhere, as democracy.[2]

The Arab legislator would be horrified to hear his initial action compared to that of the painter of ikons, who depicts common reality as descending from on high. A sun, in the upper register, gives issue to the things of this world. Their delicate bright colours signify tangible life, while its gold symbolizes the essential. *Ifâḍa*, 'an outpouring', *tanzîl*, 'descent', these picturesque words which Arab mysticism has made pregnant with meaning express also a hierarchical order. But the inevitable next step is an attempt to arouse an upward movement from below, in response to the authoritarian initiative. The more deeply implanted democracy becomes in these countries, the more it will seek to make its

[1] This paradoxical binomial is deliberately chosen.

[2] Discussed by the Congress of the Lebanese Political Sciences Association held at Beirut, Nov. 1959.

base the supreme authority. Its aim is the reverse of the *tanzîl*: it seeks to rise up from what is basic.

Such is, in any case, the explicit aim of many Middle Eastern policies, which invoke democracy with more or less sincerity; the more so as Islam, reverting to that existential immanence which, for it, is the counterpart of ontological transcendence, recognizes itself at least partially in such assertions. The theological concept of 'the people', *sha'b*, bound by subtle links to that of 'the leader', *za'îm*, permits this transition from tradition to present-day reality. Other notions, that of the 'consensus of the community', *ijmâ'*, that of 'canonic consultation', *shûrâ*, even suggest the Parliamentary system, while especially among the Shî'ites, 'categorical effort', *ijtihâd*, proclaims, in the midst of archaism, the virtues of permanent revolution. I am chiefly concerned, however, not with the political blueprints of the present, but with the movement that underlies them and goes beyond them, and which, if we avoid interpreting it too closely in the light of events, reveals the determination of these societies to 'realize' themselves in the world of today.

Iraq experienced in 1958 the dangers that might ensue if a highly concrete effort at development were made without the co-operation of its citizens. For this reason all attempts at modernization or reorganization, whether represented by a man or a class, or by some activity that has become symptomatic of social renewal—technical equipment, pedagogy, political representation, etc.—try to make contact with their material and social bases. Industrialization, mass education, syndicalism display the same trend. This throws light on many of their initiatives. Of course the most effective will not be seen as plebiscites or Parliamentary government in their present forms. We shall have to seek a far deeper level of experience, with a very different sort of authenticity, to discover what now takes the place of the traditional rule of *ri'âsa*, with all its concrete and popular implications. Of these procedures, some are still archaic, and tainted by characteristics inherited from the age of decadence. Others on the contrary give evidence of a skilful assimilation of attitudes and principles borrowed from the industrial world. Rather than enter into subtle distinctions, which would go beyond the scope of this study, I will describe at random a few significant movements.

Factories and Feelings

At the moment of writing, countries like the United Arab Republic are seeking the most obvious link between innovation and basic realities in the form of popular support. This involves speech-making and acclamation on both sides. It is thus at least outwardly connected with a genius for words which is deep-rooted, but which can only serve as a symbol for positive achievement. And indeed, behind this screen of mass-movements and oratory, the organizers concentrate on working in the economic field; and in the first place, on investment. For they propose to increase the revenue in the most orthodox fashion.[1]

Now what is the significance of such progress in countries of which large sections are still at a sub-economic level? A few years ago in Egypt the urban population, half the size of the rural population, consumed three or four times as much. Foodstuffs account for about 50 per cent of the budget of townspeople, over 70 per cent of that of peasants (if such a budget can be imagined). Clothing expenses, 8 per cent of the urban budget, are less than 2 per cent—practically non-existent—for the rural population. The rise in the national revenue, to which planners naturally pin their hopes, does not affect people's feelings. There is an increase in employment; and every Western-style financier, every Socialist planner, envisages this increase of jobs as something essential. True, indeed. But increase of employment in the industrial sector implies uprooting of the peasantry. And for a long time the effect of such uprooting will outweigh, for them, the effect of employment. Other more original methods must be found to adapt economic actions more closely to popular feelings.

At the 1959 Cairo Fair, products made in Egypt occupied 126,000 square metres. The President spent eight hours visiting them: this in itself was a manifestation of the power of number! A great number of articles bore the magic stamp: cotton goods, woollen goods, clothing, fine blankets and brightly coloured carpets, furniture, particularly of metal, fur-skins, pipes and tubes, pottery, preserved foodstuffs. And also batteries, radio sets, plastic and paper articles, medicines etc. . . . A journalist[2] criticized this exhibition on the ground that everything was written in Arabic; almost all the posters were aimed at home consumers. This struck him as a fault, from the point of view of external propaganda. But we may see it rather as an interesting sign of collaboration between the world of objects and that of signs. These two worlds were for a long time rivals in the Arab East. For a whole generation now, efforts

[1] Cf. the wishes expressed by President Nasser on the occasion of the exhibition of productivity, *Muṣawwar*, 12 Dec. 1958, and the prospects set forth by him in his speech on the Anniversary of the Revolution, 23 July 1959. More recently, *Âkhir Sâ'a*, 9 Nov. 1961. See also 'The Egyptian Economy during the Fifties', *Ec. Bull.*, 1961.

[2] 'Âdil Thâbit, *Economic and Political Review of Egypt*, Jan. 1959, p. 31.

have been made to 'acclimatize' industrial objects, that is to say not merely to use them but, at a later stage, to produce them. Now the best way of making the advent of production tangible is to raise the level of consumption. The Arab countries have not escaped the guns-or-butter antithesis. They even experience a supplementary difficulty, from the fact that consumption differs widely between the sector of the upper bourgeoisie and the aristocracy, whose tastes are Europeanized, and the working-class sector.

This was, and still is, very noticeable in most of these countries. The morning meal of beans, *fûl*, eaten by the working class contrasts with the upper-class English or continental breakfast. There is a similar contrast of behaviour in the street, in cafés and clubs; a separation, almost a segregation, between the two elements, the two social layers. But this is tending to decrease, and recent visitors to Cairo have noticed how far many of these public places have begun to assume a more democratic appearance. In Sulaimân Pasha or 'Adlî Pasha streets you can see huge crowds of men in shirt sleeves, drinking little but sitting about for hours playing backgammon. Such scenes, already common at Damascus and Baghdad, may depress the aesthete, but prove instructive to the sociologist, as illustrating the growth of a new petty bourgeoisie.[1]

Rise of New Classes

Here indeed are other phenomena, essentially 'mediatory'. They reflect the profound changes that have been taking place in the Arab East during the past half-century, in the field of social classes and their relationships. I distinguish three principal ones, all three issuing from the decay of traditional city life, and each of which deserves a fuller study than it can receive here.

At the beginning of the twentieth century, a proliferation of societies and committees, connected with the first nationalist movement, illustrated a new form of social life, *takattul*. The advent of the petty bourgeoisie, on the other hand, is related to the increased number of officials in the new States, and, since 1945, the replacement of foreign entrepreneurs; it is not connected, at least in Egypt, with the military revolution. Finally, Trade Unionism has made some progress. Muḥammad Mandûr considers as typical 'petty bourgeois' the heroes of the

[1] Cf. the lively and perspicacious articles of Simone Lacouture, *Paris-Normandie* (Rouen), 28 Jan 1959, to 5 Feb. 1959, and her *Egypt* in the *Petite Planète* series, 1962.

Najîb Maḥfûẓ trilogy.[1] The father is a middle-class tradesman, imbued with traditional beliefs and attitudes. His children, who have grown up in the latter half of the between-wars period, undoubtedly represent a different type. Yet they are still connected with their father's order of things, if only through their revolt against it. But entirely new perspectives are opened up by the rise of the bureaucrat, sometimes called by the planning authorities to important managerial tasks, by that of the army officer,[2] frequently of rural origin and predisposed to radicalism by his higher education, his relative financial independence and his more rational turn of mind, and by that of the industrial worker, although this is still more or less repressed. To a certain extent, they represent the tendency to destroy and re-make which, shattering the old set-up in country as well as in town, tries instinctively to recompose the whole in national entities; and the tendency to repel, and yet to attract, the foreigner which strives to protect the newly-reclaimed fatherland against all external allegiance and meanwhile lays its most private sectors open to influences from the outside world.

Thirty years ago, in many of these regions, tradesmen and artisans were divided into corporations.[3] The gradual decay of manual techniques, their retreat before the influx of machine-made or imported articles, have led to the replacement of this type of worker by skilled and even more by unskilled industrial workers. These, cut off from urban culture, can only foregather in groups according to their class origin, unless they reach a more advanced stage—the revolutionary form of trade unions. In general the same phenomenon is repeated everywhere in the Arab world, with varieties due to local conditions. The religious factor, for instance, has sometimes affected professional solidarity, to the point where, in a district such as Lebanon where religious feeling is strong, the guild-framework itself seems originally to have been lacking.

Foreign occupation gave rise to other movements of solidarity, grouping the citizens, irrespective of their origin, against the authorities. In many respects, during this first phase, the bourgeois leaders interpreted an unrest that was not only political but also economic and social. Thus the traditional civic order stood firm or even asserted itself actively

[1] *Qaḍâyâ al-adab al-jadîd.*

[2] Majid Khadduri, 'The Army Officer . . .' in *Social Forces in the Middle East*, 2nd edn., Fisher, pp. 162 ff.

[3] In many writings throughout his career Louis Massignon offered a profound analysis of the organization of labour in Islam. To quote one example only: his article in the *Cahiers internationaux de Sociologie*, XV, 1953, pp. 34 ff., 'La structure du travail à Damas en 1927'.

against the foreigner, while an invincible evolution was undermining it from within; the part played by the common people in the towns, by mass meetings, strikes, stone-throwing, closing of shops, street demonstrations, had become an essential element of public life. In Damascus as in Cairo, the most selfless zeal was to be found in these humble social strata. The effects of this evolution, in the form of protests by the under-privileged and even, in certain cases, of class warfare, could only be apparent in milieux where differences were clearly marked, and where a first stage of national enfranchisement had already been passed. It was only by slow degrees and in consequence of complex developments that syndicalism could escape from the bourgeois movements which had so long restrained its dynamism and exploited its potentialities.

In Lebanon[1] the trail was blazed as early as 1913 by a union of printers' workers, one of the oldest in the Middle East. Successful strikes (1926) consolidated a movement which even had its own exclusive press organ, *al-Yaqẓa*, 'the Awakening'. It was, however, vigorously held in check by the Government. 'The ideological precocity of some of its leaders and the keenness of the Communist Party to set up working-class organizations did not, however, succeed in creating syndicalism in Lebanon before 1939.' A Federation was formed, however, which energetically demanded labour regulations. Whence the attempted general strike of 1946, and several agitation campaigns between 1945 and 1948. But the resistance of the Government and of the employers, division amongst the workers and their frequent inertia, resulted in the decline of the movement. Today the Federation, 'if it can no longer claim to represent a working class and a movement whose unity it dreams of realizing, can depend, now and in the future, on unshakable and militant cadres'. It has increased its ideological acuteness. Its chances are, neither more nor less, those of socialism in the Middle East. This brief account shows what has been attained and endured by syndicalism in an Arab country with a prosperous economy, almost free from illiteracy, but whose very prosperity and whose mercantile tradition, if propitious for freedom, do not offer the best field of action for working-class demands.

It is true that industrialization in Lebanon is only on a small scale.

[1] K. Bohsali, *Contribution à l'étude de la situation de la classe ouvrière au Liban*, Paris, 1951; M. Chader, 'Action sociale,' *Mélanges* of the University of St. Joseph, 1956; see also Badaoui Zaki, *Les problèmes du travail et les organisations ouvrières en Egypte*, Alexandria, 1948.

It is in Iraq, in the Emirates of the Persian gulf, in Saudi Arabia, in the neighbourhood of the formidable oil combines, that the most decisive movements are likely to arise among the concentrations of workers. Local circumstances, for the time being, are not favourable to them, as we know. And it is not possible, either, to base any argument on contemporary Egypt, despite its seniority and the size of its population; a sort of State syndicalism is developing there, favoured by the growth of industrialization.[1] According to this country's census of labour power, the male population between 15 and 60 consists of 21 per cent industrial workers, 45 per cent agricultural workers, 20 per cent in trade, transport and various activities, and 14 per cent with 'no profession'. Among these vast forces how many are members of trade unions, and how many are militant members? The fluctuations observable in this field in France, for instance, now expanding and now contracting according to rates which are themselves variable, the proportion of inscribed members, of due-paying members and of active members, would give superabundant evidence, if it were needed, of the way syndicalism is bound up with other historic factors: the fight for liberation, the prestige of the leader, the vitality of the various parties, etc. Thus in a country like the Sudan, the whole of the early stages of syndicalism are bound up with the assertion of national claims. In Egypt the intermittent but sometimes impressive growth of the Marxist group has undoubtedly influenced working-class action. Reciprocally, repression is often deliberately aimed at militant workers, who share this privilege with the intelligentsia. However, the present work must leave aside these painful aspects to consider certain constant factors, more reassuring and more clearly distinguishable, common, moreover, to all countries in the Middle East. Undoubtedly, contemporary Egyptian history will provide the greatest number of interesting examples, when we possess enough reliable information. At present, this is far from being the case. Reluctantly, therefore, we must suspend judgment on problems of such fundamental interest as the development of classes within this society, or the relations between economic modernization and the growth of ideological consciousness, until the completion of studies at present in progress.[2]

[1] Here the most recent synthetic study is that of M. T. Audsley, 'Labour and Social Affairs in Egypt', *Middle Eastern Affairs*, no. 1, Oxford, 1959, pp. 95 ff. Cf. also F. J. Tomiche, 'Le mouvement syndical dans l'Egypte actuelle,' *Temps modernes*, no. 161, July 1959, pp. 107–123. Labour reports in *A.S.*

[2] These studies, the most interesting of which are by Egyptian Marxists, seem at present inadequate to elucidate these redoubtable historical and

Owing to the relatively archaic structure of production in these countries, personal relations between employer and employed play a more important part than class consciousness. Only a minority—some 20 per cent—of the working class can read and write. The superabundance of manpower, the widespread unemployment deprive them of the power to enforce their claims. Added to which today there are certain imperative needs of growing countries, to which the legislators of the U.A.R. have recently sacrificed the right to strike.[1] On the other hand, it is true, their Labour Code (Law no. 91 of 1959) has substantially extended the protection of the worker and social insurance. Their principal preoccupation seems none the less to be to forearm the national economy against the risks resulting from mass claims or the mobility of labour power, by increasing the State's power to arbitrate, which to the opposition seems merely arbitrary. On the other hand, since the laws of socialization, Egypt has granted her workers a substantial part of the profits of enterprise. At the Congress of Democratic Forces the '*ummâl*, having become a privileged section of the nation, were largely represented.

These latest reforms are not yet definite enough for their results to be assessed. For this reason we prefer to study the emergence of other basic forces, those of the peasantry, since these constitute a fundamental context, in all these countries, and their immemorial characteristics counteract, to some extent, the effect of political vicissitudes.

In any case, let us say, as a provisional conclusion, that the story of syndicalism in the Middle East reveals an undeniable progress, varying with different countries; that of the S.W.T.U.F.[2] of the Sudan might be considered one of the most hopeful, at the time when it was analysed by the late Dr. Fauzî.[3] This historian went so far as to conclude that the trade union movement must be associated with any economic planning. But this evolution is also characterized by specific difficulties

theoretical problems. They are too much involved with controversial contemporary issues, and are dependent on the conclusions of a study on the genesis of contemporary Egyptian society during the last hundred years which has not hitherto, to my knowledge, been undertaken with adequate documentation and objectivity.

[1] *E.F.S.P.A.*, May 1959, p. 38.

[2] Sudan Workers Trade Unions Federation.

[3] Sa'd al-Dîn Fauzî, *The Labour Movement in the Sudan*, Oxford, 1957. Cf. also the same writer's 'Manpower distribution in the Sudan', *Middle East Economic Papers*, 1958, pp. 22 ff.

and, from time to time, by setbacks due to a conjuncture of circumstances. That is why, in spite of the great importance of this type—whose inevitable, although too often repressed, rise might constitute the example *par excellence* of an upsurge from the foundations—I propose to study in greater detail the revelation of another great force: the peasantry.

The soil is indeed the most basic thing of all. Where it does not exist it has to be created. This was what 'Abd al-'Azîz ibn Sa'ûd had tried to do when he set his faithful *Ikhwân* (brothers) to work exploiting oases. This is what the Emir of Kuwait is trying to do today at great expense with his hanging gardens, his attempts to create artificial rain or even to grow things without soil,[1] so true is it that even this wealthy ghost feels like another Arab country the need to assume a body. But of course there are others of these countries which have always had their own body, and for whom the problem consists not in creating soil and man, but in providing that soil and that man with economic initiative.

The Co-operative Movement in Egypt

The co-operative movement was no new thing in Egypt.[2] As far back as 1907 a reformer, such as this country has seen from time to time throughout past ages, 'Umar Luṭfî, was known as *râ'id al-ḥaraka al-ta'âwunîya*, 'pioneer of the co-operative movement'. He founded several associations on the pattern of the Raffeisein groups. Leaders such as Muḥammad Farîd and Zaghlûl used all their skill in the face of timidity and opposition to get the first charter passed. This was an oddly theoretical one. It was only in 1923 that Decree no. 27 laid the foundations for the Co-operative Movement in Egypt. Subsequently this developed, but more in size than in efficacity; it attained figures which at a first glance seem considerable. In 1928 we find 161 agricultural co-operatives; in 1945, 1,641. At that time they comprised 776,000 members, if one includes the 361 consumers' co-operatives; for equal attention was paid to production and consumption. An 'Agricultural and Co-operative Bank' was instituted on September 23rd, 1948.

The fellah needed it badly! The economy suffered from an excess of middlemen. As its existence depended largely on cotton growing, the gap between agriculture and commercialization was filled by a whole host of professions. The road is a long one from the cotton field to

[1] *'Arabî*, March 1961.

[2] Historic account in *Majallat al-Ta'âwun*, June 1954, pp. 31 ff.

Alexandria, and all the way, speculators and adventurers are swarming. Today the State buys cotton in lots of 250 *qanṭârs*; too much for the small fellah, who has no means of financing himself and has to resort more or less, to the local money-lender (unless he can appeal to the Agrarian Reform Co-operatives, of which I shall speak later). As for the middle fellah, he is bled white by middlemen. Between the producer and the consumer, or rather the exporter, there are several kinds of trader. The *zahhâr*, who buys cotton in flower, too often a usurious operation; the *jallâb*, who acquires small quantities to make up larger 'processed' lots; but he is only a speculator, reproducing on a village level, and with a profitable increase, the movements of the Stock Exchange in Cairo or Alexandria. As for the cotton-stripper, the *ḥallâj*, who is victim and bully at once, he transmits to the people at the bottom all the sufferings endured by the big dealers and the big companies as a result of the general process of concentration which is rife in Egypt as it is everywhere else.

It is against these evils that the Co-operative Movement professed to wage war.[1] Was it successful? When in 1955, at the Cairo Congress, an attempt was made to investigate all these efforts, extraordinary malpractices, painful failures were brought to light, and are frankly acknowledged in the general report. The Co-operative Movement suffered from the selfishness of village bosses, from administrative inexperience, from the misuse of the Agricultural Credit Bank. The latter, paradoxically, but in classic fashion, had reached an understanding with the local notables to make them advantageous loans while asking them to serve as sponsors for it. It thus became necessary to start everything again almost from the bottom. Since the Revolution, therefore, the co-operatives of the Agrarian Reform, in which are grouped the fellahs who have been resettled on distributed estates, are governed by new principles.[2]

To counter the influence of these village notables, it was decreed that such groups would only include property-owners of less than five feddans. Unfortunately a three-feddan fellah is already a petty exploiter. In one of the first pamphlets devoted to Agrarian Reform, the late

[1] The information in this paragraph is taken from enquiries published in the Egyptian press: 'Adlî Barsûm, *Misâ'*, 9 Oct. 1958 and 23 Oct. 1958; 'Alî al-Shalaqânî, ibid., 9 and 25 Oct. 1958. More recently, for the problems are by no means solved, *Akhbâr*, 14 April 1962.

[2] Cf. the remarkable technical study by Gabriel Saab, *Motorisation de l'agriculture et développement agricole en Proche-Orient*, 1960, and his articles in *Commerce du Levant*, 17 and 20 Feb. 1960.

Ḥasan Abû Sa'ûd pointed out that in 1955, two million fellahs owned less than one feddan, their average property consisting of 0·30 feddans. Only 678,000 owned between one and five feddans; but the average property of these already rose to 2·14 feddans. The tendency to concentration starts right at the bottom. There is a harsh division between two strata of small producers; those who remain at the sub-economic stage, and those who have access to economic processes and who have already begun to hoard. Moreover, to assist inexperienced users, the State lavishes advisers and experts: a well-meaning effort, but a real invasion of bureaucrats! The inconveniences of the Agricultural Credit Bank are in contrast with the readily available credits granted by the Supreme Committee of Agrarian Reform; and henceforth the dangers of excessive centralism grow even more threatening.

As in any human creation, advantages and disadvantages, potentialities and perils are mutually involved. It may be said to the credit of the Reform Movement, of the books it inspires (recently, that of Sayyid Mar'î), and the often malicious reports to which it gives rise, that a sense of the concrete nature of the soil, no doubt atavistic, often forearms it against the excesses and the lack of realism to which it might be prone.

In the autumn of 1958 meetings were held in centres and Governorates, *markaz-s* and *mudîrîya-s*, to assess the results of these efforts. Here, for instance, is what happened at Sinballâwain, in the Daqahlîya. Five 'grouped units', the *waḥda mujamma'a-s*, function there, bodies providing assistance and advice to the rural population, the idea of which had been launched in 1953 in a pioneer study by Dr 'Abbâs 'Ammâr, and which are becoming widespread today. These bodies group together experts, or rather advisers, a credit branch, a stock-farming branch, etc. Here, in addition, there is a branch for apiculture and one for domestic economy. A co-operative has been founded for the development of fishing in Lake Manzala. It is hoped to extend agricultural insurance to five *markaz-s* by 1959. This association of fellahs has formulated three wishes: one refers to the Iraqi revolution, the second to Algeria, and only the third—the order of sequence shows the order of interest—expresses the bitter recriminations of the peasantry. This reversal of the immediate order of things is characteristic.

At Shibîn al-Kûm, in the Minûfîya, the Minister himself made a general report on the operations of the Agrarian Reform. At the present time, he said, 333,000 feddans have been distributed among 120,000 families. This is not much in relation to Egypt's huge population, but the figures in themselves may well seem impressive. The financial operations of the Agricultural Co-operatives have exceeded £E5,000,000 and apparently a gain of a million and a quarter has been made. Over 300,000 *qanṭârs* of cotton have been involved in the commercial activities undertaken by the co-operatives. Naturally this is against the interest of middlemen and money-lenders. The work is thus valuable, and covers a broad range of experiments, if we consider that it is accompanied by studies of the habitat and distribution of animals, etc.

Of course, bitter experience of such things in all countries makes it desirable to look a little closer, if possible, than administrative reports. This was done by a group of journalists. They went to see for themselves in two villages, Za'farân and Ada. At Za'farân the co-operative comprised 523 members. They had enjoyed the benefit of over 13,000 lb. of seed-grain—*taqâwî* or *ta'âwî*—and £E2,750 of fertilizers. At Ada, a hundred co-operators had made use of £E2,000 of seed-grain and £E4,500 of fertilizers. In each village there was a steward's office where the fellah could buy, in theory, whatever he needed; and moreover he could buy dairy cattle on deferred payment; so that the herd had grown in one of these villages from 354 cattle in 1955 to 1,495 milch cows in 1958. The other side of the picture? All new settlers were forced to join the co-operative; thus, from the beginning, they were allowed no initiative, no spontaneity. Authoritarianism is manifest at every turn, in the shape of agricultural planning, commercialization, attempted mechanization and credit. In both villages, the administrative council appeared to the Egyptian journalist, who does not hesitate to say so, as devoid of any real authority; all the power is in the hands of the *mandûb*, the administrative Commissar, unless it be in those of the Co-operative Central Commission, which is just as bad.

These criticisms are not surprising. Economic innovation, at this stage and in these countries, is introduced wholesale, with all the weight and authority of the State. Before it can be transmitted to individual attitudes, a whole set of actions and reactions will have to take place. These will be the more fertile if free rein is allowed to constructive criticism. The fellah complains that the steward's office is full of fine articles, but so fine—and to be paid for in cash—that he prefers to buy from the *baqqâl*, the small village grocer who sells on credit. He needed two sacks of fertilizer per feddan. He has only been allowed one; he had to get the second on the black market. The fellahs asked for seeds of *bassîm* and beans; in vain. The State takes their wheat at 400 piastres an *ardib*, and sells it back to them in seed at 450! In Egypt, as elsewhere, in co-operatives as in commerce, grain deals give rise to insidious abuses; and the peasant suspects the Administrative Council of more than that.

In another village, Shabshir al-Ḥiṣa, the fellah complains that in the allotment of lands, in which the poor peasants of the village ought to get priority, foreigners (meaning people from the neighbouring village) have been brought in. And above all—this is worth noting—he complains of having to pay more to buy back his land than he did as rent to the bey: over £E102, for two feddans and three *qirâṭ-s*. The fellah is quite at a loss, or pretends to be. Although he may be a careful and meticulous peasant, he is submerged (or perhaps takes refuge) in a dark haze of ideas and, above all, of figures. These are his hereditary enemies. He has always been fleeced so ruthlessly that he believes, or professes to believe, that this is still the case. A familiar situation. . . .

But other feelings, other ventures are now involved. The co-operators in one of these villages decided at their Council not to take service as seasonal workers, despite the attraction of the pay, until they had completed work on the cotton harvest for their own organization. Now such work is poorly paid, whereas they could have done better elsewhere with seasonal employment—even the poor have their opportunities. It would be an exaggeration to say these are always realized thanks to reforms which are inevitably to a large extent schematic, tentative and liable to error. Let us merely point out that the Egyptian press, with an accuracy that frequently conflicts with official optimism, lists successful and unsuccessful cases. The costly failure of the province of Taḥrîr is attributed to incompetence, or worse. Here and there are 'Potemkin' villages which delight passing tourists but distress the inhabitants, who are supposed to benefit from them. But elsewhere, particularly where agronomic planning has influenced the mass of the villagers, a development in depth can be glimpsed: the emergence of a mentality that is not merely co-operative, but possibly communal. Through uncertainties, mistakes and abuses, something is being born.

Difficult Beginnings of the Commune

Can this something be the commune? From every corner of the Arab world, from Basra to Sous in Morocco, we find the same desire: to restore the initiative to the forces at the base. But in what shape are these envisaged? Instructive divergences are revealed behind the unanimity of the assertion. Each of these countries, when it makes its Revolution, decrees an Agrarian Reform. A vast amount of literature has been produced on this theme. The Agrarian Reform has been, so to speak, the sea-serpent of all political and social thought in the Middle East for the past generation. Does not this passionate wish to grasp the reality of the soil, as revealed by men risen from the soil through force of circumstances, whether they belong to the old strata of educated aristocracy and bourgeoisie or those new strata whose sudden rise to power has somewhat severed them from basic realities, reveal a certain uneasiness in respect to these realities? They are of absorbing interest, true, but also terribly crude, indeed impure. In any case, hostile to the city culture which had profited by its alliance with nationalism in the period of emancipation. . . .

Take, for instance, the reactions of a group of students from all corners of the Arab world, mainly from remote rural and tribal regions, in 1953, when basic education was first launched in Egypt.[1] One of them gives evidence as follows (my own comments are in brackets):

'*Action in the villages.* This phrase gave rise to lengthy arguments and discussions among our group. Terrible and mysterious words! Some of them had never seen a village' (Is it possible that a tribal Iraqi could talk in such terms with his Egyptian fellow-students, whose very physique betrays their peasant origin?) 'They picture it as some wild animal' (We must make allowances for exaggeration, but even so . . .) 'Everyone was anxiously wondering: what is there to do in a village?' (They knew it only too well, having spent their dreary childhood there.) 'And above all, shall we be able to put into practice what we have learnt at our lectures?' (They are right to be anxious, for teaching in this part of the world, as elsewhere, is often more theoretical than practical.) 'The ones who argued most convincingly were not necessarily the most confident, for there is always that dread of the unknown that grips one at a first contact.' (*Dread of the unknown* in an Egyptian village, one of those villages whose oppressive presence surrounded us on all sides and blocked the whole horizon around us!) One day, they were assembled in the classroom. The lecturers had selected the aspects round which the experiment was to focus. The villages had to be named: discreetly, the names were inscribed on the blackboard. And here the difficulties began. 'Dr. X told us that the centre had chosen four villages for us; he wrote their names on the blackboard. *Diberki:* all the students laughed when they heard this odd-sounding name,' (Why?) '*Fîsha:* another burst of laughter; everybody repeated mockingly: Fîsha, Fîsha! *Qalata el-Kubrâ:* new fits of merriment and quizzical looks. And the

[1] J. Berque, 'Le comédien et les fellahs', *Cahiers de Tunisie*, 1958, p. 5.

mirth reached its peak when a fourth village was named: *Manâwahla*—the laughter grew hysterical.'

Their attitude is paradoxical. They feel that the village is something strange, that they are cut off from the reality of the soil from which they spring!

Dr. Kâmil Ḥusain, author of 'The City of Wrong',[1] was born in a village quite close to that Manâwahla whose name amused our Iraqis. He himself admits the strange cleavage that had taken place in him, severing his personality from its roots in the soil. He tells how one day, sitting by his door, he saw one of his neighbours running past to the station, as the train was about to leave. As he returned his neighbour's greeting, the writer omitted to invite him into his house. The other never forgave him for this. His *adab* was not that of the city, and took offence that such things as train-whistles should be considered worthy of attention.

In Egypt, the essence of peasant life had never succeeded in finding autonomous expression. Repressed from above by city culture, it was invaded from below by Bedouinism. Remote as the nomad ideal might be from so deep-rooted a peasant tradition, it was brought from the desert into the villages by the movement associated with Aḥmad al-'Arabî. It is particularly dominant in the Ṣa'id; patriarchal hierarchies and vendettas and the proud attitudes of Arab riders have oddly and dangerously influenced these fellahs' mentality. It is true that by a kind of revenge the obsessive power of the countryside and its particular teeming character deprive the crowded towns, in Egypt, of some of their urban distinction. A large village may number thirty or even fifty thousand inhabitants and yet not call itself a town. The contrast is a sharp one with the keen civic consciousness of so many small towns in Syria and Palestine. Nablus proclaims itself a town, but not Minuf. A traditional outlet from this oppressive state of things lay in the Azhar. The great mosque offered the rural scholar opportunities for advanced study. Reciprocally, it served for a long time as a school for popular poetry. This *adab sha'bî*, which recent trends have understandably encouraged, was one form of expression and refuge for those who had silently suffered hunger and contempt. Today moreover the fellah has gained other openings, thanks to the development of primary education, of the lower grades of the civil service, of careers in the army and, paradoxically, in the police, etc. That is why, as soon as the Egyptian Revolution broke out, it issued its decree of September 9

[1] *Qarya Zâlima.*

1952 concerning agrarian reform.[1] For the first time in history, the government of Egypt was in the hand of peasants' sons.

It is true that a revolution always raises more problems than it solves. Four years after the agrarian reforms, agricultural land was still minutely portioned out and, on the whole, underequipped, in spite of the progress of motorization. The need for land to be shared out forced the legislator to seize the domain of the *Waqfs*, the 'pious foundations'. Finally, a phase of intensified socialism began in January 1961. The maximum limit of landed property was dropped from 200 to 100 feddans, i.e. 40 hectares. Was this to prove adequate to absorb the surplus of a rural population which has already swollen the sub-proletariat of the large towns to a dangerous extent?

This phenomenon is not peculiar to Egypt. In Iraq too, swarms of uprooted people crowd into the primitive huts, *ṣarîfas*, of the suburbs of Baghdad. There, with ludicrous loyalty, they take pride in keeping up their tribal divisions and their agnatic honour. However destitute a group may be, it will not renounce the right to make its own laws. The set of customary rules now include careful clauses about motor accidents! But this conservatism is counterbalanced by an appalling degree of social disintegration. And here too the revolutionary state has sought to establish the peasant on his own ground, by bequeathing lands to him. A maximum area is decreed, according to a recognized scheme. And here too, the division which is enforced, or planned, raises problems of finance, of popularizing information and integrating the rural group. And this calls up once again the question of village life.

According to some writers, the village remains practically unintelligible for the outside observer, particularly for the bureaucrat.[2] That is why so many measures, such as Decree no. 70 of the Iraqi regulations of 1956, dealing with the construction of new villages, consist merely of so much ink on so much paper. It sometimes happened that when the houses were built the fellahs disliked them so much that they preferred living in their huts alongside the model buildings, as reformers have found to their cost, not only in Iraq but everywhere else, particularly in North Africa. The State finds it difficult to understand village life. It lays down the most absurd regulations. One of these concerned the cleaning

[1] Official report by Sayyid Marei, very clear and well documented, *Agrarian Reform in Egypt*, Cairo, 1957.

[2] Maḥmûd Nadîm Ismâ' îl, *Iṣlâḥ al-qurâ fî'l-'Irâq*, Baghdad, 1959, pp. 60 ff., 78 ff. in particular; 'Abd al-Razzâq al-Hilâlî, *Naẓarât fî iṣlâḥ al-rîf*, Baghdad, 1954.

of the village: the narrow streets must be rigorously cleared of animal droppings, *rûth al-ḥayawân.* Apparently the bureaucrat who composed this decree had never noticed how frequently, in Iraq as in Egypt, the only available fuel consists of animal dung kneaded by the women. And the author tells sadly how he recently saw, in a middle-sized town in the Euphrates region, a young girl of astonishing beauty pass by, carrying on her head a bowl full of excrement. Elsewhere her charms would have won homage. Here, in this rustic setting, she was a dung-kneader. . . .

According to the same author, such mistakes are due to a failure to grasp the inner vitality of the village. This has been misunderstood because it depends on a tribal order, *niẓâm 'ashâ'irî.* He calls it tribal for lack of another term; he understandably confuses the peasant and the bedouin. But he rightly perceives therein a rudimentary social and political initiative. Any legislation which left this out would remain inoperative. This author is about the only man in his country to have realized this at the time. He has shaken off the condescending attitude of centralist reformers. When he alludes to the long revolt of Barzânî, in Northern Iraq, he knows what he is talking about. He knows what price centralized governments may have to pay for failing to recognize the upward thrust from the foundations before it is too late.

Let us examine the Syrian Code of agricultural contracts. In the foreword, the Minister set out as his long-term objective a co-operative socialism which was to deliver the villagers from the after-effects of their past. For many people in the Middle East, country life implies the feudal system. Property there, throughout history, has been dominated by a form of regalian tenure, the *mîrî.* The system assumed that the land belonged to the *Umma,* the Muslim community. In fact, it provided a graceful explanation for all seizures by the central or local power. The landlords had collected vast areas populated by their peasants. They kept them until the last few years, since it took recent agrarian revolutions like those of Iraq and Syria to try to liquidate this structure.

The statement adds that hitherto, rural contracts were not grounded on any rights. Not in law, one must readily admit. But can one believe that rural custom itself had fallen into disuse? The legislator, in any case, considers this as subject to incessant variations. I would rather criticize it for its uniform and static character. But no doubt the arbitrary will of those in possession ruled there exclusively. A healthy reaction leads the legislator to underestimate, perhaps, the large proportion of custom that rules rural life in all countries of the world. In any case, the new code introduces substantial progress. It forbids life contracts, in order to do away with substitute forms of serfdom. It concludes by referring to the duties of the fellah, which must equal his rights. Here an authoritarian centralism is once more evident. We may note, by the way, that this code forbids the fellah to strike, and forbids trade unions to encourage strikes. True, the owner is also forbidden to lock-out. But on the whole, as we have seen, duties are closely linked with rights, a state of things which is based on reality and which no legislation can abolish rapidly. . . .

Even more stringent are ecological conditions. The Syrian agrarian reform (Law 161 of 1958) reproduced the Egyptian text without going far enough in the necessary adaptations. And it was on this issue that after the separation of the two countries, at the end of 1961, the Dawâlîbî Government based its criticisms, which eventually gave rise to a new and very complex formula. But the disappointment thus inflicted on a rural population which had been led to expect the redistribution of a million and a half hectares is not unconnected with the second military *coup d'état* of March 1962. The hectic events of today, characteristic of Syria, illustrate at least two facts: the imperative demands of the milieu, and the irreversible nature of social progress.

Another instructive case is that of the Sudan. It was subject to Arab influence partly from the North, partly from the other side of the Red Sea. And its religion owes much to the Maghrib. At the same time it exalts its African originality. It has suffered from slavery. One of its poets, Miftâḥ al-Faitûrî, recalls in 1956 'my brothers walking as slaves, weighed down with chains, while the white master followed, whipping them; I remember their cries of anguish; I remember the bloody sweat trickling from their foreheads, and how they suffered *li-abyaḍ hâdhâ'l-zamân, li sayyid hâdhâ'l-zamân*, for the White Man of those days, the Lord of those days'.[1]

And yet the African-ness of the Sudan, which has nothing to do with 'negritude', joins with Arabism to form an original blend with a 'symphonic counterpoint' (the expression was invented by a Sudanese minister, Muḥammad Aḥmad Maḥjûb,[2] the author of one of the most interesting biographies of this generation).[3] Others in the Middle East

[1] Muḥammad al-Nuwailî, *al-Ittijâhât al-shi'rîya fî'-l-Sûdân*, Cairo, 1957, p. 149.
[2] *Al-Ḥukûma al-maḥallîya*, Khartoum, 1945.
[3] *Maut dunyâ*, published in collaboration with 'Abd al-Ḥalîm Muḥammad.

had spoken of co-operatives, of concern for the fellah's welfare, of the rights and also of the duties of the fellah. The word *commune* did not appear. And it is strangely enough in this Sudanese book that we find the frankest incitement to what Western history knows as the revolution of the communes. Maḥjûb ends by saying: 'The communes' revolution' (and he has investigated what this means not only in England but also in France and in Germany) 'is the only way to help this country to constitute a nation and to realize its social hopes': national progress linked with social progress in an upsurge from the depths.

Decay and Restoration of the Rural Masses

Such a plea in favour of the communes remains rare, because it meets with great difficulties. The typical Arab village not only resists outside intervention but, we have seen it admitted, baffles understanding. In the very notion of *qarya*, a village, the downtrodden values of the peasantry mingle, paradoxically in our eyes, with the fallen ideal of the nomad. For many Arab reformers the term *qarawî*, villagers, implies *badawî*, Bedouin. Alone amongst them, perhaps, 'Alî al-Wardî, analysing the psychology of the people of Iraq, distinguishes and contrasts the rapacious liveliness of the nomad and the long-humiliated patience of the peasant. We must not forget, moreover, that all these governments have, more or less efficiently, established policies of 'sedentarization'. 'Abd al-'Azîz al-Sa'ûd himself, whom we romantically considered as a king of the desert, had concentrated his activities on the 'caravan cities' and on the oases. This supposed nomad had concerned himself with creating areas of irrigation. But such ambiguity is instructive. It goes far back, since Ibn Khaldûn included under the same heading of Bedouins the Banû Hilâl nomads and the old-established dwellers in the High Atlas mountains!

In any case, in our own day, a common destiny is once more being shaped for the two types. The peasant and the herdsman endure the same sufferings and yield to the same temptation. Both are becoming uprooted. The great industrial centres, the teeming cities are insatiably draining off the old Biblical, parasitical masses of humanity all around them. Instability is now affecting the village populations, who crowd into the wretched suburbs in their tens of thousands. In the suburbs of Cairo, the tamed Bedouin from Ḍahrân can hold out his hand to the defeated peasant from the Baghdad hutments.[1]

[1] In Egypt, the growing mass of the 'landless' must be opposed to the peasantry, however poor, and must modify our analysis, and even our judgement of

Even where village autonomy remains the most clearly marked, even where it can still establish independent structures, in Lebanon for instance where the large mountain villages form a political counterpoise to the cities of the coast, I notice the same tendency to break away from the village type. The vitality of the commune suffers both from the attraction of urban professions, of too much opportunity for cosmopolitanism, and from the bonds of religious belief which unite elements from different villages and set one against the other the various districts in one village. Émigrés, indeed, show admirable zeal in maintaining, through their investments, those symbols of village life—formerly the mulberry, now the apple tree, and always the cedar. But many developments threaten this loyalty.

In certain cases, too, the history of emancipation has contributed to cast discredit on the rural population. In spite of their participation in the Zaghlûl movement, in spite of stubborn revolts like that of the Jebel Druse at the time of the Mandate, the bulk of the resistance movement was centred round the nationalism of the cities. It is not surprising that at this stage these should reap the benefit of an independence so hardly won. It is understandable that the peasantry, with its background of Bedouinism, should appear to many Middle East Arabs as both primitive and decadent, as the bearer of ancient values but also of threats, and in any case as a prey to moral and social disintegration.[1] However, in the next stage, which has already begun in several countries, though more dilatory in others, signs are appearing which enable one to hope that the peasantry, and the many realities that go with it, will recover an important share in the national life. Unless, meanwhile, industrialization has drained its population too heavily, a phenomenon which is common to all modern countries. The peasantry would then experience, as regards its numbers, a decrease equal to that lessening of typological significance imposed upon it by the compromises of the previous era.

That is why we must greet with interest the efforts perceptible here and there, and particularly those aimed at 'basic education'.[2] Not only for the concrete results which they can already claim at Dujaila (Iraq),

any agrarian reform. Cf. 'Pression démographique et stratification sociale dans les campagnes égyptiennes', *Tiers-Monde*, July–Sep. 1960, pp. 314 ff.

[1] Whence the determined anti-nomad policy pursued by Egypt as well as by Iraq and Syria.

[2] There is an abundant literature on the subject, including a Review of the Sirs al-Layyân Centre (Egypt) and another for that of Bakht al-Rûdha (Sudan). Cf. also 'Alî Fû'âd Aḥmad, *al-Nuhûḍ bi'l-mujtama' al-maḥallî*, Cairo, 1957.

Bakht al-Rûdha (Sudan), Sirs al-Layyân (Egypt), etc. . . . But above all for the exact direction they give to youthful idealists. Hence, too, the interest of such endeavours as that of the *Waḥda mujamma'a* in Egypt.[1] A most revealing concept! It is founded on a perspicacious grasp of the whole. But it neglects the 'natural' division of the cells at the base. This is perhaps why it is so difficult for the reformer to integrate the technical culture which he is seeking to spread with the basic culture which he is seeking to maintain: the natural unity within which the union could be achieved is curiously neglected.[2] For it is a paradox—a not unexpected one—of the Arab world that, contrary to what has happened in European history, national entity is achieved before communal entity. We have already encountered such contrasts and inversions.

Any effort of this kind arouses enormous difficulties in the Middle East, to cope with which several of these countries have, to their credit, expended energies that have varied at different times, with different regimes and classes. If it is true that we find the most insistent communal demands in the remoter regions of the Arab world, in the Sudan, it might be said that this originality decreases as we draw nearer to the centres of Middle Eastern civilization: Cairo, that ancient citadel of State centralism, or Damascus, that emblem of city culture set down amidst the desert. Indeed, traditional Arab culture sublimated the basic realities to raise them to the order of religious belief, which was also that of elegance and good breeding. This hierarchy is now inverted. Today's reform aims not at sublimating crude realities but at going towards them and, better still, taking inspiration from them, arising out of them. Henceforward there is a shift of accent from the lingering aristocratic and transcendental elements in the Islamic system to those of its values which might lend authority to democracy. But such a conversion has grave consequences. I leave aside the necessary perturbations that any reconstruction devoted to justice and logic is bound to inflict on existing situations. To the risks of violence and compromise inseparable from social reform in Arab countries, as in all others, is added a conflict of ideals. Every society, and this one perhaps above all others, is today obliged to choose between rival and sometimes mutually exclusive values. It is fortunate if it is able to confine itself to

[1] 'Abbâs 'Ammâr, introductory lecture of 1953, *Tanẓîm al-qarya al-miṣrîya*, ed. A.S.F.E.C. (Arab States Fundamental Education Centre).

[2] Cf. the report, remarkable for its perspicacity and sincerity, made by Dr Hâmid 'Ammâr at the Cairo Congress on 'Technology and Society', *al-tiknulujîya wa'l-mujtama'*, U.N.E.S.C.O., 1959, pp. 64 ff.

more or less rewarding attacks on certain of these values, or to elude, more or less permanently, such sacrifices. . . .

Such are, for the Middle East as elsewhere, but more than elsewhere perhaps, the difficulties of the quest for 'the roots of heaven'.

At this point in our study let us note once again that the economic aspect, if one studies it at all deeply, implies complex relations which a purely superficial analysis cannot hope to grasp. If nevertheless I have dwelt so much on aspects of economic sociology, it is first of all because I let myself be guided, without being deceived by them, by antitheses as familiar to the Arab world as to ourselves, about the alleged idealism of the Arabs which finds it hard to come to terms with the alleged materialism of modern times;[1] this was what it was important to check, and if possible to define precisely. And moreover the economic aspect afforded the most convenient angle for analysis, and provided almost experimental indices on the evolution of the conflict between Middle Eastern man and Nature, as he gradually reconquers this from others while mastering it within himself.

But such a development involves more complex phenomena:[2] a change in the relations of the sexes, between categories of expression and meaning, and, in general, a collective as well as an individual movement of intelligence, sensibility and will.

It is this that the following chapters will attempt to assess.

[1] Is it necessary to point out that 'idealism' and 'materialism' are here used in the popular sense, and not with reference to any philosophical system?

[2] Amongst recent attempts we must quote that of Daniel Lerner to reduce all or part of these phenomena to a quantitative criterion of 'empathy', a term that might be explained as 'accessibility to the external, feeling of participation in what is external', *The Passing of Traditional Society*, 1958, particularly pp. 43 ff. where the theory is set forth. Wilfred Cantwell Smith's study, *Islam in Modern History* (The New American Library) 1959, is more traditional but goes deeper; see pp. 97–164.

CHAPTER IX

Woman's Intercession

Islamic society, more than any other, illustrates the saying of the Coptic philosopher René Habachi about woman: 'her essence is whole, her existence is disintegrated'![1] At any rate in practice, according to the tradition that pledged her to maternity and masculine pleasure. This was not without its compensations; Arab sensuality has a lavish splendour that still astonishes the West. It is true that our erotic interest has recently been replaced by anxiety at the speed of demographic growth. Nothing is more eloquent of the changing character of the world than these Malthusian fears, succeeding those quite contrary ones felt some thirty years ago by employers faced with a shortage of manpower. The theme of underemployment replaces in our essays the equally pious theme of the flight from the countryside. The West has hypocritically exchanged bucolic regrets for the learned apprehensions of the statistician. He even transmits these to the nations concerned, which take alarm at the threatening drop in their individual quotient of revenue.

The Arabs, while thus submitting to their partners' views, are not always conscious that they had already reacted against dependence by an ethnic rebound, that the fertility of their women, their sexual code and family tradition had contributed to their emancipation, both by the pressure of an ever-growing population and its increasing youthfulness, which strengthened its forward drive and forced it to liquidate its past. The married woman's contribution to national liberty is the political aspect of more subtle phenomena which we should like to try to discover. And during the same period, woman's destiny changes like that

[1] R. Habachi, 'Deux conférences sur Simone de Beauvoir et *Le Deuxième Sexe*', *Cahiers du Cénacle libanais,* April, 1960.

of man, through the reversal of what had governed it hitherto. Demographic growth, once independence has been attained, appears as a fault. The erstwhile dependent seeks to raise himself from the lower level of competition and exchange to the higher levels, those of goods, techniques and ideas. Correspondingly, woman now claims the right to be an individual.

What we know as feminism in the Middle East is thus only one form among others of a deepening of the relations between society on the one hand, nature and history on the other.

Masculinity

In spite of the facts that bring ever-more convincing evidence of development, there are other facts in many parts of the Arab world which betoken lingering archaism: the seclusion of women, the wearing of the veil, the circumcision of girls, magical practices like the *zâr*, repeated divorce which is more harmful than polygamy, and speculation on dowries. Other evils which cannot be called exceptional or residual affect society more or less openly. But these stand strongly condemned, and they tend to decrease with the spread of education and the rise in the standard of living. Their weakness, which is also their strength, is their close connection with a past which, defeated almost everywhere in principle, still persists only too commonly in the facts. Needless to say it is in the remoter regions that we must seek these traits, which distress the patriot as much as they excite the ethnologist.

An Iraqi researcher has done so.[1] In the region of the Ahwâr (the marshland of Shatt al-'Arab) many practices still reflect primitive barbarism, such as the exchange of fiancées, strongly condemned by Islam under the name of *shighâr*; or the compensatory concession of women in cases of murder. Another custom, which belongs to a common stock of institutions already recognizable in pre-Islamic days, has spread beyond the Bedouin world, since it even constitutes a sign of aristocracy in city society. This is what is known as 'preferential' marriage, which entitles the son of the paternal uncle, *ibn al-'amm*, to claim the hand of his cousin. This agnatic trend is so strongly marked among the Ahwâr that the *mahr* is duly scaled down in accordance with the parental proximity of the suitor, while the uncle has a right of veto, *nahwa*, over his niece's marriage and the right to impose penalties if this is disregarded.[2] Of course a milieu like that of Damascus is free from such

[1] Shâkir Muṣṭafâ Salîm, *al-Shibâyish*, Baghdad, 1956, pp. 97 ff.

[2] 'Abbâs al-'Azzâwî, *'Ashâ'ir al-'Irâq*, vol. I, pp. 414 ff.

excesses, which constitute an unpardonable sin according to Muslim ethics. But the great city families favour marriage between paternal cousins,[1] through custom and fashion rather than as an institution. Herein the whole of the Arab East, by contrast with the Maghrib, asserts an originality which is fascinating to the ethnologist.

Marriage with one's uncle's daughter, indeed, does not enlarge the family circle and forms no exchange circuit. Relationships remain a closed system. In so far as they confine themselves to this, the Arabs deviate from a marriage system so widespread that its exogamic principle has been considered as the most elementary addition of society to nature. This anomaly moreover is not peculiar to them. It is clearly common to a whole area of culture, of which they thus transmit to us the best preserved evidence. As in the matter of their language, they hand down to us the legacy of a very ancient 'semitism' which can be formulated thus: the 'social' assumes the functions of the 'natural' almost to the point of being identified with it. In fact the nomad group, as it has been celebrated in pre-Islamic poetry, but also as it can be observed in a more or less unaltered state, illustrates a sort of egotism of the social structure. Constantly menaced by the perils of consanguinity or simply of penury, it reacts against these by that adherence to nature, that ratifying of the immediate of which I have noted suggestions at all levels of this civilization, even in its most modern developments. . . .[2]

Arab sensuality, then, is closely and intimately linked with nature. Its joy is like a feast after famine, like the slaking of a long thirst. Man transforms his destitution into wealth, his insecurity into greatness. Amidst festivities and pleasures he still remains bounded by his pride, which isolates him in the exaltation of his lineage, just as his poetry exalts the most ancient roots of words.[3] Privation, sublimation, confer on the Bedouin's feelings a violence which is liable to sudden blossomings and fadings, but whose aesthetic distinction has made of it an impressive and enduring style. Thus the emotional intensity of the desert dweller has imposed its ideal on the opulent cities. Up to a certain point it is sanctioned by Islamic culture, which imposes on it certain legalistic restrictions, true, but provides it with spiritual guarantees. . . .

We must rest content with such impressions until a deep ethnological

[1] This tradition is being increasingly challenged.

[2] I am much indebted here to a discussion on Arab kinship systems with Claude Lévi-Strauss, whose work contains brief but suggestive references to ancient Eastern systems.

[3] Another illustration of the sociological value of Arab linguistics and of the Arabic language itself *qua* 'model'.

analysis shall have accounted for the things we notice and the things of which we are aware without, hitherto, being able to explain them scientifically. But it would surely not be carrying exegesis too far to show how the 'agnatism' of these societies, recognizable by such precise landmarks, can help us to understand their most general attitudes and their traditional behaviour. If for so many Arabs, whether Bedouins or townsfolk, the bride of their first choice is invariably the 'uncle's daughter', who represents another aspect of themselves, it is because, for the Arab male, marriage is an affirmation rather than an exchange.[1] In this sense Islam might be called the home of the eternal masculine.[2]

Naturally such a formula is too one-sided. Every society seeks to reach an equilibrium by means of contrasting institutions or impulses. In many ways Arabic poetry belongs less to this ethic of isolation than to what counterbalances it: the love of wandering and adventure, which was to take Imru' al-Qais, the dispossessed king, as far as Byzantium. Islam stands in opposition to the three champions of Bedouinism: the chief, the poet and the soothsayer—and to the troubled emotional world they represent. In his own life, the Prophet had painful experience of the inadequacy of marriage with a near relative, since the only wife who gave him a son was the one most remote by race and religion, Maria the Copt. In the cities, which in so many respects challenged the Bedouin way of life, the moral code of the great families, while considering marriage between first cousins as the ideal type, allows sumptuary excesses which scandalize the pious.

But the way of life based on this agnatic code, the proud or courtly types of citizen who represent it, are also the very opposite of those of the merchant class. The commoner will be tempted to give his daughter to the highest bidder, while the man of quality observes the rules of a subtle marriage system and prefers nobility to wealth. The nationalist movement of the interwar period, at Damascus, Homs or Hama for instance, was in a certain measure based on the revolt of aristocratic honour against the acceptance of accomplished facts. This movement mobilized the crowd through the prestige of its adherents. It supplanted, in this task, the forces of traditional religion, accusing these of

[1] *Abû'l-mar'a: zauju-hâ:* 'A woman's father = her husband' (Arab lexicographer quoted in F. Bustânî's *Encyclopedia*)!

[2] Nietzsche would have appreciated the Bedouin's aristocratic moral code, 'born of a triumphant self-assertion', and that aggressiveness founded on awareness of, and even delight in, his difference. With this, in the ancient Arab world, were connected such sciences as genealogy, heraldry, physiognomy and group onomastic.

compromise before being in its turn accused of the same fault by more revolutionary forces. Thus, in a single milieu, the various styles are intermingled, one or another gaining or losing the advantage according to the vicissitudes of history.

Mothers and Daughters

Let us try to imagine what a woman's life was like in a patrician home, shortly before the first world war. A wife was not so much a person or even a child-bearer as an extraordinary assemblage of relationships, qualifications and taboos. The extent to which her social being governed her personal life is illustrated by a well known story, the lawsuit brought against his in-laws by Shaikh 'Alî Yûsuf, director of the *Mu'ayyad*: a misalliance, in those days, was enough to justify the annulment of a marriage.[1] Undoubtedly, through the pleasure she affords in her youth, the children she bears, the food she prepares, her beauty when she has it, her capacity as wonder-worker, the Arab woman adds something to nature. There is about her an elemental vitality whose qualities of steadfastness and no doubt of serenity lay hidden from us during the Colonial period. But formidable taboos curtail her fulfilment. They isolate her both from the world and from society. Amidst the unanimity of the city's life, she remains paradoxically alienated. The veil, the gyneceum, the moral code relegate into discontinuity this creature who incarnates natural forces and who is destined to perpetuate the race.

Undoubtedly it is from the home, the place where man's strength is restored, that Muslim life spreads as if in concentric waves throughout the city. But woman is hemmed in by a barrier made up of masculine selfishness, pharisaical prejudices and spiteful gossip. The giver of life is cut off from the outside world, and cannot even find in the education of her children a means of restoring the chain of being to her own advantage. Her life, from generation to generation, always swings back to a neutral position. By an exact correspondence with the static social conditions prevailing at this period, woman becomes the repository of a past jealously sheltered from 'acquired characteristics' and the benefits of masculine experience. Thus it happened that the Colonial era, among others, passed over her without affecting her.

The trilogy of novels by Najîb Maḥfûẓ[2] has familiarized us with the

[1] Aḥmad Bahâ' al-Dîn, *Ayyâm la-hâ ta'rîkh*, 1955, pp. 45 ff.

[2] Introduced to French readers by Father Jomier, in *M.I.D.E.O.* (*Mélanges de l'Institut Dominicain d'Études Orientales*), no. 4, 1957.

7. The Garden of Eden: tapestry by Ramses Wîṣâ Wâṣif.

8. Damascus coin. (See p. 245.)

9. Revolution in the streets of Baghdad.

10. Feisal I in Damascus. Feisal is leaving the British headquarters.

life of the petty bourgeoisie in Cairo between the two wars. The mother, in her sublime humility, wears herself out in waiting and serving. The father's unquestioned authority reduces her to a sort of clandestine existence. Her son, at an early age, leaves the gyneceum for the Koranic school, then, almost abruptly, moves into masculine society. Hence agonizing conflicts and all these adolescent disturbances that psychologists study today. Many of the mental troubles characteristic of over-speedy development are here due to childhood frustration, to an initial absence of affection for which woman's exclusion is no doubt responsible. For the grave head of the house will not tolerate the counterpoise of his wife's advice. A great gulf yawns between the generations, even more between mother and daughter than between father and son.

In a play written in 1952, the secretary of the new Iraqi Theatre, Yûsuf al-'Âlî,[1] contrasts the two mentalities. The comedy is called *Ḥarmal wa ḥabba sûdâ*. It shows a Baghdad family torn by inner conflict. The mother is an ignorant woman who believes in magic. She resorts to it in any difficulty. The daughter, Su'âd, has been educated at a secondary school and is earning her living in a bank. The father, a former Civil Servant, is a disappointed man who still pins his hopes to the very things that have disappointed him. The son, Fakhrî, a graduate of the École Normale, is waiting, like so many other graduates, for the authorities to offer him a job. It is evening. The mother is fumigating the room and muttering invocations. The daughter comes in and, seeing her surprise, the mother explains: 'I went to see the mullah this afternoon. He gave me *ḥarmal*[2] and pepper. I've only got to pound them up thoroughly and use them as a fumigation, and then Fakhrî's sure to get a job.'

Su'âd longs for her brother's appointment with all her heart. Only he has unfamiliar moral scruples. He has left the business firm run by a friend of the family, the *tâjir* Razzûqî, who comes to discuss it with the father. The two old men are indignant to see the son without a job and refusing to look for one in the proper way. The contrast between the generations is brought out by countless touches: the mother sees her daughter reading a book—'But what can you find in that book?' 'I find the whole world.' 'How can the world get into such a small volume?'

Fakhrî writes for the newspapers; outspoken journalism makes up for much dissatisfaction amongst this class of intellectuals. He has written

[1] Whose importance has been rightly stressed by Dr. Ṣalâḥ Khâliṣ.

[2] 'Peganon harmala', a plant with medicinal and magical virtues found throughout the steppes from the Atlantic to the Tigris.

an article which is much in request amongst the young: 'Girls and boys have the same weight in society.' And thereupon the father, taking it literally, asks with a loud burst of laughter: 'If you put your mother and myself on the scales, which of us would weigh the more?' An allusion, doubtless, to stage by-play and the physical appearance of the actors. In the end poor Fakhrî, sooner than go back to work for the family friend, the Baghdad tradesman, adept in all the wiles of city mercantilism, chooses to work at the box office of a cinema: thus he finds a place in the superstructure, in one of those cultural professions which play so important a part in his country.

We are left in ignorance of the end. What matters is the opposition between mother and daughter, father and son. An opposition which is even revealed in their language, so that the old parents speak after the fashion of Baghdad while the children intersperse this language with words and expressions of more literary Arabic.[1] 'Modern' Arabic, in their speech as in Fakhrî's newspaper, is spreading. A new world needs a new language.

Although the picture is somewhat dated, and such conflicts are no longer found in the corresponding social milieux of Cairo, Damascus or Beirut, it is probable that they still linger, not in the realm of institutions or expressions but in more or less unconscious habits, characteristic of the contrasting ways of life of mother and daughter. The Lebanese writer Laila Ba'labakkî pities and hates her mother.[2] She observes her with horror, self-satisfied in her segregation, her only gesture of revolt an unconscious visceral reaction. 'My mother's laugh, the laugh of a creature whose throat's being cut. . . .' Nothing hitherto in modern Arab literature had been so savage in its brutality. *Aḥyâ*, 'I am alive', is the title of the book.

Now to be alive is a new concept in the Middle East.

The Women's Movement in Iraq

It is in Iraq[3] that women have had the longest way to go. Iraq had not been affected by the *Nahḍa*, the renaissance, to the same degree as Syria and Egypt, and it had not, like the latter country, enjoyed the benefit of the long pedagogical tradition starting from Ṭahṭâwî. The reformer Midḥat Pasha had indeed considered masculine education, but it was only under one of his successors, Namîr Pasha, that the first

[1] I am indebted to Albert Nader for this observation, and these facts.

[2] *Anâ aḥyâ*, Beirut, 1958; cf. passage translated by V. Monteil, *L'Orient*, 17 May 1958.

[3] Khiḍr al-'Abbâsî, *Taḥrîr al-mar'a al-'irâqîya*, pp. 18 ff., 23 ff., and *passim*.

girls' school was founded at Baghdad. For at this period a reformist, a *mujaddid*, had come forward: Jamîl Zahâwî, a remarkable figure, one of those great renovators who in recent years have scandalized Islam and have brought her greatness.

Jamîl Zahâwî was born in 1863; he was an almost exact contemporary of Qâsim Amîn. He belonged to a pious family; a mufti's son, he spent his youth at learned feasts, at floral games, at fashionable receptions and ceremonies, *maḥâfil*. He shone there with his remarkable memory and his gift of poetic improvisation. In the Parliament of 'Abd al-Ḥamîd he became one of the first heralds of Arabism. From Istanbul he visited Egypt, where he made contact with a milieu already enamoured of modernism and strongly Westernized.

Immediately on his return he urged Namîr Pasha to found a school for girls. Namîr Pasha, like a good Ottoman administrator, temporized. He appealed to the Turkish Government, which gave its approval. The governor, on receiving this reply, convened an assembly of notables to discuss the question. The 'Old Turbans' who were present insisted that the walls of the school must be high enough to prevent the neighbours watching the girls at play in their yard. At this point Jamîl exclaimed: 'But there's only one building right for you: the minaret of Sûq al-Ghazal' (where many centuries before the ashes of the mystic al-Ḥallâj had been scattered). The discussion broke up in laughter. But a house was chosen with high walls and few windows, and this was no laughing matter. The event took place in 1899, and marks the beginning of feminine education in this country. It stirred up emulation from other bodies: a Christian school, a Jewish school and then a Protestant school were successively founded. All this was before the 1914 war. At that time there were in Iraq six or seven girls' schools, at Baghdad, at Mosul and at Basra.

Unfortunately the reformer sent to a Cairo paper an article on the emancipation of women.[1] He trampled under foot almost all accepted notions: the father's power over his daughter's marriage, the wearing of the veil, on which pious people laid so much stress. When the article eventually reached Baghdad after long postal delays, there was a great outcry among traditionalists. The Synod assembled, and urged the Pasha to dismiss Jamîl, who had meanwhile been appointed Professor of Law. The affair provoked a controversy which was echoed in all the journals of the day, including the French *Revue du Monde musulman*.

[1] On the question of the veil, see *Revue du Monde musulman*, vol. xii, 1910, pp. 463 ff.

Jamîl's views, indeed, won support in Cairo from the modernists of the *Muqtaṭaf*, Shumayyil and Ṣarrûf at their head, and from the editor of the *Hilâl*, Jûrjî Zaidân, and from society people like the fashionable poet Walî Yakan. But his adversaries, curiously enough, included some women, such as Ḥifnî Nâṣif Pasha's daughter, who had conducted an enquiry into village women's life. She took a non-committal position on this matter. The time was not yet ripe, in the Middle East, for feminine outspokenness. . . .

Zahâwî, betrayed by his friends as much as by his enemies, lost his chair. If he enjoyed comparative peace it was only due to his family connections, which the Turkish Pasha respected. Eventually he left Baghdad, where satires had aroused the mob against him. But at Beirut he found an intensely receptive audience. Jûlyâ Ṭa'ma, wife of the head of the municipality, a native of Damascus, was all in favour of the feminist movement. She even edited a review, *The New Woman.*[1] Zahâwî received a triumphant welcome here, and an even more triumphant one in Cairo.

Thus began the movement for woman's emancipation in Iraq. And it assumed an intensely literary and poetic tinge, which is scarcely surprising. By a sort of inversion of the process which I have repeatedly described, the movement initially affected the higher spheres of Middle Eastern society and of the Arab psyche, where the innovation was welcomed or challenged by the strongest force which the *genius loci* then had at its disposal: speech. Despite the distortions of rhetoric, we can trace here or there, in the development of some theme, a definite historical advance in feeling.

Take for instance the theme of motherhood. We see here the moment when the relationship is revealed not only through the proud assertion of a genealogy but by the living continuity of a woman's being. The mystic, too, had felt the deep significance of this relationship. Mysticism on the one hand, modernism on the other: two symmetrical, though contrary, forces stirring the same soul.

'Where is my mother?' cries Zahâwî. 'Give me back my mother. I want nothing in her stead. I am alive and far away from her, and life is a heavy burden to me. I need my mother's love. O people, have pity on me!

'It was she who opened my eyes; her face was revealed to me in all its beauty. Give me back my mother, do not cheat me by that lying tale that patience must be my refuge!

[1] Muḥammad Baihum, *Fatât al-Sharq*, pp. 132 ff.

'If it is true, lead me to her tomb, let me be a wreath on her tomb. If it is true that my mother wishes it, lay me as a wreath, a diadem on her tomb!'[1]

From the mother,[2] inspiration moves on to other feminine types: the loved one, the wife. Most writers are actively in favour of the emancipation of women, but others admit a certain misogyny. Thus a contemporary poet, al-Nâṣirî, hates women, no doubt because they have disappointed him; he writes of 'woman's wiles . . . woman who is like a hurricane, like a tempest drowning thought . . . who is closely akin to the devil . . . who is deceitful and ungrateful . . . O woman, cyclone of the seas, drowning thought!' This misogyny is founded on a little-used argument of traditional Muslim thought, that of Eve and original sin; we have here a most important historical symptom. The Iraqi author from whom I borrow this quotation is shocked by it. He invokes triumphantly in support of the feminine cause such personalities as Mme Curie, Joan of Arc and Jamîla Bûḥirîd,[3] somewhat eclectically associated in the same sentence. He also protests against the attitude of another misogynist, a dreadful existentialist from Baghdad, Ḥusain Mardânî. But apart from these discordant voices, all writers unite to promote the cause of woman.

The first women's organization was due to Zahâwî's encouragement. His sister Asmâ, who remained unmarried—an unusual thing among noble families in this period—founded in 1924 the *Jamî'at al-Nahḍa al-Nisawîya*, the 'Women's Renaissance Movement'. After this, the history of the Middle East shows a rapid succession of such congresses: at Aleih in 1929, at Damascus in 1930, at Baghdad in 1932, and finally the great Women's Congress of 1944 at Cairo, which opened a new era.[4]

Egyptian Feminism

In Egypt,[5] the tendency has a long history. It has aroused many controversies, for instance that which broke out in 1908 around Qâsim

[1] Aḥmad Fayâḍ al-Mafrajî, *al-Mar'a fi'l-shi'r al-'irâqî al-ḥadîth*, p. 30. Zahâwî who, in the 'thirties, delighted the readers of the *Siyâsa usbû'îya* of Haikal in Cairo has clearly been supplanted, for the younger generation, by al-Ruṣâfî.

[2] Compare the rôle of the mother in many contemporary Arab biographies; e.g. that of Kurd 'Alî. Cf. his *Mudhakkirât*, vol. i, 1948, pp. 14, 36 ff. See also, concerning the rôle of women, the declarations of Manṣûr Fahmî in the *Hilâl*, vol. xxxviii, 1930, p. 629.

[3] Mafrajî, pp. 50 ff., 76 ff.

[4] Khiḍr al-'Abbâsî, op. cit., p. 64.

[5] Durrîya Shafîq, *al-Mar'a al-miṣrîya*: historical study, arguments, statistics, Cairo, 1955. Earlier, Aḥmad Badawî, 'al-Mar'a al-miṣrîya baina'l-Ṭahṭâwî wa Qâsim Amîn', *al-Majalla*, 1957, pp. 113 ff., and work by Anjâ Aflâṭûn, etc.

Amîn's book. This classic plea for women's emancipation aroused the opposition of so progressive an economist as Ṭal'at Ḥarb. On the other hand Hudâ Sha'râwî was the contemporary and the ally of the first Wafd. The feminist movement expressed itself through a multiplicity of coteries; this change in social habits was itself due to the break-up of the old framework, and such phenomena were already noticeable in masculine society even before the first world war. Today there are some hundred and fifty women's associations in Egypt. The 'New Woman' is concerned with domestic education, with that *tadbîr manzilî* which features today in all programmes of basic education. Another group is concerned with visiting the sick, another with public hygiene; yet another, the famous Red Crescent, has played a helpful rôle in the fight against recurrent malaria in the Ṣa'îd. And the great Association of Daughters of the Nile, *Bint al-Nîl*, founded by Durrîya Shafîq, has made a considerable sensation.

On February 19th, 1951, an excited troop of ladies, who had foregathered in a lecture hall, suddenly invaded Parliament, defying officials and facing the hypothetical risk of bullets. In September 1951, troops of women were mobilized; this was at the time when Egypt was shaken by a violent movement for the liberation of the Canal. Ten thousand women demonstrated in 1951 at the funeral of Egyptians who had fallen in the struggle against the British. But we must note that a pious society called 'Youth of Muḥammad', *Shabâb Muḥammad*, refused to take part in the ceremony because of the presence of women. So, at any rate, Durrîya Shafîq asserts.[1]

On January 22nd, 1952, a procession of young women, all of the upper middle class, with well manicured hands and neat coiffures, who had almost all been educated at French convent schools, gathered at the door of Barclay's Bank. Politely but energetically they prevented the staff from going in, which is one way of boycotting foreign establishments in Egypt. The crowd encouraged them, not without ribald comments. But things went rather too far when the *Ittiḥâd*, the Union, demanded the vote and based their arguments on the terms of the Constitution. This indeed granted electoral rights to all Egyptians without specifically referring to men. The matter was raised at the State Council and complicated manoeuvres ensued, in which apparently the King was involved. The final incident occurred in 1954 when the ladies assembled at the headquarters of the Journalists' Union—in the interests of discretion!—and went on hunger strike. There was a great to-do in the press about

[1] Durrîya Shafîq, op. cit., p. 223.

these incidents; the strike was disrespectfully compared to those slimming cures which American habits had made fashionable among the upper bourgeoisie. In any case the cure proved successful, for Egyptian women now have the vote, even if they scarcely make excessive use of it.

Many barriers still have to be overcome. Durrîya Shafîq, from whom I quote these facts, has attacked certain survivals, of which polygamy is by no means the most redoubtable (3 per cent in Egypt, according to statistics). The most disturbing phenomenon is that of frequent repudiation. During the last few years, the number of repudiations has risen to nearly one-third of the number of marriages. Correspondingly, second marriages, whether of men or women, account for more than half of the total number. Such instability in family life calls for legislative measures to discourage divorce. Several Muslim legislators have taken this line, thereby horrifying the devout. But such reforms still have a long way to go, although Egypt, Syria and Lebanon are already using women as doctors, diplomats, engineers and teachers, while Zahâwî's Iraq, on the first anniversary of the Revolution, appointed a woman as Minister of Municipalities (July 14th, 1959).

A Physical and Emotional Revolution

Najîya Ḥamdî describes four girls in a boat,[1] discussing the lighter psychological aspects of these problems as they glide leisurely along the Tigris. One of them declares that the soul is more important than the body. Her friend protests: 'You still believe in souls and miracles? Aren't you tired of that sort of nonsense?' A third tells a ghost story, but concludes, charmingly, that legends—*khurâfât*—must be defied. Legends and traditions have inhibited their youth. Does anything of them still linger? The names of all four begin with the letter *sh*, which is unlucky. It takes a lively discussion between them to chase away the horrid impression. How hard it is to exorcise the past! 'You'd like us to wrench out our hearts' secret ourselves! This morning I felt my eyelid twitch. My mother said it was a bad omen. But I won't believe it.'

Such beliefs are increasingly repudiated by the modernism that has invaded society, and are driven into the secret corners of personal life, together with so many other things—with the resentment due to long constraint and perhaps, too, a nostalgia for religious faith. Will American methods of investigation, by interview and questionnaire, bring them into the open! Unfortunately it seems likely that only the persistent

[1] Najîya Ḥamdî, *Arba' nisâ'*, Baghdad.

methods of psychoanalysis could achieve such a result. The investigation[1] made in Baghdad in 1957 amongst boys and girls in their fourth year at the secondary school or their second year at the University can only yield superficial glimpses. As described by Professor Ibrâhîm 'Abd Allâh Maḥyî, it seems to have neglected the most essential factor: the rôle these young people intend to assume, which will almost always lead them, in the investigator's presence, to display pontificating attitudes and express safe middle-of-the-road opinions. However, such a study helps us to discern the points by which, at the present day, modernization affects women in a country such as Iraq.

In the first place, by household furnishings. The first visible effect of the evolution is that it provides the Middle Eastern home with articles of comfort: refrigerators, which substitute the democratic ice-cream soda for the old fashioned sherbet, expensively frozen with snow; mosquito netting, which, with the help of D.D.T., may perhaps protect girls from the once-universal affliction of 'Aleppo spots'. And the poets of Baghdad will no longer sing of the ravages inflicted on tender cheeks, and love will lose something of its local colour. . . . These things have their undeniable usefulness, but also a somewhat factitious character. Doubly factitious indeed, since these are only the indirect results of a modernization accepted or endured, rather than imposed, by the male sex.

There is a deeper emotional involvement in the matter of education. Ninety-five per cent of these girls clamour for instruction. The investigator even dares to broach the question of religion. He notes a curious anomaly. There are more practising believers, whether Christian or Muslim, among boys than among girls: 25 per cent of the girls and 40 per cent of the boys. This seems to us a reversal of the usual order. With a certain subtlety the author explains that religious observance assumes the character of a challenge, in the present phase of Arab life; it forms part of the political struggle. It has the underlying character of a resistance movement. Thereby the metaphysical aspect, strictly speaking, becomes less clear cut. With considerable circumlocution this Iraqi author admits a gradual weakening, and perhaps something which would disturb a believer even more: namely that this weakening arouses no conflict between the younger generation and the old. Even pious fathers and sons quarrel over many things: economics, ways of speech, politics and so forth. But not, as far as we know, over religion

[1] Ibrâhîm Abd Allâh Maḥyî, *Mushkilât al-mar'a fi'l-bilâd al-'arabîya*, Baghdad, 1957.

or even religious observances.[1] No doubt these are growing slacker, and the arguments that centred round them thirty years ago are tending to die out. On other points these young people take a traditionalist attitude. Thus 70 per cent of the girls disapprove of dancing. This is somewhat surprising, in view of the varied and crowded clientele of dance halls in Middle Eastern towns. But considerations of propriety are here reinforced by the reactions of national pride, which condemns the frequentation of dance halls as an extreme form of Westernism and possibly as a demonstration of class consciousness.

The most important observation, undoubtedly, is that over 50 per cent of these girls, unlike the American girl students consulted by the same investigator, do not admit their own importance as girls. 'Eastern society is a society of men', as Ibrâhîm 'Abd Allâh profoundly remarked: against which these girls are not yet in revolt, even in their ideas. Hence many feel a dissatisfaction, the expression of which, for lack of adequate research, we must look for in the fiction which is itself a product of the new era.

The last novel of Haikal (who died in 1956) takes the form of a woman's biography, *Hâkadhâ khuliqat*, 'Thus was she created'. The bewildered heroine struggles painfully against the constantly renewed difficulties of her surroundings. 'I am overwhelmed', she says, 'by a perplexity which is one of the causes both of the bitterness which has pervaded my life and of the solitude that separates me from men'; the position of an introspective aesthete.[2] A generation earlier, we have the correspondence between the poet Jubrân and Mayy Ziyâda,[3] one of the first women to undertake the 'sentimental education' of the Arab East; although it abounds in irritatingly sentimental subtleties, such as are falling out of fashion even in Eastern countries, its pioneer significance must not be underestimated. The theme of amorous friendship leads Jubrân to consider that of motherhood. The poet tells how one day, when he was over twenty, his mother said to him: 'You should have gone into a monastery. If I had not chosen you, you would still be an angel.' 'But I am one still.' 'Then where are your wings?' 'Here they are', said the young man, touching his shoulders. 'But they are broken', said his mother. And this suggested the title of his first novel to the poet: 'Broken Wings', *Ajniḥa mutakassira*. Here are blended, in an effusion of morbid romanticism, Jubrân's affectionate grief for his dead mother, etherealized nostalgia, and that impetus which was to produce some

[1] Ibid., p. 22. [2] V. Monteil, *Orient*, 3 Jan. 1958.
[3] Jamîl Jabr, *Mayy wa-Jubrân*, Beirut, n.d., p. 26.

of the most innovatory work in contemporary Arabism. We see here the part played by women, and by women of a very different type from those who had inspired traditional Eastern poetry, or even from the great bourgeois ladies of Beirut, Damascus, Aleppo and Cairo who, from the end of the nineteenth century onwards, provided a feminine version of the *Nahḍa*.

What shall we say about more emancipated figures, such as those whom we meet at the Universities of Cairo and Alexandria, or whose poems (for instance, those of Nâzik al-Malâ'ika of Baghdad) rival those of Nizâr al-Qabbânî in their aggressive modernism? In the third volume of Najîb Maḥfûẓ's trilogy, which we have already quoted, we see a detailed contrast between the victimized and meditative matron of the 'twenties and a young woman walking with her lover in a park. 'The water of the pond is like a liquid emerald. A gentle June breeze is blowing, furtively. The swan swims, its beak outstretched to catch some crumb. You are happy. But your exhausting mistress is lovelier even than Nature!'[1] Lovely, no doubt, but sententious too. Here is something unprecedented! Every time the young man declares his love for her she replies by asserting her convictions. Tirelessly, she refers to principles: 'when I speak to her of love she talks about socialism'. She disapproves of the young man's links with his family, in which the father, as we have seen, is a depressing figure, a tradesman in the old town, deeply bogged down in self-satisfied traditionalism. But he and his docile wife are buried in the past. A new type has come to the fore, represented by the young couple. The aggressive nature of their problems is brought out even in the work of this middle-brow Cairo novelist.

We must seek a livelier expression of it not from novels and stories, which are always apt to stylize reality, nor from the outpourings in readers' letters on the first and last pages of magazines, but from the *faits divers*, the reports of legal cases, or those interviews in which the Egyptian press specializes and in which a great many things are laid bare. A famous actress accuses men of responsibility for women's neuroses, through their failure to satisfy them. We see the most striking contrasts:[2] we read of the first woman engineer collaborating in town-planning projects around the Corniche at Cairo, while another, with a degree in philosophy, opens a marriage bureau. At the same time a controversy reveals the persistence of female circumcision, at least among country people, while learned gentlemen defend the practice in the best

[1] V. Monteil, *Orient*, 17 Jan. 1958.

[2] Egyptian press reports.

interests of the female sex. One girl protests against the inconvenience of menstruation. She expects science to deliver her from this. An exaggerated faith in science, but a significant revolt. And we might go on indefinitely thus, collecting thousands of notes which would reveal a profound revolution, emotional and physical.

The Arab Woman and History

Transforming herself, the Arab woman transforms her mate, while their mutual attitudes towards outside things and important matters are also transformed. The young Shî'ite novelist I have already quoted, Laila Ba'labakkî, does not confine herself to asserting an exasperated individualism. True, she claims that liberty which springs from the depths of ourselves, *min aghwâr anfusi-nâ*, but also that which arises from the needs of our country, *hâjât bilâdi-nâ*.[1] She takes her own stand as regards God, her country, and the human race. There is no doubt of the sincerity and generosity of such a stand. It is not surprising that woman should simultaneously attain individual exaltation and civic consciousness, nor that she should reach these at the end of a journey that has lasted half a century.

Can one speak of the succession of a new type? The remoter regions and the lower strata of the Arab world are only affected indirectly, and belatedly, by this evolution. But, uneven though its progress may be, its reality is undeniable. It has brought to light, successively, characteristics which alter the whole aspect and significance of woman. In the last two generations woman has come to incarnate the continuity of the Arab world.

Her new rôle and status are hinted at in Mayy's emotional effusion. This was still an isolated, pioneer effort at the time. Not until the inter-war period did the new modes of feeling and expression become widespread. The interconnected development of broadcasting and Arab music, while they carried widely-diffused feelings into closed dwellings, provided the Arab woman with sentimental models which she associated with her personal emotions. Singers, today wholly forgotten, such as the mournful Sûsân with whom al-Mâzinî exchanged platonic love-letters, provide individual examples of this development. The actress hesitates between the homage paid her by flattering suitors, all prominent citizens, generous effendis, and her religious vocation. Another singer, Asmahân, towards the end of this period, inaugurates a romantic complexity which even includes the thrill of a spy-story. For all Middle

[1] Lecture given to the Lebanese *Cénacle* in 1959, *Naḥnu bi-lâ aqni'a*.

Eastern countries, between the two wars, were passionately involved in controversy with the Franco-British powers. And coincident with expressive music and an individualism whose repercussions were far-reaching, history made its entry into the heart of the harem.

This was the period to which famous authors of our own day, illustrious artists like Umm Kulthûm and 'Abd al-Wahhâb, are still linked by their youthful memories. A period which is over and done with, for woman's evolution, accelerated by national emancipation and the progress of education, has gone and is still going forward. Today this crisis of the heart and the senses coincides with a functional change. Birth control preoccupies the authorities, and is spreading among the bourgeoisie. To this we must add an economic change, in the growing extent to which woman is entering professional life, and a morphological transformation which is gradually reducing the size of groups. The descendants of the great families are deserting their homes in the old districts, which are being divided up into crowded tenements. They choose rather to live in new districts, in flats for married couples and not for patriarchal families. And these married couples are engaged in an active struggle against the hardships of a life where ceaselessly expanding needs—the demands of Western-style comfort—have to be paid for ever more dearly. Bachelors and spinsters, figures formerly unknown and still paradoxical today, are increasing. The matron ceases to be the ideal. The dancing-women, the almahs, and their traditional *danse du ventre* fall into disfavour; prostitution is repressed with increasing severity. Young delinquents, denounced by the press, haunt the pavements. But the police are on the watch. Moralists declaim against the promiscuity of seaside crowds, which psychologists, on the other hand, commend.[1] The fashion of the 'trapeze line' provoked a controversy in which even the lawyers of the Azhar deigned to join. It aroused their horror, and the mockery of the common people, who recognized in it the shape of their cotton sacks, *shwâl 'oṭn*; yet this dress served for a few months as a symbol of liberation to the smart women of Cairo![2]

For woman was conquering, and guarding ever more jealously, the right to exist as a person and as a citizen. And in so doing she was recovering that natural and social continuity from which she had been cut off by ancient institutions. Her revolution, autonomous in many respects, takes its place within man's. Man had arrogated to himself,

[1] Their number is growing. Cf. Terry Prothro and L. Melikian, 'Psychology in the Arab Near East', *Psychological Bulletin*, vol. 52, no. 4, July 1955.

[2] Egyptian press reports, July 1958.

within the traditional system, the privilege of relations not only with surrounding society but with nature itself. In many ways, man had intercepted and usurped woman's rôle. In Louis Massignon's terrifying words,[1] woman was 'the first strange guest' at her own hearth. She, the source of life, was drained dry and, at the same time, repudiated. Things are different now. Woman has renewed her own personality, and at the same time revived an undying link with the eternal flux of being and of things. History restores her to continuity, and man expects from her new and necessary mediations.

[1] Preface to new edition of V. Monteil, *Annuaire du Monde musulman*, 1955, p. xiv.

CHAPTER X

The Language

The Arabic language scarcely belongs to the world of men; rather, it seems to be lent to them. Its substance is almost always distinct from the language of life. The signs it uses disdain the things of every day. They hover above the earth, in accordance with their definition, which is to come down to it from on high,[1] not to rise up from it. Such, at least, is the principle of the language; it was also a historical fact, observable throughout Mediterranean Islam less than a hundred years ago, before the *Nahḍa*, the Renaissance, of Beirut. The alterations that have occurred since then are the more revealing. How the *lugha*, the Classical tongue, faithful to the Koran, its uncreated archetype, has tended to change from a means of attaining the transcendental and of communicating with God into an instrument for this world's communication, a means of culture, information and expression, and how far it has succeeded: such an enquiry lies at the very centre of my study.

The Initiators

The *lugha* is nobody's mother tongue.[2] It is acquired through the study of great writings and of the greatest of them all, the Koran. Traditionally, the Koran forms an integral part of any human apprenticeship. In the whole House of Islam there was no group so outcast, no region so uncultivated that it did not contain one or more scholars, however wretched their appearance and however meagre their learning, who kept up the tradition of writing and psalmody. This enables one to assert what seems a flagrant anachronism but is, in one sense, true, that primary education flourished in Arab countries before the Colonial era.

[1] Cf. *tanzīl*, the 'descent' of Revelation.
[2] Rather the reverse, since the 'illiterate' are known as *ummī* or 'maternal'.

It was less a question of instructing the child than of adapting him to the absolute. The Koran is learnt by heart, with a superb disregard of intelligibility. The virtue of its words lies in their form and sound rather than in any sort of correspondence with the facts of every day. They acquire greater power thereby, imprinted deep in men's memories. The Book, a breviary of maxims, prayers and stories, will for ever supply the adult with a tribunal to which he can submit his experience of the world, a perpetual spring the more refreshing that it flows from his own childhood, from that of his race, and from the Garden of Eden.

It is easy to see how the great language, thus preserved in a vessel that was both childlike and godlike, offers a social symbol of tremendous intensity. The moral decadence, the political dispersal, the economic decay of Islam in the nineteenth century made it, indeed, the only symbol of these nations. And it was precisely by a linguistic renaissance that their revival began. Thanks, indeed, to an earlier attack upon it. For, paradoxically, the Christians were the initiators.[1] On their lips, in their writings, the *lugha* straightway lost the Muslim part of its associations. It laid all the more stress on its social, indeed its national, aspect; it deliberately sought to be Arab rather than Muslim.[2] Herein lay the germ of many later developments.

A second characteristic fact is that the innovation, far from arising from conditions that might be described as natural, was due to pedagogues and men of letters who had and could have no direct connection with the concrete life of their country. There is no doubt some correlation, at any rate a chronological one, between the development of Beirut as a city and commercial centre and its development as a cultural focus. But there is nothing here that can be clearly defined.[3]

[1] To mention only Arab sources, let us cite the classic accounts of Father Cheikho, *al-Âdâb al-'arabîya fî'l-qarn al-tâsi' 'ashar*, 2nd edn., vol. ii, 1926, pp. 3 ff. On the general situation in about 1880, pp. 64 ff. Also a valuable history of the origins of the Press which is also that of the *Nahḍa*, by Ṭarâzî, *Tâ'rîkh al-ṣaḥafa al-'arabîya*, 2 vols., Beirut, 1913. And the bibliographies of these writers by Yûsuf As'ad Dâghir, *Maṣâdir al-dirâsa al-adabîya*, vol. II, Beirut, 1956.

[2] The part played by translations of the Bible, under the influence of Jubrân rather than that of the Koran, has been skilfully analysed by Anṭun Ghaṭṭâs Karam in an unpublished thesis.

[3] The 'nineties, which witnessed the definitive rise of Beirut, linked with that of its port, of the railway connecting it with Damascus etc., and of European investment, were also the years of its lowest cultural level; henceforward the development of the *Nahḍa* took place outside Lebanon. The irregularity of these interrelations between the social context and the cultural impetus in the Middle East might prove disconcerting to the 'literary historian', but profitable to the sociologist—always providing these interrelations, or the absence of them, are systematically explored.

Furthermore, the literary upsurge—and this is a third characteristic fact—owes much, from the beginning, to Western influence. There took place a fertilization of the old language by the intellectual themes and linguistic habits of the French language, about which no detailed study has yet been made available. How can we dissociate from the memory of Buṭrus Bustânî that of his friend Cornelius Van Dyck, or fail to recognize the important rôle of Father Belot at St. Joseph's Press? Most of these literary men managed to reconcile, in a fashion that was sometimes quaint but frequently felicitous, this cosmopolitanism with a deep-rooted love of the soil. Hence an ambivalence which might lead to a change of rite and even of religion.[1] It took the form of expatriation following the persecutions of Sultan 'Abd al-Ḥamîd; the intelligentsia of Beirut then formed a new centre in Cairo, but its representatives might be found further afield: in Paris, London, St. Petersburg, Cagliari, Tunis, Tangier, Constantinople, and even Zanzibar.

Literary expression, both form and content, gains by this broadening. To tell the truth, we must not expect from the *Jinân* the verbal brio or the emotional accent with which contemporary Arab journals have made us only too familiar. Its inspiration remains archaic. Its local chronicles are meagre, its political reports timorous, its form still hesitant. We find here a panegyric of some Khâzin shaikh, a poem by Abû'l-Hudâ al-Rifâ'î thanking the ulemas of Beirut for their flattering reception of his book about his holy ancestors; wearisomely assonanced prose; Amîn Jumayyil's versification of legal saws in the manner of Sully Prudhomme. And some distressing dithyrambs in memory of Nâṣîf al-Yâzijî and in praise of his rhetorical virtuosity.[2]

Bolder innovators were Buṭrus Bustânî, whose encyclopedia is an attempt to make contact with the world, and Louis Ṣabûnjî with his torrential flow of experiences. The former inventories long-concealed aspects of reality and endeavours to supply his brothers with things as well as with words; many of his observations are still valid, and indeed not until our own day has this effort, combining pragmatism and literature, been resumed. Our second figure—traveller, fashionable

[1] The most famous case is that of the brothers Shidyâq, one of whom was condemned as an apostate by his community, while the other became a Muslim. The *mu'allim* Buṭrus changed his creed. Ibrâhîm Sarkîs turned Protestant. Michel Mashâqqa abjured his Melchite denomination, etc. The Middle East can show many cases of such conversions, in one direction or another. But our historical and psychological approach is not subtle enough to study them deeply or to interpret them.

[2] *Al-Jinân*, volume published in 1885.

11. Egypt: work in progress on the Aswan Dam.

12. Iraq: completion of project, spring 1958.

13. Labour or liberation? Workers assembling the Ramses car in Egypt.

14. Young men and fortress. Aleppo.

lecturer, and inventor of arts and crafts—prided himself on being 'a popular writer and not a rhetorician', an unheard of thing for that time and that nation. Another Lebanese, Aḥmad Shidyâq, had contributed much to this encyclopedic apprenticeship. Unstable, rebellious, pedantic, sometimes licentious, ironic and bitter, but with a wonderfully questioning mind, he recalls the men of our own Renaissance.[1] And so, too, in a very different way, does the philologist Ibrâhîm al-Yâzijî. A grammarian, a passionate scholar, an engraver, a watchmaker, a painter, a calligrapher, an astronomer, this godlike figure was bold enough, in 1871, to enter into controversy with the terrible Shidyâq. He translated the Bible, wrote patriotic verse against the Turkish occupation, and collaborated on the review *al-Ṭabîb* which, curiously in our eyes, is as much concerned with grammar as with natural science.[2] In 1882, he sought refuge from 'Abd al-Ḥamîd's persecution in Egypt, which next took up the torch. He forms a sort of link between the first *Nahḍa* and the group we meet again in Cairo about 1910.[3]

These many-sided men strike us by their ardent desire to understand and to assimilate. While setting down in their own tongue what they have learnt of the modern world, they guard it jealously against journalistic vices. Is this an impossible ambition? In any case, they are aware of the need for change, but also of its dangers. Paradoxically in our eyes, they have little use for romanticism, of that sort which was to develop in Egypt, fostered largely by translations and popularized by journals such as *al-Hilâl* and *al-Riwâya* right up to our own day, with ever-growing success. These are conscientious and scrupulous scholars. The first evolution of the hallowed *lugha* arose from a direct contact between its linguistic arcana and the material contribution of the West. This is quite logical. The interpretation of the emotions came later, with Jubrân and the poets of the emigration. Even today Arab reformers give the priority to the communication of the exact sciences over literary expression, as they do to action over dream.

But this dream, in so far as it renders an inward experience, is itself truer, in a social sense, than technological progress. Or rather the latter is important only as a function of that inward experience. Since the time of Buṭrus the conflict between archetype and modernism has grown and deepened considerably, and the evolution of the language shows this.

[1] Cf. among others Shafîq Jabrî, 'The irony of Shidyâq', *Majallat al-Majma'*, vol. xxxiv, 1959, pp. 209 ff.

[2] Cf. in the *Rawâ'i'* the lively article by F. Bustânî.

[3] I am indebted here to discussions with Regis Blachère and Ignace Meyerson in February 1959. My opinions, of course, commit no one but myself.

And not only by the adaptation of vocabulary. The Arabs expect their language not merely to welcome new ideas and new things, but to express themselves, with all the longings and anguish of their renewal.

Discovery of Nature

Ṭayyib al-Sarrâj, of Omdurman, is an electrifying speaker. Haughty, eccentric-looking, flashing-eyed, he can recite thousands of lines of verse and comment on tens of thousands of words. For this Don Quixote of linguistics, humanity must give way before Islam, Islam before Arabism, Arabism before lexicography. He quoted for me many descriptions of deserts, of animals, particularly a lion's portrait by Ḥarmala ibn al-Mundhir. He was extremely proud of it. But it struck me that the vividness of expression in this poem contrasted with the conventionality of the feeling. I realize that this very conventionality, in this old poetry, has its own beauty because it evokes themes familiar to the group, which is essentially a form of classicism. But though it may be blasphemous to say so, in ancient Arabic literature, as in French classicism, Nature is never deeply explored.[1] The very need to interpret Nature, which presupposes both perfected methods of description and the awakening of a new sensibility, also assumes a renewal of relations between the individual, society and the world. This only took place, for Europeans, in the eighteenth century.

Let us glance at Jamîl Ṣalîba's book on *Intellectual Trends in Syria.* He devotes a chapter to the feeling for Nature. He gives several examples, chiefly poetic ones. For instance, descriptions of the Ghûṭa. It seems to him, as it does to us, that these poets, and still more these prose-writers, consider Nature only as a background on which they superimpose their own feelings.[2] And this is true of the poems inspired by the Nile at all periods![3] On the other hand, the emigration contributes in this respect a new way of feeling and writing. It seems that the Arab really begins to express Nature when exile disrupts his familiar setting and disturbs his sensibility. Jubrân, overcome with primitive emotion, identifies himself with the earth. But he knows that this earth is lost to him.[4] This is when, in the opinion of many Arabs, the old plenitude is

[1] This sweeping statement is bound to be disputed. Nevertheless there is a world between the 'Nature' of La Fontaine and that of Rousseau.

[2] The Tunisian poet Shâbbî had expressed the same opinion.

[3] Muḥammad 'Awad, 'Nahr al-Nîl fî'l-adab', *al-Majalla*, Nov. 1957, pp. 3 ff.

[4] Hence the theme of absence or departure in *The Prophet* which paradoxically recalls Shihâdî's Monsieur Bobble. Jubrân, as is well known, wrote in English. His work was only recently translated into Arabic, by Tharwat 'Ukâsha, *al-Nabî*, 1959.

shattered, to make way for the divided activities of modern times: meditation that is exclusively meditation, specialized art, industrial pragmatism. The poetry of Fauzî Ma'lûf, Elie Abû Mâḍî is as remote, in feeling and imagery, from the spirit of the ancient lyric as their bodies are from Bikfaya or Zahle. Before them, Rîḥânî had written:

'I have come, O Mother Nature, to renew in you the hopes and joys of life. In my heart today I have something of my neighbour's heart. In the heart of the forests there are impulses that arise within me. There is something of my own heart in the mind of this peasant, and something of this peasant's mind in the secret places of my heart. What he sees of the earth, of the universal light, I see it in the curves of the rose or the jasmine bud. The leaves of the mulberry tree tell me an ineffably divine secret. Among the terebinths, under the spreading ilex, I build the apse of faith.'[1]

But these effusions spring from a heart which has lost the calm faith of its ancestors. In Europe, the expansion of the romantic cult of Nature preceded the transformation of technique and society, although it was part of the same revolution. The *Nahḍa*, which was contemporary with the Victorian era, experienced the same upheaval. But this came to it from without, not from within, and Arab minds, in consequence, underwent painful distortions.

The Rehabilitation of Popular Art

The Arabs took a long time—two generations at least after the *Nahḍa*—to become aware of their own wealth. It is only in our own day that a whole intellectual class has begun to take an interest in popular art and poetry which is consciously and deliberately revolutionary.[2] Folklore, indeed, was traditionally disdained because it was alien both to Classical culture and to foreign models.

One of the journalists who has striven most keenly for its rehabilitation, Badr Nash'at, practically asserts this. In contrast with modern music and painting, which are closely governed by the imitation of the West and filled with the complexities of a new urban existence, village folklore derives from what is eternal. Nature springs up freely in it. Folklore is what underlies culture. But folklore implies dialect. Now

[1] *Hitâf al-Audîya.* The poem was written about 1910 at Firaika, a hamlet depending on the village of Bait Shabâh.

[2] The most important effort in Egypt is that of Rushdî Ṣâliḥ, *al-Adab al-sha'bî*; the Government has founded a Council and a whole office of Popular Art under the direction of Yaḥyâ Ḥaqqî. Cf. Dr. Ḥusain Mu'nis, 'al-Fûlklûr' (with glossary), *al-Majalla*, Nov. 1958, pp. 93 ff.

this dialect had hitherto been despised or suppressed. Folklore implies, too, a protest against the exorbitant attitude of the *adab* (literary culture), of urban ways, of religion itself, it implies the application of principles, attitudes, a whole ethical code contrary to those of the city.

The fact remains that it has now become fashionable.[1] Quite recently, two delegates from the Department of Popular Arts went to Port Said to record folksongs. But it so happened—and this shows how deeply popular art is involved with the life of the group—that nobody was singing at Port Said. The families of the two leading bards had quarrelled. Our two officials were obliged to use a subterfuge. They put on military uniform. They visited each of the two families in turn, saying that they had been sent by the mudir (the Governor) or by some even higher authority, and that this dignitary insisted on a reconciliation, in the name of the State and of the Nation. They used promises and possibly even threats. In any case they succeeded in patching up the quarrel between the two clans. Then they gave a huge fête. And it happened that one of the two so-called officers was fond of music and had spent two or three hundred pounds on a tape recorder.

Apparently the harvest was magnificent. It sprang from an inexhaustible soil. But the effort to gather it contradicts many conventions. The resurgence of popular art implies the overthrow of many taboos. Hence its subversive character. It rehabilitates values hitherto suspect or at least repressed. The upsurge of folklore is that of the downtrodden classes against literary academicism and social conformism. It is easy to understand how, in Egypt, such movements were often fostered by socialists. Elsewhere, in Lebanon for instance,[2] popular poetry comes from mountain people, Maronite or Shî'ite, who thus take their stand against the cities of the coast. Although this poetry attains a remarkable degree of elaboration, is published in a number of magazines and inspires great writers (such as Rashîd Nakhla), its literary promotion does not suppress its revolutionary intention. Folklore has long played a political rôle in Lebanon. History is its element. The different parties in their controversies wrangle in the style of popular verse. During the last war, Left wing supporters celebrated in *qarrâdî* the advance of the Soviet army. The Trade Union movement itself goes in for verse. And all this is closely linked to its mountain origins, for Beirut is somewhat sterile in this respect. The Sunnites prefer classical versification. They

[1] Numerous investigations reported in the press.

[2] Cf. the thesis of Jabbûr 'Abd al-Nûr, *Étude sur la poésie dialectale au Liban*, 1957, particularly pp. 60 ff. I am much indebted to this.

can only boast of the popular song-writer Zi'innî. And he, indeed, writes chiefly in Egyptian dialect, perhaps out of contempt.

The same is roughly true of Iraq, its songs, its *abûdîya,*[1] its great popular poets like that Ḥâjj Zâyir of whom I have already spoken. And I should mention, in the same vein, on the further side of the Arab world, in the Sudan, the *shaikh* Ḥârdallu,[2] singer of the glories of his tribe, the Shukrîya, the pleasures of love and those of the hunt.

Invention of the Theatre

If the folklore movement has to overthrow many hierarchies, aesthetic and social, before it can revive a poetic reality independent of Classicism—which is, after all, for these nations, a new way of taking an interest in themselves, indeed of accepting themselves—the effort to create a theatre which is not merely a scholarly exercise meets with difficulties that are even more severe. For the Arab theatre is a creation *ex nihilo.* The great translators of the Greek classics, for instance, when they tackled the *Poetics,* had rendered 'comedy' by *hijâ'*, 'satire', and 'tragedy' by *madîḥ*, 'panegyric'. The commentators recently edited by 'Abd al-Raḥmân al-Badâwî made the same mistake. Averroes himself went to great pains to find examples in support of these misinterpretations.[3]

Not until the middle of the nineteenth century do we find any attempts to create real theatre. And here I must not omit a reference to two innovators: a Lebanese and a Syrian. The earlier of the two was Mârûn Naqqâsh. He belonged to a family of Albanian origin, which played a leading part in the rebuilding of Beirut. In 1848 a comedy of Mârûn's was staged: *al-Bakhîl,* 'The Miser', closely inspired by Molière and scarcely naturalized. The language is a blend of Classical Arabic, Turkish, Lebanese and Egyptian. The Syrian Qabbânî went somewhat further, artistically. But his attempts were frustrated by the reaction of the conservative element. He was drummed out of Damascus and his works were banned, so that he had to take refuge in Egypt. And there is a considerable lapse of time before we come to the purely literary experiments of Shauqî.

This poet, who has been called 'the Emir of poets' but whom the

[1] Cf. the remarkable article by Nâzik al-Malâ'ika, 'La personne de l'Autre dans les chants iraquiens,' *Âdâb,* Aug. 1957, pp. 11 ff.

[2] Mubârak Ibrâhîm and 'Abd al-Majîd 'Âbidîn, *al-Ḥârdallu, shâ'ir al-Buṭâna,* Khartoum, 1957.

[3] Muḥammad Mandûr, 'al-Masraḥ al-ḥadîth', *al-Majalla,* Cairo, July 1958 pp. 162 ff.

younger generation unkindly describe as 'the Emirs' poet', was at that time in France, where he was much impressed by theatrical experiments. At the turn of the century he had already drafted several plays, which remained unpublished till after 1927. All are learned works, except for one, *Sitt Hudâ*, intended for popular audiences in Cairo.

Let us skip yet another generation. *Sitt Hudâ* is performed in Kuwait, by the actor-manager Ḥamarrûsh. He is obliged to wear an enormous turban and to veil his actresses from the neck down, for the citizens of Kuwait are more fastidious about theatrical performances than about their income from oil. In any case the play did not last long. Its enduring result, however, is shown in the development of comic operas, which genre enjoyed a tremendous vogue in Cairo between 1920 and 1925. To create a genuine theatre, there had to be achieved a fusion between this popular tradition and the learned models. Save for a few happy exceptions, the attempt cannot be said to have succeeded.

And yet what enthusiasm has been displayed in this direction! Egypt created a National Theatre Company, which is neither better nor worse than the rest. It founded an Institute for Dramatic Studies, and in 1948 a Popular Theatre which, by 1957, enjoyed a budget of some fifty million. At which the critics raged. They pointed out that 95 per cent of the credits were spent on salaries and sinecures, and the actual cost of production took only 5 per cent; that as regards subjects, out of 37 plays only 8 were tolerable. All dealt with one or other of three themes: revenge, the Bedouin theme *par excellence* (*tha'r*); women's wiles; youth frustrated. Not one left the beaten track. Why not broach themes of topical interest, of patriotic significance?

To which it might be objected that, in Europe at any rate, the best feelings don't always make the best theatre, as we have known for a long time! However, there was an undoubted florescence, a vast number of productions. Every method was used to develop a popular interest in the theatre: puppet shows, comic operas, classical plays adapted or translated to suit local taste. At the present moment over a hundred actors are involved in this enterprise.[1]

Among the most prominent figures, whose endeavours and whose whole personality would have seemed incredible to a previous generation, we must note 'Alî Bâkathîr. He was born in Indonesia of a Malayan mother and a father from Hadhramaut, who brought him home to be educated by a traditionalist shaikh. He continued his studies in Hejaz, and came to Cairo in 1933. He seems to have been strongly influenced

[1] Press enquiries.

by Shakespeare at the University; he wrote a host of plays, historical, legendary, lyrical, political, more remarkable for quantity than for quality.

Far more significant are the plays at present being put on in the Azbakîya Public Square. These are completely popular entertainments, in which the actors' voices are often drowned by the sound of the cracking of dried fruit pods. At the time of the Suez affair, all sorts of patriotic playlets were enthusiastically received: about Danchway, about the resistance against Bonaparte, and other more topical subjects, as we may well imagine. Here were produced Yûsuf Idrîs's *The Republic of Farḥat* and *The Queen of Cotton*, and Nu'mân 'Âshûr's *Top and Bottom People*. These novelists' realism finds a promising means of expression in the theatre.[1]

Other plays are more closely related to the literary vein inaugurated by Shauqî. The questions arising from a broader humanism are debated there. They are meant to be read rather than acted. This applies to most of the plays of Taufîq al-Ḥakîm. These gave rise recently to a most instructive argument between a young candidate defending his thesis, and his jury. When Taufîq criticizes indolence and fatalism, this young Aristarchus retorts that unemployment is to blame. When he advocates an intenser idealism, the young man replies that the Middle East today needs economic rather than spiritual reform. Muḥammad Mandûr, who was on the jury, notes that 'aspiration towards a better life has irresistibly overwhelmed our younger generation. They seek, by means of voluntary efforts—*irâdîya*—an art which may appease their hunger and set their eyes gleaming with hope for the future.'[2] And a long article, already quoted, by Maḥmûd Amîn al-'Âlim, one of the most prominent theorists of the tendency, recently attacked Taufîq al-Ḥakîm and the prudent compromises of his *Riḥla ilâ'l-ghad*, exalting technique and machinery as the only true means of restoring completeness to man.

The work of Taufîq al-Ḥakîm, like that of any great writer, inevitably provokes controversies; and the interest of these goes beyond differences between generations and rival schools. In an appendix to a play called *al-Ṣafaqa*, Taufîq al-Ḥakîm expresses his theory of dramatic language. And this is of great importance for our study. For what interests us in the Arab theatre is the way it represents a victory of the world over the Word.

[1] Muḥammad Mandûr, *Qaḍâyâ*, p. 145.
[2] Id., ibid., pp. 133 ff.

From the Word to Language

Arab tradition knew nothing of dramatic expression, for it could not have conceived of such a use of language. For the word *theatre* implies a public, and a language that can be understood by all. In Europe in the sixteenth century the learned genre of plays in Latin died away to make room for a popular theatre, which, in France, was gradually to become that of Corneille and Racine. The same problem has arisen in the Middle East. But it is harder to solve, in view of the considerable distance between the classic language and popular dialects. Therefore Taufîq al-Ḥakîm proposes a third language: *lugha thâlitha.*[1] It is to consist in a sort of compromise. It can be read and pronounced, in turn, in a dialect accessible to Cairo porters and also in a language satisfactory from the grammarian's point of view: what a *tour de force*! Only the critics, who are touchy folk, begrudge Taufîq al-Ḥakîm his achievement. One reproaches the 'third language' for its artificiality: this Esperanto will not take on, any better than the other. A second accuses him of flying in the face of concrete evolution; all languages, he says, arise through historic evolution and not through arbitrary invention. No doubt there is some collaboration between the scholar's efforts and the collective reality. But your 'third language' reduces the popular share too drastically. Moreover, says a third critic, a language consists not only of words having each its meaning, taken separately, but of the associations, the suggestions they evoke. Now only the past can supply these evocations, can provide their spiritual and aesthetic values. You are going to produce an artificial, bloodless monster. Your 'third language' will be neither truly literary, nor truly a spoken language.

The same criticism might be levelled at many curiously parallel experiments in the Arab East: that of the Lebanese Anîs Fraiḥa, for instance.[2] He, too, proposes to give general currency to a language which is that of cultured people, midway between the literary and the vernacular. Another attempt is made by 'Abd al-'Azîz al-Ahwânî,[3] one of the most daring opponents of the classic tongue as well as a leading Egyptian scholar. From time to time, many such experiments arouse sensational controversy. Generally the defenders of the classic tongue recognize the paradoxical connection by which modern Arab history is at the same time the result, the occasion, and the reason for a renaissance of the *'arabîya*. They perceive, too, the religious background

[1] Id., ibid., pp. 133 ff. [2] Anîs Fraiḥa *Naḥwa 'arabîya mutayassira.*
[3] *Âdâb*, April 1956, pp. 20 ff.

which gives it strength, so long as the Koran remains the prototype of good speech. Finally they denounce, accurately but sometimes excessively, the misdeeds of a Westernizing trend which leads to bilingualism, if not to a loss of personality. However, they cannot ignore that growing secularization of the most hallowed concepts, that of motherland or nation, for instance. And on the other hand they display great zeal in finding Arabic equivalents, as far as possible, for the terms and statements of foreign science. Their attitude is certainly not deficient in self-confidence.[1] But hitherto it has lacked a systematic historic explanation of rival necessities.

The language has incurred the major part of those tasks of expression and incitement which are imposed on, or assumed by an evolving society. Other arts remain outside this colossal mission. The plastic arts, in the Middle East as elsewhere, require a physical realization, for they form part of our 'imaginary museum' without leaving the world of objects. Their progress, in the Arab world, has suffered from material obstacles. It is too dependent on external influences not to remain, in certain respects, superficial. Music, on the contrary, has a deeply intimate character which makes its rôle in the contemporary Arab world, as we shall see, that of a sort of mourner over social change. In both cases the significant medium and the techniques suitable for perfecting it are so much indebted to the West that they are scarcely compatible with the quest for modernism combined with authenticity. Language, on the contrary, with its suprasensible references, its communal values, its infinite resources of vocabulary, its semantic flexibility, could perfectly fulfil this rôle.

Already its exacting grammatical logic, steeped in rationalism, provided an apprenticeship for the struggles of modern times. Although endowed of old with powers of demonstration, it did not shed its powers of incantation. The struggle for independence was bound to develop both of these. And the Arabic language has proved itself capable of everything: of competition with the cultures of the world, subtleties of political bargaining or the technique of stimulating oppositional fervour. It has provided expression for the consciousness of the Arab East.

Mass Communication

But for this it has had to renew not only its style but its implement, not only the material but the spirit. Through the press, the radio, and the

[1] As we can see from recent studies such as those of Amîn al-Khûlî, Amîn Nakhla, etc.

ever more frequent contacts between Arabs of different speech, the so-called 'modern' Arabic language has come into being: what I call *median* Arabic, *'arabîya wusṭâ*, mediating between nations, and between letters and life. This mediation brings its own failures, this power demands its ransom. Not without resistance does public opinion admit changes so radical. Therein it shows ingratitude, for it is in order to serve it that the Word has become language. But also perspicacity, for the process involves a disturbance of functions and values from which the community instinctively feels it cannot emerge unscathed.

Thus the Arab press has played its part in that subtle dialogue between the efficient and the authentic, in which the whole of contemporary Arab history is summed up. I mentioned earlier the remarkable lack of synchronization in the early stages, between the communication of knowledge and that of imagination, between information and expression. Even today an Arab daily paper takes infinitely more interest in the outside world than in internal news. This disproportion is noticeable even in the amount of space allotted to one or the other.[1] But this passionate obsessive attention fixed on others provides the guarantee of its functional accuracy. The major rôle it has played for half or three-quarters of a century, and which it plays with ever-increasing intensity, has been to appropriate and explain the world to the Arabs, and thereby to assume for them, and in their own fashion, that task of providing information[2] which hitherto was only available to them through the oppressive technique of the West, integrated in a new type of humanism.

This is why communication is achieved today through the press and the radio rather than through literature. The old 'unanimism', of the *umma*, the Muslim nation, can be recognized in proclamations, speeches and articles better than in poems or novels. The press and radio acquire prestige as well as duties. They are felt to be the rivals of tradition. When modern methods of diffusion began to become general—printing first, then the newspaper, then the microphone—many conservative spirits were loath to admit that they might serve as vehicles for

[1] This is only true of daily papers. The proportion is reversed in the weeklies, some of which, which I have consulted freely in this study, display genuine historical and sociological curiosity concerned above all with local things. This tendency was already marked in the Dâr al-Hilâl weeklies in Egypt as early as 1925. Why such a difference in attitude? Another subject for future research!

[2] The Arab press has played the vital rôle of helping to restore the human element in a world thrown out of joint by mechanization, cf. G. Simondon: *Du mode d'existence des objects techniques*, 1958, pp. 119 ff.

the sacred Text. In this they were reacting not only out of fear of novelty but also by an unerring foreboding of profanation. Language, and the communal exaltation which it foments and which supports it, were indeed beginning to change their function and their meaning. These reactionaries had at least the merit of recognizing it.

The time is long past when such controversies could arise without seeming ridiculous or hateful. The time is long past when learned men, miserly of speech, made their parsimonious glosses on the sacred Text and in their Friday sermons never exceeded the strict limits of a homily written once and for all. The orator, the journalist, with their incredible fecundity, their tremendous capacity for amplification, can stir up, far better than the *khaṭîb*, the preacher, that proneness to collective feeling which still persists in the populace. Every great leader knows how to make the *umma*[1] thrill with a sense of solidarity. His leadership retains some of the prestige of the immamate. And he partakes, in some respects, of the ambiguity of sacred things. This master of words represents now good, now evil fortune; in the latter case, applause will give way to curses. His magic power will have changed its meaning. At a lower level, at crowd level so to speak, the publicist partakes of the same ambiguity. Admired by some, he is denounced as a scoundrel by others. The persuasive magic of his editorial, the cunning pointedness of his articles seem to his opponents mere machiavellism and demagogy. To how many of these journalists might one not apply the epithet adopted by one of them: *tâ'ih*, 'the wanderer', in every sense of the word? This excess of honour or shame does not mean that the Arab journalist is necessarily more vicious or more talented than his European colleague. Only he represents, and profits or suffers from, the paramount importance attached to the communal exercise of language. This is why in the Middle East, at the present day, the controversies between politicians and even between publicists often have the fanatic character of religious wars. There is a battle between symbols, and between those who carry them, serve them or make use of them. . . .

This ambiguity, this ardour, these prohibitions initially launched against the use of new methods which might increase the powers of the language at the level of the masses, illustrate the singular power of that language. If theologians, without admitting it to themselves, feared lest the radio should emit a sort of magic adverse to Islam, it was because

[1] Renan, in his *Histoire des langues sémitiques*, could assert in 1855 that 'the art of oratory, in the classical sense of the word, has always been unknown in Semitic civilizations' (1958 edn., p. 159). Would he dare say this today?

the unleashing of collective emotion still retained a certain religious element in their eyes. And that is why in such societies all the processes of recognition and rediscovery, those which create a sort of symphonic agreement between all the component parts, are so much stronger and more binding than in our own. That is why their sense of propriety, *ḥishma*, is so strong. True, the words of the innovators hold a strange power of arousing passion and winning support. But these words themselves must conform to a sense of decency which may foster moral pharisaism. Just as textual conformism, *taqlîd*, shackled religious reformers, so does the respect for time-honoured collusion obstruct political daring with ever fresh impediments. Arab intellectuals are well aware of this.

Realism and Symbolism

The need for public approval still restrains the impetus of innovation in the Arab world. This is the case in the artistic as in the economic sphere, in language as in the way of life. The practical use of words does not always coincide with their significance. That part of language which is devoted to utilitarian communication, and which becomes more necessary and more unquestionably legitimate the more these societies recover their position in the modern world, is overwhelmed, dominated and sometimes hindered by that part which is concerned with the signs—religious primarily, and then social—which the community needs to recognize itself. Hence a conflict between information, expression and meaning, the effects of which could be traced in the evolution of Arabic style and in the functional division which is increasingly evident between different genres. Hence, too, the fact that although it expresses the new turmoil of feeling, and although, thanks to its foreign models, it is endowed with subtler techniques of expression, modern literature has a smaller audience than that of old, which expressed less but had greater significance.

In poetry notably, the élite, like the crowd, remain faithful to the great 'Lights', although the evolution of society and its feelings contradict them more profoundly every day. Ṭaha Ḥusain accuses the younger generation of murdering the *lugha*, while 'Aqqâd blames the symbolists for breaking with the genius of the language. And simultaneously we witness the spread, through the press, broadcasting and education, of that 'median' Arabic, which is still Classical in its grammatical structure and the major part of its vocabulary, but less and less so in its spirit. For it has lost those associations with sacred ritual which made of it the herald of a world of plenitude; it has drifted away from the unifying Message—such is the sense given by mystics to the Koran, the *qur'ân*, by contrast with *furqân*, division.

Arabic, we must insist, still retains some of these powers, in so far as it remains faithful to its revealed archetype. But a tremendous mutation has taken place in it. The unity it foretells is no longer a metaphysical one. It refers ever more definitely to the encyclopedic discovery of the world and the secular struggles of mankind.

Nothing provides a clearer illustration of this development than two contemporary literary efforts, which differ in statistical importance, in aesthetic interest and in political significance, but which are both aspects of the same tendency.

The realistic school in Egypt recently produced the two vigorous novels of Sharqâwî, the stories of Yûsuf Idrîs, already mentioned, and those of Rushdî Ṣâliḥ, the folklore theorist. I must now draw attention to a genuinely working-class writer, Muḥammad Ṣidqî. He was born in a poor family of Damanhûr. He was expelled from his primary school because he could not pay his contribution. For a while he studied at a religious institution, playing truant every afternoon to earn his living as a labourer. During the war he worked on the land; for several years he watered fields, carried manure, exterminated boll-weevils. Carpentry, textiles, oxyacetylene welding, manufacture of tin lanterns, he tried a bit of everything. Meanwhile he had become a militant trade unionist.

He felt at last the urge to express the anguish of contemporary life as he had experienced it, the arduousness of toil, the hopes that spring from struggle, the sudden surges of joy caused by men's friendship or by women's beauty. Such are the themes of his stories, collected in two volumes: *al-Anfâr*, 'the Lads', and *al-Aidî al-khashina*, 'horny hands'. In a bus, an old workman confides to his neighbour his distress because his son, a clerk, is ashamed of his father's profession. A metal worker, trying to earn enough to pay for a pretty frock for his daughter, wields his sledge hammer too violently as he attacks a piece of iron tubing; he wrenches a muscle, and will henceforward remain a cripple; a profound warning to his young comrades. A student leaves the city for his country home. His mother, in her black peasant dress, embraces him, and he is aware of his mother's odour. She offers him a little low table covered with a dish of *mlukhîya* and round rolls of bread. But why are these rolls a different colour? And moreover, where is the boy's father? A painful silence falls. The young intellectual begins to guess a horrible truth. At last the father returns, carrying a shabby bag from which he flings out the bread for which he has been begging. And the son, with a sob of anguish, imagines his father's horny hands, those honest peasant's hands, outstretched for alms.

Such painful themes can obviously not be rendered in the classic vocabulary and style. The conversation is shot through with dialect. For which such young writers are taken to task by established authors. Strangely enough, a collection of stories published in 1955, *Alwân min al-qiṣṣa al-miṣrîya,* opens with a critical preface by Ṭaha Ḥusain, berating the new school for its grammatical errors and ends with a postscript by Maḥmûd al-'Âlim, which is a manifesto as well as a speech for the defence. In reaction against all that has gone before, and following the example of Zola, Maupassant and Chekhov, Egyptian realism rejects all art that has selfishly withdrawn itself from social problems. Something decisive has taken place: the sense of the concrete, the urgency of the object—the weight of a hammer,[1] the poverty of the fellah, the yearnings of the artisan—have invaded the ivory tower in which literary tradition and the prestige of Classicism had imprisoned the writer. 'The essence has mingled with the object.' This profanation is, needless to say, revolutionary. It stirs up these young writers—some of them under thirty, many of them political militants—to iconoclastic attitudes. One such is Rajâ' Naqqâsh, 'who has lived as we all live, torn between village and city, culture and nature, dream and experience, impulse and action'. Naturally he chooses the second of each alternative; the contrary would have surprised us in view of his age, his country and his time.

Very different, however, is the choice made by the *ramzîyîn,* or 'Symbolists'. But it proceeds from an equally powerful reaction against the poetry of the preceding generation.[2] 'Society' poetry, an arid waste of rhetoric, panegyric and occasional verse, still dominant in the 'twenties, was succeeded in Egypt by the 'School of Apollo', so called after its leading magazine. It extolled a sentimental subjectivism inspired by the *wijdân,* 'breath of life', which is condemned today by realists for its remoteness from reality and by avant-garde aesthetes for its shallowness. And these learned poets, most of them adepts in French culture, aimed at an 'alchemy of language' based on the message of Baudelaire combined with that of Rimbaud and the Surrealists, or else

[1] Here, probably for the first time, there appears in Arabic literature that type of feeling catalogued by G. Bachelard in *La terre et les rêveries de la volonté.*

[2] An interesting historical account in Muḥammad Mandûr's *Qaḍâyâ jadîda,* pp. 78 ff.

with that of Mallarmé and Valéry. This is not the place to point out how far, in the work of such a writer as Nizâr Qabbânî, this art deviates from the Classical tradition. It rejects prosody and rhyme, stresses the unusual rather than the basic, new conjunctions of sound and meaning rather than the associations arising from the permanent roots of the language. But the challenge is an even more radical one when metrical and grammatical correctness, together with richness of vocabulary, conceal a complete change in the relations between words and meaning: such is the case with the Symbolists.

Jamîl Ṣalîba has defined Symbolism, philosophically, as the act of transforming sense values into abstract values, and vice versa. But is not this rather allegory? That genre is no new thing in Islam. However, we should not seek Symbolist models in the verses of Ibn Sînâ on the soul, nor in those of Ibn 'Arabî,[1] nor in those of the Syrian poets of the preceding generation such as 'Umar Abû Rîsha, nor yet in the *Dîwân* of the Palestinian Ibrâhîm Ṭûqân. Symbolism, in the precise meaning of the term, does not make itself felt until about 1935.[2] And even then it remains sporadic, limited to artists in small literary groups such as Bishr Fâris or Sa'îd 'Aql. These were two highly cultured writers, familiar with Western literature as well as with the subtleties of their own classicism. 'Symbolism', wrote Fâris,[3] 'is the discovery of that which lies behind sensation, the exposure of sealed secrets, the notation of lightning flashes, the rejection of everyday reality.' Sa'îd 'Aql, in the 'Philosophical Enquiry into Poetry' which prefaces his tragedy *Cadmus*, contrasts prose with poetry, the conscious with the unconscious. 'Consciousness is the prose of unconsciousness.' And in a lecture given to a Lebanese literary society he tries to bridge the gulf between the hedonism that lives for the moment—'every moment is our bride, our wife'—and history.[4] Symptomatically, this 'perfect magician' of Arabic literature, this learned thinker and scholar, this promoter of a revolution in the concept of Beauty, advocates the use of dialect. Although in this respect he conflicts with the views of a scrupulous philologist like Bishr Fâris, the two are allied in a common endeavour.

Herein they are joined by the Tunisian Mas'adî, who in his Ibsenite play, 'The Dam', *al-Sudd*, sets forth in faultless language the most

[1] Ṣalîba, op. cit., pp. 227 ff.
[2] Anṭûn Karam, *al-Ramzîya*, Beirut, 1959, particularly pp. 118 ff., 154 and 183.
[3] Bishr Fâris: particularly his play 'Parting of the Ways', *Mafraq al-ṭuruq*.
[4] Sa'îd 'Aql.

violently modern message.[1] But the most subversive effort is that of the Beirut group connected with the magazine *Shi'r*. They practise systematic dislocation of language. In quest of future syntheses, they sharply denounce fakes and compromises, or at least what appear to them as such. Hence many controversies, in which the underlying political conflict can be discerned. None the less, two or three of them are true poets. Perhaps their attack on the *lugha* will be rewarding. For it is a fact that their inspiration goes beyond what is merely Arabic; as in the *Songs* of that Mihyâr of Damascus, recently published under the signature of 'Adonis', which suggests an orphaned Lautréamont.[2]

Sacred and Profane in the Language

Their outrage consists in demanding an expressly symbolic value from the language, whereas from its divinely inspired origins to its present-day rôle as medium for unanimity, it has always been *in itself* symbolic.

True, this language tends increasingly to lose the original undividedness by which the word of God was identified with man's fate and with his daily behaviour. It has begun, in poetry and in prose, to describe Nature, precisely in so far as it was growing detached from Nature, thus following the way shown by Western literature in the industrial age. It has extended its powers of stimulation and adaptation, welcoming in its vocabulary, in its aesthetics and, gradually, in its spirit, ever-increasing foreign influence. Simultaneously it has volunteered to act on and against external forces, to make or to re-make Muslim history. The press, the radio, a whole mass of controversial writing, the formidable powers of public eloquence have armed it effectively for political struggle. Meanwhile its old incantatory function, the magic inherent in the legacy of a mighty past have been and still are laid under contribution, in conflicts that are increasingly secular. But these require an exact correspondence between the word and the object, now seen as distinct from one another. And the Arabs at the same time denounce 'verbalism' and endeavour to incorporate in their dictionary the contribution of

[1] Ṭaha Ḥusain has praised this work. Mas'adî, being a man of the Maghrib, has experienced the even more radical disturbances of a native genius whose energies are even more vigorous. I only quote his work here because it is one of the few that represent real Arab symbolism. It reflects, however, processes somewhat different to those which I analyse in this book.

[2] Adonis ('Alî Sa'îd), *Aghânî Mihyâr al-Dimashqî*, 1961. On this school, called the *Thammuz Group*, cf. my article, 'Expression et Signification dans la vie arabe', *L'homme*, 1961.

the West, which in their view is chiefly a technical one. The characteristic alliance between the magic power of language and concrete action, which had been prominent in these struggles, is now called in question. An increasingly uninhibited interest is taken in dialect and in popular literature. The novel, the theatre, do not merely bring new life to old genres, they are causing a revolution in the function of literature, itself of course linked to a revolution in the way of life. Strictly stylistic researches are being undertaken, but these deviate ever further from true classicism even, and especially, when they proclaim their adherence to it. For every attempt at verbal 'alchemy', whether of Symbolist or of purely formalist inspiration, constitutes—just as much as does realism, with its cult of dialect—an attack on accepted values.

Language tends more and more to assume the function of conveying information, of practical communication; it seeks to confine itself to providing signs whose neutrality guarantees their exact correspondence with the concrete object. Some, like the Egyptian socialists, defiantly adopt this evolution; others, like the Symbolists, react against it, trying to endow the language with new powers of suggestion; but in either case there is the feeling that the language is doomed to lose such powers. And thus these two literary experiments take their place, together with the expansion of the Press, technological research, and the spread of translations, amongst the signs, factors and consequences of increasing secularization.

Meanwhile, however, such an evolution is far from complete. And we ought, here as elsewhere throughout this book, to draw a distinction between geographical and psychological zones, between individuals and masses. The whole of the Arab East is up in arms in a struggle for political recovery, an effort towards material and mental self-equipment, a desire to adapt Western ideas that implies both docility and hostility towards the West. This cannot take place without creating divergencies between nations at unequal stages of development, and, within one nation, between social strata, between individuals, even between different phases in the mind of one individual. A general rhythm is all the more difficult to discern in that, even part from all these varieties and unevennesses, the movement is complicated by strange twists and contradictions.

The Arab East, and its language with it, are passing today from the phase of ritual to that of history; this evolution is unquestionable. But having gone a certain distance on the road to emancipation, that is to say to self-realization in conflict with, by means of, and in the midst of, the outside world, the Arab East experiences the need to reconstruct itself from within. It begins to fear lest in its efforts to recover from dispossession, it has lost something of its authenticity. And it is through its language that it seeks to re-establish continuity with itself, just as it had made language its chief weapon in its adaptation to the world of others. This is why in contemporary Arab history the use of the word precedes all other forms of expression and all categories of behaviour. This precedence creates a paradoxical situation. The language, while undertaking a tremendous effort towards modernity, intends to remain faithful to its ancient vocation. In so far as it succeeds in this, these societies can still subsist in a sphere unbroken by the centrifugal impetus of social conquest and critical objectivity.

Thus the Arabs have begun to profane their own symbols. But they seek to counteract this profanation by sheltering under fresh symbols, of which the language is one of the strongest and most enduring. They require of language that it should give them both a means to grasp the outside world and a spell to bind themselves, both a practical method and a way of escape.

CHAPTER XI

Music and the Plastic Arts

The façades of Khartoum, that summer, were adorned with expressive emblems, a bull, a hoe, representing such and such an electoral candidate. Symbolism thus played its part in the Parliamentary game. Remote from such topical interest, here and there small heaps of stones crested with tufts of reeds and many-coloured rags, the *bayân-s*, signified an epiphany, a divine apparition. On the further side of the Nile the Mahdi's cupola, with a horrible coating of iron-grey, recently replaced the one that Kitchener destroyed. The conqueror had made profitable use of the technical advantage he enjoyed over the dervishes. However he also made use of psychological weapons, and sought to attain the magico-religious level of his adversaries. On a renegade's advice, apparently, he bombarded the mausoleum. The population of Omdurman was smitten with a *ṭambos*, a sacred panic which the old folk still remember. Since then, the neighbouring ground, a vast square esplanade, has been turned into a stadium. Football was played in the very place where the Mahdi, under a light roof of leaves, had assembled praying crowds. But a spell still lingered on the consecrated spot. Sport proved a failure there, and there is talk of re-establishing a sanctuary.

It is in this very African atmosphere of violence and religious faith that a great scholar, a collector of rare manuscripts, Dr. Tîjânî,[1] carries out his experiments. He rightly attaches great importance to those exorcising ceremonies of song and dance which are known as *zâr*

[1] Dr. Maḥy al-Tîjânî, author of *Muqaddima fî ta'rîkh al-ṭibb al-'arabî*, Khartoum, 1959; see particularly his article on Mental Health Work in the Sudan', *World Mental Health*, vol. ix, no. 1, Feb. 1957. And many papers given at the Congresses which he has attended as regional representative of the W.H.O. in Alexandria.

throughout the Nile valley. He considers them as a barbaric form of psychological drama. The conflicts between traditional cults and orthodoxy, between 'Sudanism' and foreign powers, confer precise historic references on the cases he has discussed. He is searching for others, more archetypal, in oneiric experience and even in the metaphors of the Koran. Already seven centuries ago Ibn Sîrîn had noted curious connections between dreams, religion and the ancient learning of the East.[1]

Dr. Tîjânî's great merit is to have confronted this old teaching with modern therapeutic data. His attempt is no doubt one of the most advanced as well as one of the best integrated in the Arab world, where the transformation of the social milieu inevitably involves a whole train of neuroses and psychoses. Hence the widespread growth of clinics and, all too frequently, of psycho-therapeutic centres: a hundred and fifty in Cairo alone![2]

One can understand, in the case of the Sudan, that this region, with its visionary genius and its startling contrasts, offers more clearly than others an illustration of both the correspondences and the discords that reign between the world of practical things, that of religion, and that of beauty. Dream experience, states of ill-health, inspiration itself merely provide supplementary evidence, bridge the gap between different categories. Although perhaps less easy to read, these correlations recur on the plane of normality. Even so, we should have to decide as exactly as possible, for each milieu and each phenomenon under consideration, at what level, in what direction and with what force they come into play.

The reciprocal evolution of language and society in the Arab world has brought us convincing evidence on this point. I shall now examine how in the Middle East today—in a psychological trance, for all its material progress—two other forms of expression and meaning are developing in relation to one another, and both in relation to history: music and the plastic arts.

Anti-figurative Nature of Arab Art

The European Renaissance loved symbols so intensely that it collected and catalogued them; but it sought their reference and their

[1] Ibn Sîrîn, *Ta'bîr al-ru'yâ al-ṣaghîr*, 2nd edn., Cairo, 1936; a probably apocryphal work.

[2] With corresponding advances in the study of psychology: e.g. Drs. 'Abd al-'Azîz al-Qûṣî, Yûsuf Murâd, Zîwar, Horus Wîṣâ Wâṣif, 'Abd al-Mun'im al-Malîjî, etc. See the useful index by E. Terry Prothro and Levon H. Melikian, 'Psychology in the Arab Near East', *Psychological Bulletin*, vol. lii, p. 4., July 1955.

end in the human body[1]. Everything assumes a face: or rather, the body, in its fullness, becomes a temple. It is within the body, through it and for its sake that the Renaissance strives to solve the anxious problems raised by the impetus towards exact science and the scientific interpretation of the universe. Remember Dürer's *Melancholia*.

Contrasted with this vast wealth of imagery Islam surely represents the negation of the image: a pool of black light, or rather of green light, since green is the colour of the intercessor, that *Khiḍr* who through history, but outside history, goes to and fro between man and the Divine. Western art competes with reality. It has become a demiurge. It may be, as Malraux calls it, an art of 'appeasement', but it aspires, too, to remake the world. This remaking of the world, and particularly of living beings, is rejected by Islam. And therein lies the cause of that old and undying dogmatic hostility of all Islamic thinkers towards figurative representation. Has man the right to represent life, and above all to represent the human body? That is the theme debated in the quarrel about *taṣwîr*.

Let us examine this word. Its root is a rich one, far richer even than those from which, in English and in French, words like 'image', 'representation' are derived. For *ṣawwara*[2] is even more meaningful. *Al-Muṣawwir* is one of the names of God: 'the Fashioner'. How can man call himself *muṣawwir*? According to the terms themselves, if we refer to etymology, it is an act of impiety even to raise the question of *taṣwîr*! This capacity, or this art, cannot, by essential definition, belong to man.

And yet we notice, throughout the artistic history of Islam, a large number of representations, some of which show figures in movement. Thus I note in the Arab Museum of Baghdad a vase that looks almost Pompeian, with griffins and canephori: ornaments with stylized fruit, gargoyles with birds, and even, from the town of Wâsiṭ, figurines of dancing girls and waiting maids. It is true that these are two-dimensional; this had already struck me on looking at figures of popular art, wrought iron work in Cairo, ivory in Khartoum. And the contrast between this sporadic representation and the colossal figures of the Mesopotamian Museum in the same city is most striking. Such studies of movement

[1] Cf. for example *Umanesimo e Simbolismo*, Proceedings of the Congress of Venice (1955), and Hélène Leclerc, 'Du mythe platonicien aux fêtes de la Renaissance', *Revue d'histoire du théâtre*, April–June 1959.

[2] *Lisân al-'Arab*, q.v. Cf. R. Ettinghausen, *La peinture arabe*, 1962, where the admirable illustrations show how fortunately the ban was disregarded!

as one can find in Islamic art are rare and seem curiously constricted: imagery that implies a guilty conscience. . . .[1]

In the Arab Museum in Cairo I admired a bronze door of the Mameluke period, with magnificent curvilinear arabesques, purely ornamental in our eyes, but if you look more closely at them you notice that, as in puzzle pictures, they conceal animal silhouettes: doves, lions, peacocks, gazelles. The animal has hidden behind the alibi of the arabesque. Exactly the reverse of Gothic art, which strives through the real to suggest the spiritual. True, if we go even further back, the contrast dwindles between an Eastern art that still carries on ancient tradition (as in Coptic textiles) and a Western art still itself somewhat remote from the figurative. Egyptian archaeologists quote the example of ceramics of the Fatimid period,[2] in which they discover plentiful imagery. It is true that there seems to have been a retreat subsequently due to the growth of rigorism. A sinuous development can thus be anticipated, rather than a straightforward and persistent refusal.

Difference in genres must also be taken into account. The manuscript of the Wonders of the World, *'ajâ'ib*,[3] of al-Qazwînî, unhesitatingly depicts the human figure. Naturally it is in this type of work: handbooks of medicine, of veterinary art, of tactics, bestiaries, herbals, books on chivalry, that we are most likely to find realistic illustrations. In this kind of technique the West was frequently indebted to the

[1] It might of course be possible to counter this view by quoting many collections of facts. The West may even have imported from Islam representations of human and animal figures on textiles. Cf. the twelfth-century 'Chasuble of St. Thomas Becket' reproduced in the article by D. S. Rice, *The Illustrated London News*, Oct. 1959.

[2] 'Abd al-Ra'ûf 'Alî Yûsuf, *al-Majalla*, Sep. 1958.

[3] Ṣalâḥ al-Dîn al-Munajjid, *al-Majalla*, March 1957.

Opposite: 'From Kufic to Abstraction'. (*Drawn by Lucie Berque.*)

Top right: Fragment of gourd. After J. Sauvaget, 'Poteries syro-mésopotamiennes du XIVe siècle', *Doc. d'Études Orientales de l'Institut français de Damas*, vol. i, Paris, 1932.

Top left: Mosaic, marble and mother of pearl, from the Mausoleum at Qalawûn. After Weit et Hautecoeur, *Les Mosquées du Caire*, vol. ii, plate 78.

Middle right: Inscription, sketches on paper, Vienna, Archduke Rainer's collection. After Adolph Grohmann, 'Floriated Coufiq', *Ars Orientalis*, 1957, vol. ii, p. 214, plate 6.

Bottom: Tiraz fragment made for the Caliph Al Muṭî' Lillâh, Cairo Islamic Art Museum. After Adolph Grohmann (same article).

Background: From rectangular band on a window of the Madrasa of Baibars I. Wiet and Hautecoeur, *Mosquées du Caire*, vol. ii, plate 53.

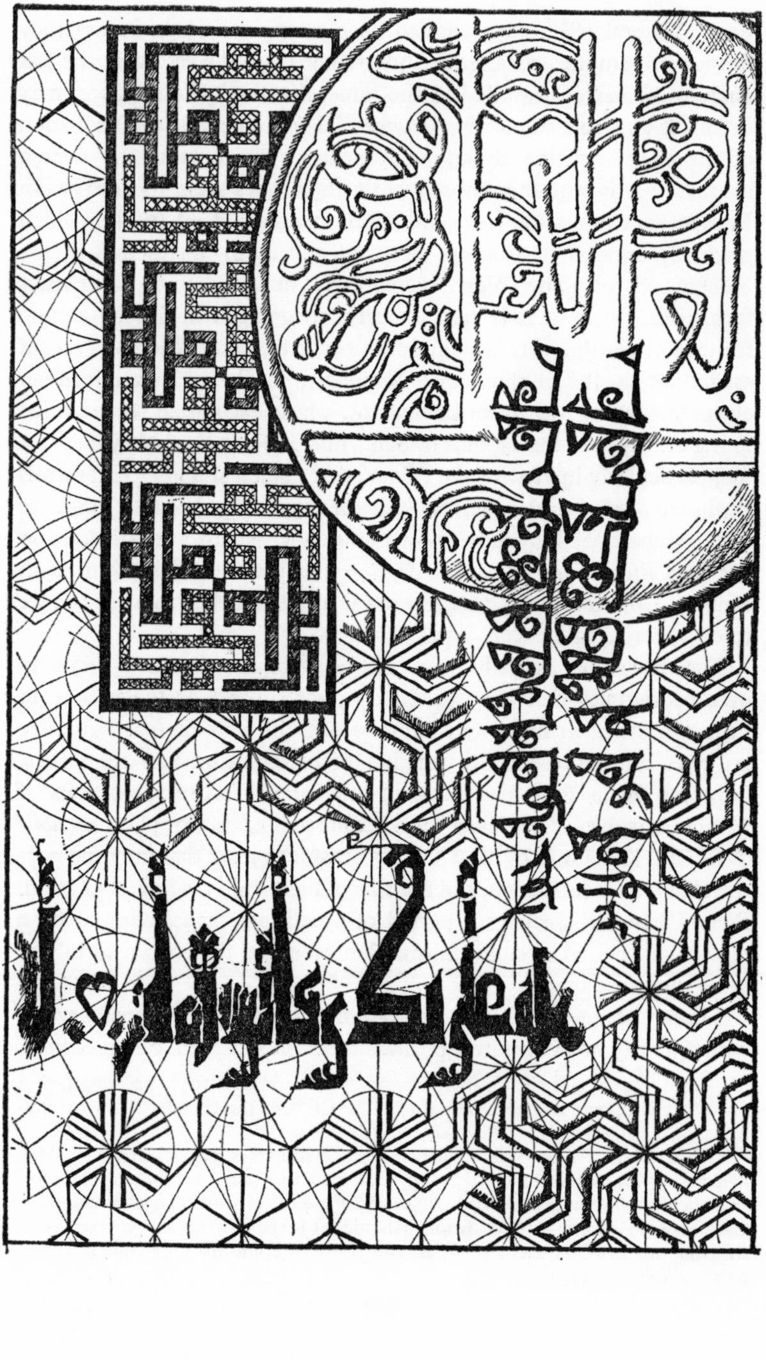

East. Bilateral influences seem to have come into play. Or are they not rather genuine exchanges? And are not these the result, in the last analysis, of having travelled in the same direction? For instance, may there not be seen a connection between Islam's dogmatic condemnation of the image and the Byzantine iconoclasm which lasted for over a century?[1] It is true that subsequently their ways seem to diverge. In Europe we witness the slow and subtle invasion of art by life, which gradually appears in Russian ikons as well as in the themes of the Sienese school. The West increasingly outstrips and contradicts formalism. But is it not, paradoxically, encouraged in this by certain features of Muslim art? The question occurred to me when at a recent exhibition in the Bibliothèque Nationale, in Paris, I examined an eleventh-century MS. from Languedoc, whose decoration was ascribed to the influence of the capitals of San Vitale in Ravenna.[2] Now it struck me, particularly in view of the colour, that golden shimmer that recalls the lustre ware of Andalusia, that it might simply have been the influence of the arabesque? Remember how minutely Orientals were depicted in the *Très Riches Heures du Duc de Berry*, at the end of the fourteenth century. Does this interest merely imply a taste for the exotic, or can we trace an actual influence?

The discussion, actually, can only be concluded when it ceases to invoke examples that are isolated by their context or too remote in time. On the other hand we cannot be sure that this Eastern figurative art does not represent the reaction of certain Christian minorities. However, Bishr Fâris has made an interesting discovery: portraits of Muslim lawgivers.[3] He even found a portrait of the Prophet, *horribile dictu*! and also a text by Abû 'Alî al-Fârisî, asserting that only the portrayal of God is forbidden, and not that of men, even the holiest of them. Bishr Fâris thus assumes a period of artistic tolerance followed by a reactionary period of conformism. Henceforward the chosen form was to be the arabesque.

The arabesque combines decoration and prayer. Nature survives within it only in an infinitely purified form: in some curve suggesting a

[1] From 730 to 843. Cf. Grabar, *L'iconoclasme byzantin*, 1957, pp. 103 ff.

[2] What is known as the *Gradual of Albi*. Cf. also the themes listed by Baltrusaitis, *Le Moyen Âge fantastique*, 1955, pp. 75–150.

[3] Bishr Fâris, 'Philosophie et Jurisprudence illustrées par les Arabes', *Mel. Massignon*, Damascus, 1957, p. 109. See also the same author's *L'art sacré chez un primitif musulman*, Cairo, 1955; and *Vision chrétienne et signes musulmans*, Cairo, 1961. According to M. Brion, Islamic art is the abstract art *par excellence*, *Diogène*, no. 24, Oct.–Dec. 1958; cf. the study of Kandinsky by Shâkir Ḥasan Sa'îd, *Âdâb*, Beirut, 1958.

flower stem, some fanlike shape hinting at the acanthus. But the Kufic imposes an even more scrupulous geometry on workers in stucco. Panels of plaster and wood, fine sheets of copper, pages of manuscripts display linear patterns whose beauty lies in the incomparable splendour of the sacred text. The illustration is subsidiary to the writing, and the writing to the truth. 'It is as though Islam, and Arab Islam, and, within Arab Islam, Sunnite Islam in particular, proclaimed an ideal of abstract transcendence, without idols, in which social forms and aesthetic forms must only be concise allusions to the ineffable name.'[1]

Traditional Musical Feeling

Ṭaraba, the dictionary tells us,[2] is connected with *ḥaraka*, that is to say 'to set in movement'. *Ṭaraba* is to make one's voice vibrate, while *khajja'a* is to produce in it a guttural reverberation conducive to enchantment or incantation. One is aware of the 'mystic' possibilities of such a root. In the root of *laḥana*, we recognize again the characteristic ambiguity of the concept. If *ṭaraba* can arouse either grief or joy, *laḥana* can mean either successful chanting or, on the contrary, a mistake in pronunciation. A dictionary such as the *Lisân al-'Arab* devotes several pages to distinguishing these meanings. According to whether it is pronounced *laḥan* or *laḥn*, the meanings are antithetical: the root suggests, for instance, an 'error' of syntax, but may also mean 'the language' in the sense in which they say, for instance, 'the Koran has come down to us in the language of Quraish'. In short, an equivocal conception which the grammarian cannot master easily through philological methods alone. We may resort to sociology, which has familiarized us with the rich notion of ambiguity. *Laḥan* means 'the second language', just as *ramz*, 'symbol', also means a second language, hence one conducive either to error or correctness. It may be the song in which Eastern sensibility delights; or again it may be the solecism that distresses the scholar's ear. . . .[3]

The appeal of Eastern music is not confined to its listeners' sensuality, innate and profound though that may be. It could not reach such innermost depths without involving complex effects on body and mind. In certain towns, mental patients were treated by listening to special

[1] L. Massignon, *Ishtar*, Paris, 1958, no. 1.
[2] *Lisân al-'Arab*, q.v.
[3] This is one of the *aḍdâd* of the Arabic language; but it can be explained as many others are, if not all. *Song* is that part of speech which has *significance*, but does not impart *information*. Cf. Fück, *'Arabîya*, pp. 203 ff., 232.

melodies. Mystical schools chose their own rhythms. A subtle correspondence united words and music, as Louis Massignon, in a memorable article, has pointed out. The same structure underlay the semantics of music and the semantics of speech.[1] The language postulates fixed, three-letter roots, to which the voice imparts functional modulation. Music is based on rhythm, stressed by drum-beats and given colour by the modes, *anghâm*: more numerous and diverse than ours, each holds a definite emotive value. Thus the 'ear of the heart' perceives 'spiritual sounds' in different melodies. Their modulations, said Sayyid Darwîsh, 'are expressed by quiverings, *ihtizâzât*, to which the heart responds like a needle to a magnet'.[2] Religious feeling can thus sometimes compete with profane emotion.

Thus when radio was first developed in these countries, there was a campaign to prohibit the broadcasting of the Koran. Orthodox jurists foresaw dire contamination of traditional reading by contact with the new modes of utterance. The rivalry between different methods of expression involved a semantic conflict, highly characteristic of the period. One such controversy affected the West as well as the East.[3] Following the appearance of one number of a Middle Eastern review devoted to the chanting of the Koran, *talḥîn al-Qur'ân*, the ulema of the Tunisian Zaitûna seized the Egyptian mufti, Shaikh Hasan Ma'mûn. He retorted with a denunciation, *taḥrîm*. The affair was sensational! One side quoted arguments from the *Ḥadîth* proscribing chanting; the other side, with equal erudition, argued the contrary thesis.

The debate is far-reaching. All we ask of it here is to show the extent to which, in these societies, the stirring power of music—*ṭarab* or *laḥn*—can arouse emotions and involve impulses.

The journal *al-Bilâd*, of Baghdad, published some time ago an interview with a Syrian musician. He had begun as a shopkeeper in the markets of Damascus and gone bankrupt, then roamed from Jerusalem to Cairo, from Cairo to Beirut, trying various employments, including those of musician, singer and teacher. He specialized in playing the theorbo, *qânûn*, the favourite instrument of Northern Syria and particularly of Aleppo. At one time, apparently, they used to group together orchestras of sixty theorbos all playing in unison amidst a vast circle of ecstatic connoisseurs. Things have changed greatly since the

[1] L. Massignon, 'Voyelles sémitiques et sémantique musicale', in *Encyclopédie de la Musique*, Fasquelle, Paris, 1958, pp. 77 ff.

[2] Reported in *Âkhir Sâ'a*, 11 Dec. 1957.

[3] Egyptian press.

triumph of broadcasting, in which our theorbo player now takes a modest part. Asked whence he derives his inspiration: 'The musician', he replies, 'cannot control the duration of his inspiration, whatever its nature. Inspiration is not circumscribed in time. It comes when it chooses.' Thus our man may be playing at a concert. He feels himself possessed. He steps aside from the orchestra and improvises for an hour or even two. It was thus, they say, that the future star 'Abd al-Wahhâb first shone in an orchestra at Ṭanṭa, some twenty or twenty-five years ago; he began to improvise, to modulate in that manner which disconcerts the Western listener but which brought the singer his fame. Moreover this inspiration has no clear content. The Syrian, asked whether he was inspired by love, wisely replied: 'I am a married man. I draw my inspiration from the music itself, and from music alone. Young men may be inspired by love, but I am not'. In fact, he was governed by his technique alone; without knowing it, he produced pure music. His instrument, the theorbo, is said to play a part in Arab orchestras comparable to that of the piano in our own; and this theorbo-player was a pure musician. Sound, above anything else, inspired him. His art was a purely inward one. It stopped far short of any intellectual plane, or any contact with the outside world. He seemed to be taking refuge in his own inwardness. Arab music may thus be, or become, a sort of *kitmân*, of intimate withdrawal.[1]

The East-West Conflict Again

For it is not the only form of music in the picture today. Many music-loving Arabs who have had a European education despise it, and its old primacy is increasingly diminished as cultured people discover Mozart and the young discover jazz. Hence new controversies, reflected in a recent issue of the *Majalla*.[2] Dr. Fû'ad Zakarîyâ writes despairingly of Arab music, judging it inferior to Western music as regards composition, performance and audience. He is used to musical analysis; he has himself published a book on musical expression, *al-Ta'bîr al-mûsîqî*. He has no difficulty in showing what inequalities are revealed by a comparison between the inspiration of the West and that of the East. 'We need a new generation of musicians.' He despairs of the present. This is, curiously enough, a fairly common attitude among many Arabs. As regards performance he goes further still:

[1] Such 'intimate withdrawal' is characteristic of Shî'ite Islam, but also of any comparable system in similar circumstances.

[2] 'Mustaqbal al-mûsîqâ fî Miṣr', *al-Majalla*, June 1957, p. 102.

'How dare you try to interpret Western song?' (note moreover that he makes a certain confusion between song and music, and that this confusion reveals a whole state of mind), 'how dare you confuse these songs with cries? For you render a large proportion of Western sounds as mere cries.' And as regards Eastern recitative, *kalâm*, 'your voices are far less skilful than the educated voices of the West. They are for the most part microphonic voices' (this neologism applies probably to that 'Abd al-Wahhâb who had lately been criticized for an ominous weakness in voice production). 'Basically, what we need is science, and ever more science.' His pessimistic opening leads to an ultimate faith in science.

The answer given by Muḥammad Fatḥî, however, refers, as we might have expected, to the profoundly specific character of Eastern music. 'How can you expect our music not to correspond to our own tastes and needs! This is so true that we prefer to listen to Western music pure and simple than to bad Eastern adaptations of this Western inspiration'; wherein he is probably right. But he might find it difficult to answer the attack as regards execution; weakness and lack of variety in instruments, voices untrained, which do not yield their full power as Western voices are taught to do. We may note this definition of musical pleasure, which is threefold, according to this author, being connected with the ear, the mind and the heart. The ear because of the touching 'sweetness', *ḥalâwa*, of the song: this might strike us as a limitation. *Al-'aql*, the 'reasoning mind', responds to eloquence, to the oratorical splendour which brought Umm Kulthûm fame. Now European music, even more than European poetry, has long ago rejected such eloquence. Finally, the heart: 'it perceives the soul, *rûḥ*, of the song, and all the delicate sentiment and subtle emotion instilled therein by the artist.' On the whole, this is the weak point of the definition. M. Fatḥî is undoubtedly right, speaking of Westernism, to maintain that music must primarily spring from personality. But, probably from ignorance, he does not make the same far-reaching distinctions as his opponent. He is right to insist on the special content, the *thing signified*, in Eastern music, but he cannot or will not see the mediocrity of the *significant* medium, which is indubitably less accomplished and less well equipped than is that of the West, owing to the latter's tremendous technical tradition. In the sphere of music as in every other, the West differs from the East by the way it has turned technical progress to account.

It might even be questioned whether the traditional *thing signified* really corresponds to the present needs of the Arab world. For this is

'The Westernizing of Arab music', as seen by the cartoonist of *Fukâha*, Cairo, 1930.

basically the point at issue. The controversy would not be so acute did not many Arabs question the expressive value of their own music, whereas they have never before felt so acutely its functional necessity.

In Kuwait, the decline of the fisheries, rendered obsolete by the growth of the oil industry, has reduced the number of sailors from 30,000 to 3,000. But at the same time it has produced a considerable florescence of songs.[1] These, it is true, belong to an artistic level and a social milieu remote from those of the cultured class. There is an immediate transition from work rhythms, as in the case of the fellah, or nostalgic longing for those rhythms, to their expression in sound. Such effects naturally ensue from any alteration in social conditions. More subtle, of necessity, is the evolution of an art bound up with the city way of life, with evenings in the garden on the banks of the Baradâ, or great gatherings of listeners spellbound by a loudspeaker. Searching psychological studies are needed to distinguish between the different sources of emotion or release whether in the listener, the composer or the performer. Here is a typical observation.

The working-class writer Muḥammad Ṣidqî, in one of his stories, depicts a hero with toil-worn hands. This young mechanic, sprung from a poor Cairo family, is one of those 'who remain close to the basic reality in which they live'.[2] They are rooted in the Egyptian soil: a reminder of peasant origins from which the working class cannot easily free itself. Now the young man aspires to become a musician. He hurries after his day's work to the People's University in Qaṣr al-'Ainî Street, and takes his place in a class learning the elements of music. Only he comes in rather late, still wearing his worker's overalls. The teacher, stiff and supercilious, a typical figure of this transitional phase, berates him inordinately, considering this manual labourer out of place among his intellectual companions. Next day, as the worker arrives late again, the teacher, who is writing on the board, in pretentious jargon, the musical significance of the terms *do*, *re*, *mi* . . . breaks off to flare up at the newcomer. 'What's your job?' 'Sir, I'm a welder.' There is a general burst of laughter, and the teacher sneers contemptuously. But one girl in the class takes our hero's part; eventually they go off together. In the companionship of this girl, of working-class origin like himself, he finds a promise of relief and fulfilment—and the hope of a

[1] According to my friend Bishr Fâris. Dr. Ḥusain Fauzî has a similar impression. It is true that this development is linked to an old work-tradition: in every fishing-boat the crew includes a *nabhâm*, a singer.

[2] Muḥammad Ṣidqî, *al-Aidî al-khashina*, pp. 28 ff.

music which is not that of the petty-bourgeois teacher, but the expression of a nation reconciled. . . .

At the other end of the social scale we find Dr. Ḥusain Fauzî. This Sinbad of modern times,[1] doctor and oceanographer, deliberately goes much further than did the mechanic from Cairo. The latter had sensed in Western music a revolutionary significance unguessed at by the *ustâdh* 'Abd al-Wahhâb. The great professor sees in it the substance of a universal humanism. He denounces the traditional music of his own country for 'its total incapacity to express or to construct'. His little book on symphonic music strives to defend this thesis against objections and prejudices. Many Arabs, who respond emotionally to their own music, are disconcerted by the complexity of Western music, and ascribe to it a purely descriptive capacity. They consider it a figurative art. Dr. Fauzî has no difficulty in demonstrating that a symphony rises above mere description, even psychological, and that its appeal to the mind and soul goes, in every way, far beyond that 'titillation of feeling', *daghdagha li'l-shu'ûr*, of Eastern melody.[2] The latter, in fact, is only expected to provide emotional stimulus, itself ambivalent; that *ṭarab* which is equally conducive to joy or grief.

Since 1958 the Cairo radio, on its second circuit, has undertaken an experiment which is of great interest in this connection, giving a programme of Classical music and meanwhile trying to find out listeners' reactions by means of questionnaires. The newspaper *al-Qâhira* conducted a meticulous enquiry on the subject. Almost all the cultured class, the *muthaqqafîn*, approved of the endeavour. Others, on the contrary, protested in the name of national tradition. They considered this music alien, out of keeping with Eastern taste. A professional psychologist like Yûsuf Murâd grasped the potential depth and importance of the experiment. 'We badly need a world culture, one which will take us out of ourselves. We must study and assimilate the contribution of all nations and all languages.' For one of the severest indictments brought by certain sections of the public against such efforts is a lack of Egyptian-ness, a tendency to internationalism. And there are times when the broadcasting authorities are bound to take such criticisms into consideration, for they may become dangerous.

[1] This is the title of one of his books: *Sindibâd ilâ'l-Gharb*, *Sindibâd 'aṣrî*, *Ḥadîth*, *Sindibâd al-qadîm*. Cf. interview with the author, *Âdâb*, no. 4, 1962, pp. 17 ff. This work has been criticized, at the same time, for 'Westernism' and for 'Pharaohism'.

[2] Dr. Ḥusain Fauzî, *al-Mûsîqâ al-simfûnîya*, p. 17.

The reactions of the young are even more interesting than those of the learned. One girl student from the University, from whom one might have expected some acquaintance with Western music, replied: 'No, I don't listen to these broadcasts, because I only like songs. I only want to hear songs broadcast, and that's all the people want, unlike the cultured classes.' This divorce between the tastes of the élite and that of the common people is a pernicious one; this is the sort of obstacle that inevitably confronts any initiator or reformer in the Middle East. 'Less classical stuff', says another. 'You don't give our national music a chance', says a third. On the other hand a fourth demands more Western music, particularly Russian music, which is fashionable, if only because of its foundations in folklore. The Director of Popular Arts, Yaḥyâ Ḥaqqî, is more cautious; he is an Egyptian nationalist as well as a man of culture. No doubt he does not recognize in Mozart and Chopin that local authenticity of which the author of *Qandîl Umm Hâshim* is rightly appreciative. But can he get it from 'Abd al-Wahhâb?

The fact is that a truly national music should seek its inspiration from the richly vital themes and sounds that folk art can supply. In Egypt, particularly, the fellah lives in an atmosphere steeped in song, while his most secret fibres bind him to the soil. At Ḥarrânîya where, in a tiny bulbous house of Coptic style, Ramses Wîṣâ Wâṣif fosters the inspiration of boys and girls who, without premeditation or preliminary sketches, gradually bring forth on their tapestry brightly coloured plants and animals, one is not surprised to hear them singing. They seem linked by some obscure correspondence with this work, which brings fresh life to the ancient imagery of their race, and with their limpid, flattened landscape. . . . In Cairo today a Council of Popular Arts is doing all it can to exploit these enduring sources, where the most 'Westernizing' composers now consciously seek inspiration. But it is not our purpose to study these intimate correlations, and the promise of future developments which they contain.

Let us return to Dr. Fauzî's enquiry. His endeavours meet with even more unexpected reactions. A leading University scholar admits: 'The music you offer us is beyond me, it is above my cultural level; your commentaries, on the other hand, are below that level! . . .' We can imagine the wry smile of the 'well educated' man, reflecting the mingled attraction and repulsion which, with unexpected cleavage lines, Western music exercises on the Arab mind. For it conflicts not only with an old tradition, with an inherent taste, but also with exigencies which it cannot satisfy until it has been more deeply integrated to the needs and feelings of these nations.[1]

Main Stages of Egyptian Music

This is not to imply that Arab sensibility has not evolved during the past generation, or that it has ceased to do so. At the beginning of the twentieth century there were two main musical genres: the *mawwâl*, with its roots in popular folklore, continuing the inspiration of the peasant—love songs, gnomic verses, political or satirical themes—and the *durr*, an essentially aristocratic thing. For this, the orchestra would assemble in the bey's home. A refrain, a theme, *madhhab*, recurred at regular intervals in a fashion that strikes us as extremely monotonous, though it has a powerful charm for those that love it, resembling that felt by traditionalists on hearing the last echoes of Andalusian music in the Maghrib. The *durr* derived its strength from its indefinite repetition or ritornello, the *dullâb*. Significantly, it is pure, *ṭarab*, that is to say it blends grief and pleasure in an intoxicating ambiguity. Some surprise is felt today at the indifference it displays towards content or story. Its charm operates at a level underlying that of the intellect: the level of the 'eastern' attitudes of a bygone period, difficult for modern minds to appreciate, and expressing a sated and yet restless sensuality.

The old *takht* orchestra has undergone colossal transformations since that time. The most evident of these is connected with a specifically Egyptian genre which became popular about 1920 and reached a kind of apogee in 1925: the popular theatre based on recitatives and satires. In Cairo in 1925 we know of about a dozen companies, all of which have retained their celebrity: that of Ramses, in which the famous Wahbî made his first appearance, as did also Rosa al-Yûsuf, who gave her name to an opposition magazine; the company of Salâma Ḥijâzî, which specialized in operetta and in which 'Abd al-Wahhâb made his debut; the company of Georges Abyaḍ, a pupil of the French actor Sylvain, who was considered by himself and others as a local substitute for the *Comédie française*, until his recent death; the company of the 'Ukâsha brothers, in which that great innovator Sayyid Darwîsh began his career; that of Najîb Rîhânî, etc.

Many artists' names form a link, during the 'twenties, between past and present. For instance Kâmil Ḥaljî, who, during the first part of his career was still concerned with melodies of the old type with indefinitely

[1] Cuttings kindly provided by the Egyptian Ministry of Culture.

repeated refrain, and in the second part composed popular airs. We may also mention Sa'ûd Ḥasanî, Ibrâhîm Fauzî, etc.

Sayyid Darwîsh speaks in terms which recall Molière's when he appeals to popular inspiration and the collective will, and turns to nature for inspiration rather than to art. He listens to workers singing on their way home from work, and exclaims: 'What are we compared to these? Nature is above art.' After his death in 1923, 'Aqqâd wrote of him in striking phrase: 'Sayyid Darwîsh lavished forth his melodies in stage plays, in odes—*qaṣida-s*—or in brief lyrics. They re-echoed in every part of the country. They were hummed on sports grounds. Women sang them at family festivals. The younger folk echoed them in back streets and market-places. Listening Egypt, *Miṣr sâmi'a*, had become like some huge orchestra, which he conducted from his desk.' How was his revolution accepted? 'It was he who introduced life and simplicity into musical composition and song. Whereas formerly this art, like all the rest, was crushed by conformism—the dreadful *taqlîd*—the enemy of life, this inspired genius came, and established a link between words and meaning, between verse and the moods of the soul.'[1] Under his influence Arab music ceases to be mere entertainment and aspires to true expressiveness; and the states of mind which it expresses are not only those of an individual but of a whole society. Hence the importance of this symptom. Darwîsh launched Eastern music into history. He made it an instrument not merely of delight, but of action. He was thus the first realist, the first *waqi'î*, and as such, the present generation hails him as a forerunner. In 1922, with the help of a craftsman, he invented by himself a piano which could convey those quarter-tones by which the Eastern scale differs from our own. He also wrote a book of introduction to music, which the journal *Nîl* published as a serial. His technical reform, which I cannot define in detail, is said to have been extremely daring. He brought logic and movement into the sequence of couplets and refrains, and he gave articulate structure to the melody which formerly wound endlessly about.

Many other famous musicians followed Sayyid Darwîsh; I shall only cite one already mentioned, the famous *ustâdh* (teacher) 'Abd al-Wahhâb. He was the son of a muezzin, and thus connected with the religious roots of music; and of a muezzin at the Mosque of Sîdî Sha'rânî, which takes us deep into the history and mystique of Islam. He began his studies at the Azhar; his father wanted to make a lawyer of him. Then he became apprentice to a tailor, but failed in this profession. He was forced to

[1] 'Aqqâd, *al-Balâgha*, 27 Sep. 1925.

turn from the external world to his private universe, which was music. Here he brought about a revolution in the orchestra; he borrowed the sounds of European orchestras and adapted them to a certain type of Oriental music. This style reached its peak about 1927, when he himself took up an opera about Antony and Cleopatra which Sayyid Darwîsh had left unfinished. At this point 'Abd al-Wahhâb found a Maecenas: none other than Shauqî, the aristocrat, the bey *par excellence*, steeped in French culture and adept at Classical verse. It was he who helped 'Abd al-Wahhâb in his difficult beginnings and took his side in certain acrid controversies, and against attacks from the press; the musician, indeed, has managed to hold his own, but he is subjected to ever-increasing criticism. A woman has taken his place in public favour, an artist of even greater renown, Umm Kulthûm; she is a remarkable social phenomenon.[1]

Like all heroes and heroines, she rose from humble beginnings; her family were poor, her health was frail. But from early childhood she astonished her village neighbours by her promising talent. Gradually she became noted throughout her *markaz* and then throughout the whole province for a voice which, little by little grew irresistible—a heartrending wail in the upper register, cooing sounds in the middle range, and that sort of huskiness, *buḥḥa*, as though the voice were bruised, at the touching climax. Serious study of the Koran initiated her into the noble language. Meanwhile she had become a professional artist. She went from one family feast to another, at that period invariably dressed as a boy. She settled in Cairo in 1924; her first appearance on the radio was in 1934. In the meantime the East had discovered America—I mean the use of broadcasting, which Sûsân had inaugurated in 1932. And gradually Umm Kulthûm became the sacred wonder, around whom crowds foregather. She would sing for whole nights at a time for fees of two or three thousand pounds, and she charged a thousand for making a record. But she remained ever observant of the proprieties, *ḥishma*. She was a moral symbol as well as a fabulous artist. When she made a film she always stipulated that she was not to be kissed on the lips; at most, she would allow her hand to be kissed. Thus she combined everything: an inexhaustible voice, skill in the use of the *lugha*, virtue and modesty! And the synthesis grew even more perfect

[1] Newspaper articles; personal observation; an unpublished study by Dr. Muṣṭafa Shak'a, *Umm Kulthûm ka-ẓâhira ijtimâ'îya*. It would be fascinating to compare the 'classical' singer Umm Kulthûm with the delightful folk-singer from Lebanon, Fairûz.

when, after Farouk's departure, she revealed herself as an authentic descendant of the Prophet, a *sharîfa.* Then she summed up, to the mass of the Middle Eastern people, the most sublime elements in womanhood, the very essence of their society.

The 'Night of Umm Kulthûm', heralded long beforehand, brought together the whole gamut of classes and individuals, from the University professor to the peasant. Radio sets were borrowed from the black market. If you had no electricity you stole a bit of wire to connect yourself with the current from the next-door butcher's shop. People of standing would issue collective invitations, thus borrowing some of the great singer's prestige. Wives, consumed with jealousy, would go off to sleep at a neighbour's house; young girls would take an extra hour's siesta so as to be able to stay up late. Certain addicts, who had been listening to wireless for twenty or thirty years, acquired thereby a reputation for enlightened fanaticism: such as one well-known landed proprietor in Upper Egypt who could not resist uttering howls at the more pathetic moments.

New Musical Trends

But with the passing of time the great artist herself has begun to date. Take the writings of young Socialist critics: Rajâ' Naqqâsh does not spare Umm Kulthûm.[1] He takes a different view of her from the older generation. He accuses her of cutting herself off from her roots, of giving false expression to her country's spirit, of becoming a professional, greedy for gain.

A controversy broke out in 1955 on the subject of backwardness of Egyptian music—described nowadays as *takhalluf*, underdevelopment. Progressive people deplore this backwardness in music, as in technical or political matters. And remedies in plenty are proposed. Naqqâsh suggests that no prescription is valid, although the nation is sick. This sickness, this problem is due to the fact that the Egyptian people, the Arab people in general are not living in a state of grace as regards music. Their relative inferiority in this sphere can only be corrected by general progress in all other spheres.

Artists, too, ask the same questions. Should they opt for Western or for Eastern inspiration? The problem is still that which confronted Dr. Fauzî's listeners. Now most musicians incline towards Westernism, foremost among them 'Abd al-Wahhâb himself. True, this sort of Westernism seems to us sickly-sweet and narcotic. Umm Kulthûm on

[1] Rajâ' al-Naqqâsh, *Fî azma al-thaqâfa al-miṣrîya*, Beirut, n.d., p. 76.

the other hand takes her stand against Europeanism, particularly against the imitation of Europeanism: 'I do not respond at all to Western operas and operettas. What we need is to base ourselves on our ancestral heritage, to cultivate voices with greater variety more apt for further development, and to confine ourselves to Eastern instruments.' She is alluding here to the instrumental experiments of 'Abd al-Wahhâb. But she is becoming an increasingly isolated figure.

The press reflects ever more urgent questionings. Thus a young Alexandrian journalist touches on the heart of the problem: 'Eastern music is nothing but languor, the lowest form of sexuality. Western music describes, represents, makes reference to intellectual movements and schools.' This young writer is already affected by what one might call centrifugal curiosity. External currents have touched him. I need not mention the sharp criticism at present rife in cultured circles concerning a traditional form of art, which to the tourist represents Arab art *par excellence*—the *danse du ventre*. It arouses ever-increasing indignation among cultured people. The musician Maḥmûd Sharîf himself, during a controversy with 'Abd al-Wahhâb, denounced this bogus Arab style, this suspect Orientalism, as being as harmful as pseudo-Westernism; it is basically a legacy from the Turks and Persians, rather than a return to true national art. There is a salutary tendency to look for this national truth in folklore, in the inspiration of men at work. Reporters have been recording popular songs, even the rhythm of the tabors that fishermen beat over the lake to track fish, with a special rhythm for each fish. Here again, when Egypt casts aside the accumulated contribution of centuries—her glassware in Turkish style, her Italianate decorations—she dazzles us by the glimpse afforded of immemorial treasure. The *zâr* itself, the exorcist ceremony, arouses musicians' curiosity. There may be in these incantations a psychological therapy that Plato knew well, whose strange powers the modern symphony may attempt to recover.

Egyptian intellectuals have begun to interpret the whole of this evolution in terms of those convenient historic patterns provided by the chronology of their country's emancipation. Fatḥî Ghânim, for instance,[1] discerns a first phase of traditionalism: the period of the *durr* and the *mâwwâl*. It corresponds to an aristocratic way of life, with refined pleasures. A second phase begins with what he calls the advent of the petty bourgeoisie. Ṭaha Ḥusain in literature, Mukhtâr in sculpture, Yûsuf Wahbî in the theatre, Umm Kulthûm display, in his view, the

[1] Articles in *Ṣabâḥ al-khair*, Oct. 1957.

common characteristic of having escaped from village society, and of fighting on two fronts at once: against old conformist traditions and against the aestheticism of the aristocracy. They have set up a sort of Third Estate of art. But their vigour has been enfeebled by their very success. Professionalism, publicity have invaded everything, at the same time as conventionality. People take pride, now, not in nobility of birth or behaviour, but in owning a big car or being a member of the Gezireh Club. 'Abd al-Wahhâb, with his selfish individualism, Farîd al-Aṭrash with his affectation of youthfulness, are retrograde in respect to Sayyid Darwîsh.

Everywhere else music has evolved, say these critics, indulging in characteristic pessimism: with us it has remained stationary. Our so-called great composers are those who have failed to gain admission to our Institute of Music: for instance Ibrâhîm Ḥajjâj, Anwar Mursî, 'Aṭîya Sharâra. The system must be a bad one. We ought to seek our inspiration more from folk songs from the songs of peasants and artisans. We should revive our native folklore, by methods adapted from the West. The problem is thus, once again, that which confronts the Arab world in every sphere: how to restore its own individuality by means borrowed from an alien source. We must be grateful to these critics. Even if they display a certain injustice towards their nation's taste, even if in their zeal for what is modern and universal they sometimes go so far as to mutilate what is specifically their own, yet they face the problem squarely. Its solution, however, will depend on a movement from the depths. A folklore exploited according to Western recipes will have merely propaganda value. But an original art which has undergone profound and searching scrutiny, and which has developed according to the laws of great aesthetic creation, would do much for the advancement of art among these nations, and for the advancement of these nations through art.

On 19th January, 1959, at the Opera in Cairo, already famous for its long tradition of *bel canto*, there was performed a symphony by a young, Western-style composer: Abû Bakr Khairât. His biography is interesting. He began his studies in traditional style with a Turkish master. Then he turned to architecture; in Paris, he won prizes for architecture, and meanwhile discovered orchestral music. In this symphony, his op. 21, he endeavours to elude the burden of tradition while restoring, thanks to the resources of Western instrumentation, the authentic character of his country and his society. 'Its oriental nature is clearly marked: thus at certain moments it recalls the famous peasant dance with sticks, the *taḥṭîb*. Another movement suggests the Alexandrian handkerchief dance, which is part of a marriage ceremony; and then there is a description of the course of the Nile. After a long passage for strings indicative of a journey upstream, the brass rings out to celebrate the journey's end in the Sudan.' And a martial hymn suggests, no doubt, for the composer and many of his listeners, the prospect of the High Dam.[1]

Experiments in the Plastic Arts

It would be futile to seek too close a parallel between the evolution of music in the Arab world and that of the plastic arts. And yet here, too, modernity has imposed its demands. And perhaps even more radically here than in the sphere of music; for here, in its technique and in its inspiration, in the aims it pursues and the audience to which it appeals, it is predominantly indebted to the West. The Arab painter and sculptor need considerable ingenuity to establish their connection with their own past. True, they may seek remote precedents for their refinement of line and colour in the work of miniaturists and illuminators, and claim Islamic iconoclasm in support of abstract expression. But the notions whose relationships I am endeavouring to examine are governed both by the fluctuations of history and by enduring attitudes. Artistic activities cannot be considered except as part of a whole which involves the demands of action as well as the needs of sensuality. Pictorial classicism, or the lessons of the school of Paris, which most of these painters have learned, or the experiments of surrealism and abstract art, provide a constantly renewed interpretation of the whole pattern, and suggest apparently unprecedented methods. Their rôle cannot be understood without reference to the way in which industrialism has affected the relation between nature and society in Arab countries.

A 'realistic' approach, in the commonplace sense of the word, would consist of a simple alliance between social practice and an adequate expression, both inspired by that rationality which is mother and sister to machine civilization. The object, under this definition—whether technical or aesthetic—represents the impact of rationality on a world whose unity it has shattered, and on a society in process of differentiation. Now the present period inspires in Arab countries, as in all others, a formidable impulse towards transformation. Dams on the great rivers, soaring factory chimneys give evidence of changes which any art of direct expression, which is committed to the community, must

[1] We might also mention here the researches of the Lebanese musician Taufîq Sukkâr, and the Egyptian Yûssuf Grais (died 1961), etc.

strive to interpret and to serve. Other trends, on the contrary, reject this intelligibility. They will seek subtler exchanges between the object —whether an object of the outside world or a work of art—and a world in depth. By this the surrealists imply the world of the unconscious; but one might also say the world of pure poetry, of ideas. For in their relation to ordinary life, the unconscious and the transcendental have a certain symmetry, harbour certain correspondences. The real contrast lies not between a higher and a lower form of art, but between this uncommitted exploratory art and one of practical contribution: between art that is primarily significant, and art that is primarily functional.

This explains how, in the Arab world, the plastic arts, as well as literature, are seeking renewal in two divergent directions. Against the *waqi'îya*, the realistic movement in Egyptian novel and story writing, we must set the timeless quests of symbolism. And the experiments of Arab artists in painting and sculpture each take their place, according to contemporary fashion or individual vocation, somewhere between the two extremes of abstract or figurative art.

At Cairo in 1908 an Academy of Fine Arts was founded, thanks to the patronage of Prince Yûsuf Kamâl.[1] To this generation, which is already a past one, belonged such artists as Maḥmûd Sa'îd Pasha, to whom Dr. Henri al-Kâyim has devoted an enlightening essay. Maḥmûd Sa'îd appears as essentially one who interprets the world, but who furthermore seeks to transmute it: a realist who tries to go beyond realism. 'The gardens are there,' writes al-Kâyim, 'the blue of the sky has endured every sort of violence, the quietness of midday is weariness, and if the painter lies asleep in his first-floor room his dreams carry him back to the ancient landscape, where women stand breasting the wind, proud of being nurses to this land.'[2]

These precursors, or rather these now matured artists, were followed by others. And many schools arose, some more lasting than others. The group of independent artists founded in 1939 under the aegis of Georges Ḥinain seems to have been inferior aesthetically. 'We cannot feel that in the plastic arts surrealism has opened up any new prospects to Egyptian artists. The painters who have allowed themselves to be seduced by this school only adhered to it in a superficial manner. Their subconscious has certain subtleties which surrealism cannot absorb as it has done in the West.' Here I must protest: it has its subtleties, but

[1] Cf. Dr. Arschot, *Peintres et sculpteurs de l'Egypte contemporaine*, Brussels 1951; Aimé Azar, *Femmes peintres d'Egypte*, Cairo, 1953.
[2] Henri al-Kâyim, brochure on *Maḥmûd Sa'îd*.

the transcendental or sub-rational world which surrealism probes in European countries has its own subtleties too! If the surrealist approach seems hitherto not to have called forth any successful plastic art in the Arab world, it is due to lack, not of inspiration, but of its material support—forms and images. In the Middle East, the object has not yet asserted its rights. At the present time it is through industrial manufacture, rather than through artistic creation, that these are being won. First things first!

True, it can boast one privilege which makes up for all its backwardness: the arabesque, which Théophile Gautier described as an Eastern equivalent to romanticism. A compound of language and line, a 'heavenly material' if ever there was one, the arabesque was naturally conducive to abstract enquiry. This, as the Iraqi painter Jamîl Ḥammûdî has pointed out, does not preclude the play of colour, particularly for Eastern people who have never learnt to dissociate form from flesh. Ḥammûdî practises what he preaches. He re-creates an arabesque with broad contrasts of tone. A literal meaning is conveyed through labyrinths of line and stretches of colour; but this is only a pretext and a result. The significance of the work goes further. Innovation is achieved through loyalty to the past.[1] For the Arab world, with its hieratic tradition, can shield its artists from the difficult conflicts involved in all Western experiment between a too-easily handled medium and the world of meaning.

At the opposite pole from Jamîl Ḥammûdî we find the venture sponsored by Ramses Wîṣâ Wâṣif,[2] to which I have frequently referred. In the neighbourhood of Cairo he has set up a weaving factory employing only children. Through their spontaneous art he approaches nature directly. No models are used. These child-craftsmen often depict living creatures: last year's Zürich exhibition of the finest of these tapestries displayed naively-coloured peacocks, geese splashing in the water, a cock in a garden of flowers, herons watching a herd of oxen, hoopoes and ravens, birds in bushes. The masterpiece is the Garden of Eden.

[1] We ought here to sketch, *mutatis mutandis*, the story of the Iraqi school; cf. Jamîl Ḥammûdî, *Arts*, 28 April 1950. The influence of Turkish miniaturists was followed by that of students home from abroad (school of Paris, English teaching, even Polish impressionism!). V. Hakim, in the *Revue du Liban*, Beirut, 9 Nov. 1957, gives a striking description of some of these developments, which were not limited to painting but affected sculpture too. The exhibition of Iraqi art at the U.N.E.S.C.O. palace at Beirut (cf. *Orient*, 8 Nov. 1957) attracted interest above all by the statue of Sharjawîya by Khâlid al-Raḥḥâl.

[2] See account in *Renouveau*, illustrated supplement; *al-Kullîya*, vol. xxix, no. 2; 'A propos d'art copte', in *L'art sacré*, Sep. 1956.

In a tangled thicket recalling pre-dynastic art, animals are shown moving around a scarlet patch—the bodies of two stags. The Coptic youth who wove this scene drowned himself shortly afterwards in the Nile.

In April 1959, on the occasion of an exhibition of Nada's paintings, a small group of leading intellectuals set forth in a pamphlet, *Still Unknown*, some of the most illuminating points of view on the question at issue in the Arab world today. Nada himself writes:

'An art empty of surrealism is no art. I mean that spontaneous expression, of whatever sort and trend it may be, cannot be dissociated from the artist's essential being, in so far as it is sincere. And this link with the essential is to some extent a link with the subconscious.

'There are two sorts of abstraction. One makes use of forms derived from our daily reality, while the other produces forms which only exist in the artist's innermost sensibility, forms of a freer sort. At present I follow the former trend, but I am sympathetic to the latter, although I feel it may be unrealizable.

'Absolute abstraction is the summit to which abstract art seeks to attain when it severs connection with all customary forms, geometrical and others. All plastic art which reproduces common reality fails on the plane of the imagination.'[1]

For Nada and some others, the Arab world can thus regain an authenticity too long frustrated by outmoded traditionalism and superficial Westernism.

Music and Action

We may accept the augury. But it must be admitted that these arguments, in the Arab world, interest only an élite—an important élite, but a tiny one. The great phenomenon, which excites controversy among the learned as well as the feelings of the masses, is that of musical progress, which claims to be part of history. Such a connection certainly defies summary explanation, and it takes the form of a psychological conflict

[1] Extract from the catalogue issued on the occasion of this public demonstration of the Egyptian intelligentsia, in which the influence of Georges Ḥinain was decisive. It would be most instructive to compare this exhibition with that held at about the same time in Damascus, centring round the master-craftsman Abû Sulaimân al-Khayyât, decorator of the Syrian Parliament and faithful heir to the ornamental style of the Ayyubids. And also at the same time, at Damascus, the Minister of Culture was organizing a spring *Salon* for painting and sculpture, where figurative art predominated! In 1959 I came across the son of Abû Sulaimân working in the same style as his father in the new rooms of the Damascus Museum.

rather than a succession of chronological phases. Positive motivations can be made out, none the less.

The shock of contact with industrial civilization produced a wealth of song in the Arab East. From a source of delight to the senses, music has become an expression of feeling. It has thus acquired, with the help of the radio, an immense collective significance. It is obviously notable for its popular appeal to a mass audience rather than for its quality. And many controversies indicate that since the last war, it has been more valuable as a compensation than as a testimony. To many Arabs it seems to lag behind the other arts, such as literature. Many criticize its languorous obsession, its facile sensuality. Socialists have begun to call it bourgeois and reactionary. Arab music, born of Arab history, proudly sharing in the internal development of a whole generation of Arabs, is now in its turn repudiated by history. As it developed it begot the necessity for its own replacement by more adequate forms. And yet if, despite valuable achievements, Western music has not yet supplanted it, this is because it does not correspond to the same spiritual needs.

Our scale recognizes no smaller interval than a semitone. It climbs the ladder of sound by degrees which shock the Eastern ear by their crudity. But the rhythmic discoveries of our great musicians have perfected it as an instrument wherewith to grasp not only the world of dream but the real world, the one confirming the other. And to Eastern minds, it seems turned too much outward. It disappoints him by its angular logic, its affinity for the concrete. Eastern music is wholly emotional. The *ṭarab* is basically ambivalent: the traditional *mawwâl* brought joy or grief, sensual rapture or even more sensual longing and deprivation; and these are still conveyed by the singing of Umm Kulthûm, despite its excess of anecdote or sentimentality. This music has an oppressive 'viscosity', to use Sartre's term. And it has a profoundly moving effect upon the Arab listener, whom his whole education has subjected to antithetical concepts of *ḥalâl* and *ḥarâm*, that which is allowed and that which is forbidden!

For musical emotion stirs those parts of one's being that the ethical code leaves in darkness. Thus in the vast realm of sexuality, whatever cannot be confined within the notions of licit and illicit, that whole voluptuous twilight which is shattered by the rigid distinctions of speech and traditional morality. Such music fosters an inward life which is the more secret because each of us has to protect it against the limitations of language and the classifications of jurists. These do not underestimate its powerful appeal, and with just cause. They dread it the more because it is so profoundly moving. They repress it as far as possible from the sphere of moral consciousness. And by so doing they set a barrier between man's inward being and his outward-looking self, between his intimacy and his activity. Music and speech are complementary, so to speak, on either side of the norms they have set up.

And thus the Arab seeks to grasp the world through speech, while his spirit withdraws in the secret depths of his music. If one were not afraid of falsifying the symmetry by exaggeration, one might recognize in the contemporary development of political eloquence on the one hand and sentimental music on the other the two main reactions, the one inward, the other outward, of the Arab to his new historical situation. Only in this new situation all sides are equally inculpated. History accuses speech of ineffectiveness in action, music of failing to satisfy newly-recognized needs, the ethical code of idealism. And this indictment implicates a whole structure, and all the elements of security and happiness which it has hitherto afforded these men.

CHAPTER XII

Political Values

Today, the thing that most forcibly strikes the foreigner about the Arabs, and that fills the major part of their conversation and their writings, is their re-establishment in international life. This re-establishment, which has as great an interest for the psychologist and the historians as for the politician, is gathering speed today. There was less distance between the semi-colonial Arabs of 1914 and those who in 1920 began to assert their rights, or between the latter and the insurgents of 1925, than there is between the emancipated Arabs of 1945 and the citizens of 1960, or, no doubt, than there will be between these and the Arabs of tomorrow. Over the whole southern face of the Mediterranean, an increasingly radical independence—which is, however, frequently constructive and sometimes co-operative—has spread from Morocco to Iraq, that zone which, only a third of a century ago, was completely in a state of dependency. It would therefore be paradoxical, in a study of these countries' development, to neglect the political movement which either heralds or reinforces that development—unless it causes it to deviate. Only this raises certain practical and theoretical problems for the analyst.[1]

[1] In this chapter I have incorporated and recast a certain number of passages taken from my article in the *Encyclopédie française*, vol xi, 1957, entitled: 'L'Univers politique des Arabes', which includes a bibliographical section (drawn up with the help of N. Tomiche) that seemed unnecessary in a purely interpretative essay. I must cite, however, amongst the more recent publications which have either contributed to the general picture or have brought me useful factual elements or suggestive cross-references: the last volumes of the *Cahiers de l'Orient contemporain*, inspired by N. Tomiche; W. Laqueur, 'Communism and nationalism in the Middle East', *Journal of Modern History*, Sep. 1957, pp. 280–281; P. Rondot, *L'Islam et les Musulmans d'aujourd'hui*, and *Destin du Proche-Orient*; A. Hourani, 'The Middle East and the Crisis of 1956', in

Arab Politics and Social Progress

In the first place, the problem of current events and the disorders that ensue from them. The scarcity of objective documentation, the difficulty of judging calmly, a predicament which seems here more than elsewhere bound up with man's wisdom or folly, with internal or external competitions, with the accidents due to violence or the subtleties of intrigue, forbid one in this sphere to make assessments which are liable to be contradicted tomorrow. Only history, with its broad rhythms, its long threads, interests the sociologist.[1] Its deep-rooted logic can, to some extent, adjust the chaotic oscillation of facts. Its general theme, which for the past half-century, and ever more emphatically, has been the liberation of colonial peoples, can be reconciled, if envisaged in broad masses and great phases, with the liberation of man: as a political subject, of course, but also as a human being. And for this reason we must give it our help. But the concordance does not always hold good for any particular time and place.

Trade unionism, the emancipation of women, although moving in the same direction as national enfranchisement, sometimes come into conflict with nationalism. A party whose central cause is the assertion of social rights, such as Communism, has thus for a whole generation followed lines which bring it now into alliance, now into conflict with the leaders of the nationalist struggle. As we know, the disagreement frequently flares up into open strife. Militant communists have been exiled, such as the Syrian Bikdâsh, or imprisoned like so many members of the Egyptian intelligentsia, or even hanged, like the Iraqi al-Fahd. Conversely, if during the preceding period religious congregations and religious sects in general were open to reproach for their solidarity with the established powers, which were then more or less dependent on the foreigner, it must be admitted that the civic bourgeoisie of Islam had shown itself quite as capable of forming an opposition as the purists of the reforming movement. Islam had come to symbolize, together with its language, that which makes the Arabs *different*, that is to say, in many respects, that which they essentially *are*, at a time when they

Middle Eastern Affairs, Oxford, 1958, pp. 9 ff; Qusṭanṭîn Zuraiq, *Ayyu ghad?*, Beirut, 1958; Ḥasan Sa'b, *al-Wa'î al-'aqâ'idî*, Beirut, 1959, which aptly introduces the expression *ṣairûra 'arabîya*, Arab growth or 'becoming', pp. 63 ff.; and Morroe Berger's account in *World Politics*, July 1958, of several recent works in English.

[1] F. Braudel, 'Histoire et Sciences sociales, La longue durée', *Annales* (*E.S.C.*) 3rd year, no. 4, Oct.–Dec. 1958, p. 725.

were mainly *against* imperialism. But conversely, in the between-war generation, attitudes of unbelief frequently demonstrated the younger generation's rebellion against a subservience which the old creeds had not effectively exorcised. Then new movements, deliberately secular, replaced piety, allegiance to the caliphate or Panislamism in the task of maintaining Islam's personality against the rigidity and uniformity of modern life.

A study of the types of resistance would thus have to characterize successive reactions to the installation of foreign powers. The first of these were identified almost everywhere with religious and social conservatism: 'holy war', tribal risings, citizens' rebellions. The decisive, although timid, contributions of the first phase of dependency: civil security, administrative reforms, the exploitation and expansion of an industrial culture and a European language, deprived these initial forces of significance. Thenceforward, as was to be expected, the assimilation of these new contributions, consciously by the intelligentsia and indirectly by other classes, gave rise to the decisive teams: Zaghlûl and his comrades of the Wafd in Egypt, the heralds of the Kutla at Damascus and Aleppo, etc. The terms which describe the two most famous of these movements, the Syrian 'assembly' and the Egyptian 'delegation', indicate that at the time these were merely associations without clear-cut ideologies. This lack of sectarianism is indeed the chief merit of the whole period of militant nationalism.

Meanwhile, however, such a resistance movement, marked by the struggle it has waged and by the attraction, as well as the horror, it feels for the alien, the 'Other'—in any case by the urge to follow its example—is naturally governed by the requirements of its tactics, as well as by the hazards of repression. It has displayed no brilliant powers of analysis, any more than its adversary.[1] Hence the irregularity of its reactions towards strictly social phenomena, which are what count in our eyes, but which often only appear important in retrospect. And this irregularity may go so far as a change of symbol. Although liberty is indivisible, men often take a long time to understand its unity, and even longer to realize that unity. In Europe, it is customary to contrast economic and social democracy with political democracy. Similarly, Arab nationalism displays, together with many other youthful faults, certain sometimes disconcerting hesitancies about things that it does not discern closely enough, because they seem too remote from actual events.

[1] The relative backwardness of sociological analysis in the Arab world is still very striking, whatever its cause. But a fertile reaction has begun to be apparent.

Many of these traits can be explained by a hasty and constantly accelerated tempo. A state of dependence explains even more, in so far as it leads to irresolution or excess in behaviour once the threshold of independence has been crossed. True, Middle Eastern Arabs no longer have foreign High Commissioners. But they are too often considered by foreigners, even important ones, as mere human accessories to oil wells! At all events, as objects of competition between East and West. As long as this is the case, their history remains out of centre, and being denied their individuality, they seek to compensate by a self-assertion which takes opposite forms, alternately or simultaneously. Excess of passion or opportunist manoeuvres, metaphysical detachment or down-to-earth intrigue, prevail over positive effort, which is accomplished nevertheless, only at a cost of human bewilderment and suffering. Hence the splendour and squalor of what is known as Arab nationalism, a movement which grew between the two wars and reached its peak after the second, and led the Arabs, by way of postponed successes and grievous failures, of disappointments overcome and incomplete triumphs, to complete political emancipation. But this emancipation, for lack of a renewal of method or any searching analysis, is liable to fail in its responsible tasks.

It is clear from this that the two great conflicting themes in the Arab world, which I have tried to trace on many levels in this study—the symbol against the machine, the sense of the cosmic against the sense of history—are implicit in the most urgent of current problems. But also that the development of the political set-up, although superficial and misleading, can influence and determine a deep-rooted reality. Hence the great danger of mistakes in interpretation, as well as in action. The key lies in an understanding of the Arab phenomenon. The Copts have their own special character, no less than the Kurds; the delicate point is that they can both be associated in a generalization which, at certain moments, disregards all barriers. This was what our mandatory policy in the Levant did not recognize. A correct, although suspect, appreciation of Arab unitedness certainly made British policy superior to that of France until after 1945; a superiority which was soon cancelled by the upsurge of those elements on which Britain had previously banked. The revolt in the desert brought the Hashemites to power, and then cast them down when it came into conflict with other revolts whose roots lay deeper. Leaders grow out of date and so do ideas, because logic becomes keener and situations change.

It is not the separate elements or details that count in the latter, but the totality and the trend. The existence of every social whole is made up of infinitely complex internal relationships between human beings and things; it is almost impossible to elucidate scientifically, and it understandably eludes the politician. Or rather, the latter is only a true politician in so far as he instinctively perceives and expresses it. This is why the Middle East has hitherto expected so much from its leaders; they must sum up in their own person, and interpret in their actions, the underlying conflict in all its living reality. And it is this conflict that interests our present study.

Close Groupings

Many problems grow clearer, many apparent dilemmas vanish when, leaving the plane of generalities, we study this social reality in its minuter aspects. Over the vast extent of the Arab world we find samples of every sort of form, and within the same society, we must unhesitatingly repeat, phenomena that differ in depth and age. The upheavals that have shaken it have not been uniformly violent, and it discloses not merely an extensive range of types but often every phase of development of the same type; it offers not merely a museum, but a laboratory.

Among the elementary forms of political association, that which is based on individual prestige is particularly flourishing here. Not that the sacredness of a chief's authority is a concept particular to Islam. On the contrary, the conduct of the democratic leader is here confined by fairly stringent rules dictated by tradition. Ancient values and definitions are the more keenly respected because society is intentionally traditionalist. But no sort of rule or stability are conceivable in the Arab world save amidst a sort of balance of fluid forces where, here and there, the strength of some personality, the success of some venture suspends for a moment the uncertainty of things. This is still true on the tribal scale, and sometimes on the national scale too. Of course, these relationships reflect particular situations and forces, and may indeed derive their importance from these. But their power of suggestion and temptation is weightier here than elsewhere. Political action, in Arab countries, consists too often in what elsewhere would be called intrigue and finesse. This is so true that foreign specialists are frequently led to dangerous distortion; they see things only from the angle of human relationships, or what used to be called 'native politics'. Such reprehensible features of French or British public life as the influence of powerful personalities, the appointment of chosen individuals, can be found in germ in the conduct of the Arabs themselves. And although this is concealed in a romantic penumbra, we should not have far to seek, even now, to find illustrations of methods which are 'human, all too human', flourishing despite their anachronistic character.[1]

Family solidarities stand out in contrast to this fluidity. Business interests assemble powerful groups around patriarchs, political leaders or at least electoral agents. The Parliamentary system in Iraq was for a long while dominated by the force of such associations; it was quite recently denounced in Syria. In Lebanon, the events of the summer of 1958 revived their hitherto dormant power. It conflicted with the sectional interests of cantons and of rival religious creeds. In Egypt, these time-honoured periods showed a marked regression at various periods, with an occasional recrudescence. Turkish and Circassian governors were succeeded by the aristocracy, the *abnâ' al-dhawât*. From 1923 onwards, under the Wafd, peasants' sons occasionally rose to positions of authority. But most frequently the ruling class was still recruited from among the top members of the liberal professions, who differed in every way, at that period, from the mass of the people. Long after Zaghlûl, a leader like Ismâ'îl Ṣidqî remained in power for as long a period as all the first ministers of the Wafd combined. Now he governed solely through his prestige and his aristocratic connections. Military dictatorship did away with this state of things, and brought to the top men of humbler origins: authentic Egyptians, indeed, from rural backgrounds. But even in these rural milieux there survived, together with the increasingly unpopular institution of village chiefdom, something of the old patriarchal order. The Egyptian village preserves not only its coteries but their institutional organs, of immemorial origin: the *duwwâr* for instance, the 'great house', 'house of honour', where prevailed a way of life that was both authoritarian and generous, hospitable and tyrannical. These hierarchies are falling into decline, assuredly, and the Egyptian '*umda* (village chief) has as bad a reputation as the Algerian *caïd* (*qâ'id*). But it is still unwise to oppose him openly. In 1962, the Egyptian revolution still had to reckon with him.

The remarkable fact is not that such factors should operate (where do they not?) but that they should do so under relatively complex conditions, and in a fairly advanced state of culture, without shedding

[1] Of which all fallen leaders are unfailingly accused: Shishiklî in Syria, Naḥḥâs in Egypt, and above all Nûrî Sa'îd in Iraq. But without resorting to these polemical concepts, it is significant that the period following the second world war witnessed the development, indeed the 'success', of the paradoxical anachronism of American oil expansion and British 'penetration' in the Middle East, from Aden onwards.

their ancient patriarchal style. In Syria for instance the Popular Party, *Hizb al-sha'b*, owed much of its authority to the *gens* of the Atâsî dominant in Homs: whereas it retreated before the jealous sectionalism of Hama. A company of five big business men could express, while distorting, the spirit of Damascus. Lebanon, seen from outside, displays an enlightened and complex political life; it sometimes has great difficulty in prevailing over religious sectarianism, that *ṭâ'ifîya* that is universally condemned but seldom relinquished. It must be admitted that it is in Lebanon that the history of local families, and indeed local history in general, are the best known. In recent years we have had no chronicles comparable to those of Shidyâq or Ma'lûf for any other Arab country, except perhaps those of the Maghrib. But neither do we find anywhere else a constitutional life as narrowly and openly linked to the balance between rival rites and rival clans. Of course this balance is sometimes uneasy. The power of lordly families over such or such a district, the rule of a religious creed over its congregations, sometimes assume aggressive forms. The sad happenings at Ehden (June 1957) are well known. Other incidents, in 1958, have revealed the persistent virulence of religious factionalism in this enlightened country. However, common sense usually prevails, and the spirit of mutual concession, revived from the National Pact of 1943. But once calm has been restored, it is piquant to read in the memoirs of a respected leader high praise of the support given by his own clan, and bitter condemnation of the opposing faction.[1]

Of course these are isolated examples, which are almost always disowned by the responsible authorities. Often the conflict is settled almost immediately, which is to the credit of the country's political maturity. But what makes such incidents characteristic, and of particular importance for our study, is that they are liable to coincide with such a state of maturity. These internal contradictions are not rare in Arab countries: religious sectarianism in Lebanon, Syrian impulsiveness, the archaic mentality of the Egyptian masses, tribal aggressiveness in Iraq, for instance, can be observed simultaneously with other characteristics which evince an impetus towards enlightenment, an evolution that is already well equipped, and a growing critical spirit.

For this sectionalism, so tempting to those who wish to exploit it, whether feudal lords, demagogues or foreigners, reigns not only among rural clans but over urban districts. Each district frequently displays an almost total autonomy in its way of life. The layout of the town itself is

[1] Kamâl Janbulâṭ, *Ḥaqîqat al-thaura al-lubnânîya*, p. 76 and *passim*.

conducive to this: a warren of complex lanes, bewildering to the stranger. Neighbours associate in a community dominated, on the one hand, by the prestige of a few old families and on the other, by the turbulent rule of gangs of swashbucklers: the *abaḍây-s* of Beirut and Damascus, the *fitiwwa-s* of Cairo.

Modern Egyptian novelists have familiarized us with this atmosphere, which has its own sufferings but also its joys.[1] By the side of the local bully, prominent in all political demonstrations of one sort or another, we see the local beauty, *fatât al-darb*, whose smiles brighten the dreary texture of daily life. And there are the delights of gossip, neighbourliness, local festivities; and the allurement of this way of life is such that the younger generation, feeling the pull of other forces, are torn between a repulsion that is usually powerless and a familiarity which will gradually extend their revolt. In this closed circle the electoral candidate will, from time to time, intrude. He sets up a platform, *sirdâq*, and holds forth, anxious to win over the forces latent in this circumscribed existence. But he can only touch it superficially. A more cunning method of agitation is able to call forth from it more redoubtable forces.

This is the aim cherished by leaders and parties. In Syria, the old *Kutla waṭanîya* was able to retain its vigour for a long time thanks to the attention it paid to the *ahyâ'* of Damascus. District meetings were often organized, and provided the opportunity for speeches profoundly imbued with the tradition of Damascus. No one has better realized this than Luṭfî al-Ḥaffâr, who collected several of these speeches in his Memoirs: 'We draw fresh inspiration from visiting each of the city's districts. Each of them suggests an idea to us; we extract this from its local setting and combine it with those we derive from other districts the idea of a city, vigorous and exemplary.'

In these Memoirs he makes frequent reference to an achievement which fulfils one of the most ancestral needs of an Arab city: the provision of water. Ten years' efforts enabled him to carry out the scheme of bringing the waters of the Fîja to Damascus without any contribution from foreign capital. He was inspired herein by the efforts of the Miṣr group. But what interests us here is less this financial nationalism than the deep, and deeply felt, connection between this enterprise and the order of the city. An immemorial connection! A Roman medal from Damascus depicts the river Fîja under an almost identical name:

[1] Cf. for instance what is said of this by Najan Maḥfûẓ in *Âkhir Sâ'a*, 16 Aug. 1961.

'Damascan coin, with the effigy of the Empress Otacilia, wife of Philip of Arabia (244–249 A.D.). Conventional representation of a grotto, from which issue the waters of a river. In the grotto a nymph is lying, holding in her left hand a horn of plenty resting on her shoulder, and in her right an ear of corn, symbols of fertility. To the left of the grotto a small altar for offerings, whose presence implies the sacred nature of the place. Above the grotto, probably on the slope of the mountain, a tiny building containing a statue of Marsyas standing on the left, holding his waterskin on his shoulder. The statue of Marsyas was the symbol of Roman colonies, of which Damascus had attained the status under Philip of Arabia. Inscription: COL(onia) DAMAS(cus) METRO(polis), i.e. capital of the province. Under the grotto: ΠΗΓΑΙ, the Springs.' (Commentary by Henri Seyrig, who kindly showed me the coin. See plate 8.)

Meanwhile, clienteles and factions have quite rightly been subjected to intensified criticism. Already those who make use of them, whether cynically or with genuine sympathy, tend to consider them as residual forces not to be served but to be exploited in the service of larger ideas. And at this point they begin to disintegrate; but the process will take a long time. It cannot be said to have been completed even in the most advanced of these countries. Everywhere, even now, it is the complex transition from one set of forms to another which accounts for the psychological diversity and the unexpected element in political affairs in rural and particularly in urban regions. These transitions form the background of the political scene; they can be studied, but they must above all be felt, and, in their picturesqueness, observed. Obsolescence and renewal, radical changes together with a redundancy of the familiar: such features, among others, of Arab life give it its particular savour today.

Anyone who tries to analyse it must take into account the most familiar pictures. Already in 1850 Flaubert[1] had enjoyed watching the effendis of Damascus bustling about the first billiard table. And in fact cafés have played a great part in the construction of the Arab nation ever since that time. The memoirs of 'Abd al-Raḥmân al-Râfi'î stress the importance of café life in Egypt. It is there that between the backgammon tables, under the lively influence of their beverage, they plan the future, read the news, discuss the latest scandals. The segregation of the sexes, which is still the rule, thus keeps men for long evenings out of the company of women; yet another way of escaping from their

[1] *Voyage en Orient*, Budé edition, Paris, 1948, vol. ii, p. 245.

original cell, of detaching themselves from the old family solidarity. For at the café one meets people of widely different origins. Their only link is a common interest in some idea, a common preference for some leader. An obscure Alexandrian, humbly employed, who was later to become 'the preacher of the Revolution', *Khaṭîb al-thaura*—'Abd Allâh al-Nadîm, found his first audience at the famous café of Matâtyâ in Cairo. Here he met Jamâl al-Dîn al-Afghânî every evening. The latter, it was said, distributed tobacco with his right hand and spread revolution with his left. Scores of disciples surrounded him, among them a tall Azharite called Sa'd Zaghlûl.

But not all these gatherings produce personalities destined for such an impressive rôle. Far from it. Some cafés attract none but failures, those whom life has defeated. Others, infinitely humbler, are found in villages. These were to play their part in the first Wafd movement. On all sides there has arisen an unprecedented desire for group life, a 'committee spirit'. Men shake off the bonds of their tribe, their coterie, their sect or their village, to foregather with other men under different symbols. The most varied and sometimes the most abstract of symbols, although appealing keenly to the emotions: noble concepts to which a fine Arabic name would add further dignity.[1] And groups flourished: *nadî* (plural *andiya*). The word is ancient, the thing itself too, since even in the Prophet's Mecca *andiya* were already functioning, under the aegis of the leading families of Quraish. But now their objectives were totally new. In Syria, the adversaries of the Young Turk movement created centres everywhere. A profusion of groups were formed—for religious or charitable ends, in defence of such and such an ideal, such or such a symbol of the questing nation.

The club where people meet to kill time, often somewhat sordidly, in the capital may on the contrary in provincial towns be a centre for associations destined to an important future. Hence the proliferation of gatherings which reflect all fashionable trends, or on the other hand tendencies which are still clandestine: for among other advantages, clubs and committees can shelter political activity under the alibi of good works, art or piety. There is a noticeable growth of religious organizations in Egypt from 1927 onwards. The most important is that of the *Shubbân al-Muslimîn*, which was subsequently connected with the later movement of the Muslim Brotherhood. We must also mention the development of Freemasonry, which in Egypt and particularly in Lebanon exerted some political influence. Finally we must consider this

[1] Yet another reference to religious tradition. . . .

sociable trend in its wider context: that of a transition from one conception of the world to another.

Naturally all this energy had sometimes to take refuge in clandestine movements. Conspiracy is its temptation and its risk, while the very fact of being banned increases the warmth of brotherly relations between members. The contribution of secret societies to the growth of the Arab movement today is thus an important one. An old militant tells us, in somewhat blasé tones:

'In those days, which were so unfavourable to any national movement or to any freedom of thought, we schoolboys were full of enthusiasm for restoring the glory of the Arabs and their language. Amongst ourselves, in the depths of our homes or on the mountain tops, we always reverted to study of our Arab fatherland and of its great men, its great poets, the need for regrouping in a national faith. All this was then considered as a serious and terrible crime.'

Such movements took part in the Arab Revolt, during the first world war. Their unquestionable effectiveness seems to contradict their emotional and oratorical content. It may be surprising to anyone who does not know, or who underestimates, the original forces which from time to time bring forth a *za'īm*, a leader.

Broad Groupings

The *za'īm*, on a national scale, enjoys a certain prestige which turns to his advantage the old unanimity of the *umma*, the Muslim nation. He retains a theological dimension, although his significance is wholly secular. Now there is a growing divergence between the supreme authority, which is inevitably modernist and concerned with the outside world, and the basic elements of the nation. The latter are still more or less bound by the familiar and restricted forms of social life which I have described. The village, the district, the town, of course, each have their own life, so do the tribe and even the community; but there are still no municipal courts, no provincial administration of the modern type. Everything takes place as if some powerful impetus, while remaining faithful to traditional ideals, was soaring up towards ever-higher summits, but neglecting the moderate slopes of development. What the Arab world lacks most notably is, as I have said, the intermediary stages of modernity, of institutions, or even of moral impulse. Integration only takes place at the level of archaic customs which their authenticity cannot save from obsolescence, or else at the national level, itself influenced by the struggles of the Colonial period and moreover disturbed by the appeal of even vaster conceptions, Arab unity, Islamic unity, Afro-Asiatic unity, etc. . . .

Everything at the basic level seems to radiate from the focus of power:[1] the traditional prestige of an ancestor, the heroism of an innovator who is at the same time an almost eponymous founder. As though in concentric circles, reality spreads until this system of waves, so to speak, meets with a rival system to thwart it. And Islam confronts this efflorescence with its violent antitheses, its radical classifications, its interdicts which allow 'free passage' to Nature provided she accepts the rules.[2] How different from what seems to underlie the social and moral life of the West: a construction based on external factors, geographical and historical, which seeks to translate and institute a concrete reality drawn from far afield; whereas in the domain of ethics, the law is imposed not from without but from within, and seeks to track down into man's very heart the sin which contaminates its most secret crannies.[3] The West, with its intimate moral code, aims at objectivity in action. The Arab East is legalistic in its moral code, but remains subjective in its behaviour, which is almost always a matter of nerves and intuition, like riding a horse.

And we can understand how the integration of political forms is the more enduring the closer it keeps to the central tradition, the more creative the more faithfully it adheres to its ancient specificity. And the more risky, on the other hand, the further it moves away from these in scope or in conception. I have already noted the organizational weakness

[1] It is not by chance that the most frequent *motif* in Arab decoration is the polygonal star. Cf. accompanying figure: a star *motif* of carved wood: Minbar of the Madrasa of Ghaurî, Cairo; from Wiet and Hautecoeur, *Les Mosquées du Caire*, vol. ii, plate 211. Already in 1921 L. Massignon, in *Les méthodes artistiques de l'Islam*', *Syria*, p. 150, had pointed out this 'negation of closed forms', characteristic, in his opinion, of Islam. Cf. our article on the social motivations of Muslim aesthetics, *Journal de psychologie normale et pathologique*, 1962.

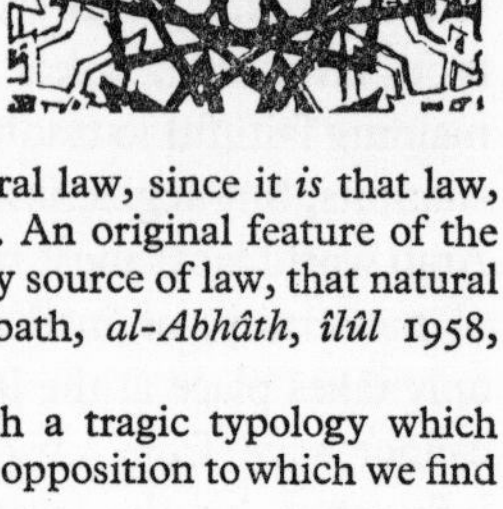

[2] This is why the *fiqh* makes no reference to natural law, since it *is* that law, being at the same time natural, divine and revealed. An original feature of the recent Syrian Civil Code is to mention, as a subsidiary source of law, that natural law which the *fiqh* formally ignores. Cf. Ed. Rabbath, *al-Abhâth*, *îlûl* 1958, pp. 339 and 373, no. 15.

[3] Cf. its theory of concupiscence, bound up with a tragic typology which L. Goldmann has analysed, *Le dieu caché*, pp. 50 ff. In opposition to which we find the Muslim notion of *fiṭra*, 'innateness'.

of its communes; the same might be said of its departments or provinces, always remembering that one cannot apply these labels to peculiar local structures of persistently archaic character, which have hitherto proved impossible to transform into administrative entities of a modern type.[1] So that the intermediary elements are always either excessive or inadequate: excessive so long as their out-of-date autonomy is allowed to persist, or is even encouraged, inadequate when it comes to interpreting their peculiarities in terms of genuine variety rather than sectarianism. These observations may explain a major part of the failures of the Mandatory in the Levant, and conversely the deficiencies of regional or local organization in Arab nations up to our own day.

At a certain stage in the process of expansion and generalization, the national entity suddenly emerges. But this is felt to be a halting-point, more or less provisionally imposed by the foreigner. The Arabs want to be Arabs rather than Egyptians, Syrians, Iraqis etc. And this, in spite of their awareness, indeed their assertion, of obvious differences of speech, manners, appearance, let alone interests. The fact is that hitherto, republics or monarchies, a prey to the strains imposed by current events, and subjected to the caprices of leaders and the pressure of mob feelings, could only give, in spite of their varying successes, an exaggeratedly pessimistic and in any case an incomplete idea of political institutions in the Arab world, if the picture were to leave out other elements which promise more considered constructive efforts, and sounder prospects.

At this point we might mention that sense of federal unity which finds such eloquent expression, and which was reflected in the creation of the Arab League, if this did not, through its emotional appeal, far exceed the bounds of concrete achievement. But is it not in fact this difficult adjustment between the impulse and the form, the ideal and the result, which most closely concerns our theme? The League, as we know, has experienced bitter controversies amongst its associate nations. For in it, and through it, all their tendencies, appetites and rivalries confront one another. Hence manifold expressions of impatient opinion, and the disillusioned realization that the League, since its difficult birth in 1946, has not succeeded in saving its members from the loss of Palestine, nor from internal intrigues, nor from the Baghdad Pact, nor from the tension between Iraq and the U.A.R. on the one hand, the U.A.R. and Tunisia on the other. Brother countries are lavish of mutual accusation. The

[1] The recent agrarian reform of Syria does not apply to the Jebel Druse, which is not a 'Druse department'.

disaffection of a large sector of opinion sometimes leads one to apprehend that the League will break up, or be irrevocably discredited. It was after a particularly disorderly session that the representative of Morocco, 'Abd Allâh Ibrâhîm, made the following answer to a Lebanese reporter:

Q. 'Do you think as an Arab or as a Westerner?'

A. 'I am not sentimental and I always keep calm. Without wanting to offend anyone, I consider that opinion in the Near East tends to be abstract. People indulge in utopian speculation and lose sight of present realities. I do not believe in the stability of any country when its power is not founded on scientific data.'

Westernized Islam here incriminates an attitude rather than a policy. The emancipation of Algeria was to produce even more fruitful contrasts. None the less, the League has powerfully contributed to the strengthening of Arab feeling. The initial good offices of foreign powers were naturally repudiated by a body which owed its first inception in part to Anthony Eden, then British Foreign Secretary, but which very soon became independent of its mixed origins. If its vicissitudes have sometimes aroused, in its members' minds, irritation and suspicion, disastrous rivalities and frequent disappointment, they have by that very fact laid the foundations for useful self-criticism, and strengthened the sense of an Arab entity superior to its component nationalities. Paradoxically, the League was responsible for the progress both of universalist Arabism with its background of Islamism, and of the modern concept of nationality or even of internationalism. And I am not only referring to the strange aggregates assembled in that Afro-Asian group of which Cairo is the most active centre, nor of the uncommitted nations which at Belgrade in 1961 expressed their cautious reaction to the echo of atomic explosions. For after all our time is conducive to vast groupings. The coal-and-steel community, the Common Market have caused the Arabs understandable anxiety, because they display the same impulse towards unity on very different bases. It is piquant, in this connection, to compare the European discussions on the price of potatoes with the passion for unity professed by the League countries at the very moment when they were quarrelling over the resources of Kuwait, and by Syria at the very moment when she was breaking with Egypt.

Finally, the Arab League has accomplished one unquestionably good work, its efforts for the progress of Arab culture and scientific investigation.[1] The Institute of Arabology in Cairo, with its microfilm section,

[1] The late Dr. Shafîq Ghurbâl, Ṣalâh al-Dîn al-Munajjid, etc., and the valuable series to which this work is largely indebted.

its frequent congresses on problems of pedagogy, technique or nomenclature, displays the most promising efforts. The League, like many things and institutions in this period of development in the Arab world, offers a very human mixture of hopes, failures, weaknesses and successes. Subject to internal rivalries and to the excesses inevitable at the present stage of development of these populations, it constitutes none the less a historic step forward. In any case it occupies the forefront of the picture, to an extent that far exceeds its real efficacity. This change of focus in itself indicates the progress realized by the Arab sense of citizenship, since the days, not so long ago, when it could only be displayed in clandestinity or at the cost of exile.

The League thus proves to be, undeniably, a form of adaptation of the ancient *umma* to the multi-national or international combinations of modern times. A transitional form, whose weakness lies in that which makes its worth; namely the working out of a compromise between that which is peculiar to the Arabs and that which, in order to survive, they must borrow from others. The same might be said of their parties, their parliaments, even of their governments to a large extent. It would thus be unjust to deny that, in contrast with the solid but primitive forms of their home policies, they have produced other institutions which are broader, more self-conscious, and recognizably more modern. But these seem to lose their spontaneity as they grow broader. For in so doing they are subject more urgently to the influence of the West, by which they are both attracted and repelled. The fact that the growth of political forms denatures them, that any modernization must strive to keep an increasingly difficult contrast with the masses, that efficiency may conflict with fidelity, this faces the Arabs with a problem which they can only solve by continuous maturation, or by periodic readjustments. The second way is known as revolution. In such a case the *za'īm* is entrusted with the task of restoring the authentic within the framework of what is adapted or imported. He achieves this, with a greater or less degree of success, supported by the people's unstinted enthusiasm and faced with all the perils of omnipotence. In any case he is a significant rather than a representative figure, and through his rôle, his actions, his very appearance and language, he appeals from a drab reality to a better future.

The virtual, in the Arab world, is always truer than the actual, more profoundly experienced and more fully accepted, and this explains many phenomena characteristic not only of parliamentary life but of power and political institutions in general in these countries. The ever-swifter replacement of one generation by another; the primacy of enthusiasm over wisdom, of hope over experience, of the hoped-for over the acquired; the disadvantage of what is, compared with what is to be; all these traits can doubtless be explained by a sort of shift of time. Since the end of the nineteenth century, whole nations, once entirely and even today partially orientated towards a past which is, strictly speaking, their point of contact with the absolute (the 'descent' of the uncreated Koran) are now bringing to bear on the future an energy made keener by long privations. The disadvantage is that between this past, which is steeped in myth, and this future, which is steeped in dream, there has intervened, by means of Europe, 'historic' time, that time whose laws must be obeyed by whoever wishes to speak its language. Hence misunderstandings, grave risks, and from time to time violent upheavals. But also, access is gained to history, through the Other, the Alien, and in opposition to him.

Presence of the Alien

The Alien is a familiar figure to the Arabs. Without going back to the *ḥadîth* of Heraclius, let us recall the contribution of protected minorities, the *Ahl al-dhimma*, in the transmission of the Romano-Byzantine heritage. In many respects, as René Habachi has pointed out, the priority of Western thought, philosophical, theological or juridical, already faced Islam in the ninth and tenth centuries with problems of adaptation and transcendence. The same chronological precedence presents it today, in the sphere of technical modernization, with the same difficulties and the same possibilities. Only since the point of departure of the period coincides with that of imperialist expansion, the generation of the second *fitna*[1] (revolt) was subjected to industrial civilization long before it could exercise it. It endured humiliations, some of which at least were due to the fact that Islam, as represented by itself, Islam with its sense of immanence or at any rate of adherence to the world, was primarily experiencing the world as something inventoried, possessed and remade by aliens. At the darkest moments of Islam's subjection, it had itself become *a thing* for others. Everything within it and around it had been *reified.*

At that moment the Arab lost his warm contact with beings and things. He was cut off from everything: from the landscape around him, being transformed by 'exploitation' to which he contributed only as a labourer or, at best, as a customer; from the sequence of cause and effect, whose

[1] Cf. above, end of Chapter I.

internal law escaped him, since another handled it or invented it; from the knowledge of his history, of his language, of his very soul, since the Colonial period imported its efficiency and its prejudices into ethnological investigations. All things considered, the Arab retains very few autonomous sectors of his own existence; and even in these, function and content are altered. Religion, become a symbol of irreductibility, oscillates between the two poles of popular piety and the practice of the law, or flares up in visionary fanaticism, until reformism suggests some compromise with the modern world more or less concurrent with nationalism. The family, become the reserve which the foreigner himself is reluctant to violate, is concentrated on the rôle of woman; it is his authoritarian and sensual possession of the latter that provides the Arab male with the last remaining exercise of his sovereignty.

I am well aware that this picture is exaggeratedly dark, and that nowhere in the Middle East has the ubiquity of the foreign dominator penetrated far enough to drive humanity into so extreme a position. But the very latitude which here, contrary to North Africa, is left to the local system, sharpens its resentment and its fear. The dominant system, especially in the case of the French, does not merely foster this fear and this resentment; it motivates revolt and provides it with a language and an ideal. As early as 1925 a young lawyer of Aleppo, Edmond Rabbath, pleaded for the restoration of Syrian integrity in the sphere of mind as well as in that of politics.[1] For once—he was to become one of the leading Arab lawyers—his eloquence was fruitless. The Mandate ran its course, amid a deplorable display of missed opportunities and 'useless service' . . . In Iraq, in spite of the cunning bluff and shrewd counterstrokes in which British policy excels,[2] the same depersonalization takes place. It is felt as a crushing blow by intellectuals,[3] such as those depicted by the novelist Dhû'l-Nûn Ayyûb, striving to reintegrate their nation and expose the treacherous compromises of the Government. Many other examples might be shown for all these countries. What they all reveal is the atmosphere not so much of alienation as of frustration that surrounds all feeling, militant, or thoughtful elements in the Middle East. And it is against this state of being cut off from history,

[1] Ed. Rabbath, *Unité Syrienne et devenir arabe* (1937), and an earlier pamphlet, *Les Etats-Unis de Syrie*, Aleppo, 1925. See also *L'Evolution politique de la Syrie sous mandat*, 1928.

[2] On the parallel experiences of French and British policy, see the two recent works of Longrigg. But everything is not yet known. . . .

[3] A. Hourani, *Syria and Lebanon*, ed. 1954, speaks aptly about that reintegration of self which is the chief aim of nationalist movements. Cf. pp. 70–2, 96 ff.

the world and themselves, that the younger generation have been rebelling with increasing violence ever since the second world war.

For the resistance movement is primarily a youthful phenomenon. It is directed against the older generation as much as against the foreigner. The former, it is true, had stood out tolerably well against European interference. But they quite understandably dissociated the alienating intervention of the newcomers from other forms of oppression. The comfort they derived from their ethical rejection of external civilization was too often concomitant with a submissiveness expert in mental reservations. Their resistance, which was frequently admirable, was founded on the obsolete motives of religious conservatism and aristocratic honour. The world of essences, to which they were so deeply attached, seemed to them scarcely affected by the material usurpation with which the Gentiles professed to be satisfied. A few concessions regarding worship, the harem, paternal authority were enough to conciliate, at least from a secular point of view, these metaphysical opponents. From 1930 onward they saw, to their displeasure, the authority pass from their hands into those of their sons, who had been educated in European fashion and had scant respect for the old *mores*.

The new generation instinctively transferred its rebellion to the secular sphere. True, it had the backing of sanctions inherited from a recent past. Fostered by that fierce vitality which acquired explosive force through repression by the political and social system, it none the less referred to the authority of that world of essences which this younger generation, sometimes unconsciously and unintentionally, were championing in their turn. What could they achieve, indeed, without that popular support which in the last resort mobilizes the *umma* in their favour? Their strength lies, precisely, in reconciling what seemed unreconcilable: Islam's authenticity and the efficiency of the West: allegiance to the *sha'b*, the 'chosen people', and recourse to the principles of democracy. A difficult art, an almost impossible wager, which contains within itself the inevitable alternance of violence and compromise, of impetus and failure.

The politician tries to reconcile or confront these rival forces to his own advantage. But he has to reckon with highly emotional public opinion, quick to follow but unforgiving. Moderatism is suspect; 'leftism' finds cunning exploiters. Excess leads, occasionally, to disaster. Most frequently the line taken is not backed by any positive data. For lack of analysis and for lack of doctrine, all parties act, to a considerable extent, on impulse; sometimes unrealistically, sometimes with opportunism. Hence their weakness, which would make success impossible to account for were it not that, underneath and beyond the action of politicians, a whole world is struggling to be transformed.

The Three Stages of the National Movement

The first upsurge of nationalism, thwarted by external and internal forces, generally calls forth broad-based associations that combine bourgeois and popular elements. It leads to resentment and violence, but also, frequently, to inspired improvisation. Everywhere, it has called forth outstanding men. Ibrâhîm Hanâni, Sa'ad Allâh al-Jabrî in Syria, Riyâḍ Ṣulḥ in Lebanon and many others are outstanding examples of this period of heroic improvisation and transaction. The Wafd was originally, as we have seen, not so much a party as a 'gathering'. One of its first friends compares it to 'a lake into which all streams, all canals, all rivers are to pour'. For the first time, militant activity united great landed proprietors, tradesmen, civil servants and intellectuals. The excitement spread even to the peasantry. There were some Copts among the leaders' right-hand men. 'Learned men, ulemas, from the Azhar spoke in the Churches, Coptic priests spoke at the Azhar.' Even princes joined the common cause. This whole-hearted popular support was the pride of the party, but also constituted its ideological weakness. Correspondingly, the vitality of such groupings reflects a balance of forces which is related to the unhealthy condition of the present rather than to the dynamic quality of emergent nations. Competition between individuals stirs up stubborn hatreds, under the deceptive similarity of programmes and the vociferation of impressive words. There is an increasing dissociation between the form of political life and its substance, which is made up of growing anger and awareness, both in quest of an effectiveness which has too long been denied.

I quote from an Iraqi writer a few disillusioned, but scarcely pessimistic reflections. 'It is characteristic of the Arabs', he says, 'to understand swiftly and grasp the underside of things. But this quality can lead to disaster if the latter is not averted by the wise attitude of their leaders. The Iraqi did not fail to perceive what was being attempted under colour of representation. The people stood by watching, applauding the fall of their rulers in the hope that those who were to follow would do better. The nation had lost all hope of improving its lot by its own efforts. It felt only revulsion for these parliamentary groupings. So that the politicians became convinced that they could deal as they chose with the nation's affairs and that the Iraqi were nothing but cattle to be bought and sold, milked or slaughtered, and whose skins could be sold for the benefit of foreigners or the friends of the authorities. And this went on until events demonstrated that the people of Iraq would no longer endure oppression, nor refrain from voicing their just claims, even temporarily, save at a risk of violent upheaval. . . .'

Now the progress of self-assertion, the first successes won through negotiation or through revolt, shattered the amorphous unity of the resistance movement. Personal and doctrinal dissensions came to light. Hitherto, militant patriotism had provided a sufficient spur. Henceforward, differences of background, culture and belief were to play their part. The long history of the Wafd reflects, from 1919 to 1953, the curve followed by a group which was revolutionary at its outset but which was subsequently worn out by discord rather than by the power which in fact it shared with other parties. Its illusory electoral triumph, in 1950, was no doubt, partly responsible for its leaders' loss of critical lucidity. From being a great gathering inspired by patriotic enthusiasm it had become a mere parliamentary association. It included persons whose reputation was tarnished or who had fought against the movement in its heroic phase. The Palace intensified its grip on external affairs, on the army, on religious institutions. The governing clique displayed a subservience which is in striking contrast to the ruthless struggle waged by Zaghlûl against the king on the subject of the choice of the royal cabinet, or the granting of decorations. Then a disquieting phenomenon occurs: the lower strata of the party detach themselves from the ruling stratum and even begin to attack it in pamphlets and newspapers. Another significant incident is the refusal of a Minister of Finance to resign, when called upon to do so by Naḥḥâs. The party henceforward wins its victories only by intrigue or compromise. It is considered more or less as in collusion with the excesses of the Palace. The end is well known.

Similar dissensions broke out between Iraqi parties after General Qâsim's *coup d'état*. Here, a veteran patriot, Rashîd 'Âlî al-Gailânî, was challenged by younger opponents. Things had altered since the Colonial era. The situation had grown complicated in proportion to the concessions wrested from the foreign power.

Youth proclaimed its growing dissatisfaction. If the immaturity of the masses still obliged their leaders to resort to risky techniques, yet the education of the country had progressed. Here and there, élites of the modern type had begun to emerge. The defects of the system were felt

1910; the book is full of an ardent scientific and positivist spirit, and it constituted a real challenge in its time.[1] Understandably it met with much opposition. His poem *al-Rujḥân* extolled man's integration with earthly Nature, from which any attempt to dissociate him is futile. And he ended on a note of optimism: 'Compare the religious centuries with our own; they were far worse!' A revolutionary position, not only with respect to the academics of the Azhar but also to the exponents of bourgeois liberalism, the type of cultured Arab combining loyalty to the East with open-mindedness towards the West represented, from that time to our own, by such men as Aḥmad Zakî, Luṭfî Sayyid, Ṭaha Ḥusain, Taufîq al-Ḥakîm and many others of our friends.

In 1912 there appeared the 'Views of Dr. Shiblî Shumayyil', a study of modern civilization which recalls the philosophical attitude of Herbert Spencer. Religions, it claims, are merely a social fact, open to observation and criticism like any other. The Arab countries are in the throes of a precipitate evolution which is by no means near completion. 'Our renaissance, our *nahḍa* has triumphed chiefly in the sphere of abstraction, of oratory, of the imagination. When we want to assess our concrete achievements we have to seek the aid of a microscope.' He attributes this backwardness to the tyranny of literary culture. He condemns the type of humanism which is based on pious and learned reference to the past, in favour of the exact sciences. Shumayyil may have been an unbeliever; in any case, after his death in 1916, his adopted son, Gabriel Bûlâd, lamented the 'terrible responsibility' assumed by him and offered himself as an expiatory victim.[2]

This proves the profound character of a conflict which hardly any one in Europe was able to understand in time. It pervaded the consciousness of those minority groups which henceforward, far in advance of their brethren, assumed responsibility for the Arab East, a historic act of will which the nationalist struggle and the adherence of Muslim majorities was to disfigure with passionate strife and bloodshed but which might, given a little more understanding on our part, have saved us from deadlock. If the linguistic revival of the *lugha* offered a common denominator to Christians and Muslims, the rationalist fervour of such men as Shumayyil, Ṣarrûf and Anṭûn extended the same offer to Eastern and Western opponents. What opportunities were thus lost

[1] Particularly as the term *rujḥân* itself, meaning literally the factor that makes the arm of the balance lean one way or the other, has a canonical flavour.

[2] L. Massignon, 'Un ancien: Gabriel Boulad-Schemeiel', in *Annuaire du Cercle de la jeunesse catholique*, Beirut, 1928–9, notes these developments, which were closely studied in the *Revue du Monde musulman* at the time.

on both sides! In Egypt itself, Shumayyil's example was slow to bear fruit.

A young collaborator on the *Muqtaṭaf* of those days—he has recently died—passed on to our own day its precocious message, while deploring the scarcity of apostles. In fact, not until after the second world war did the quest for exact thought develop in the Arab world. Thus, meanwhile, Egypt's potential Romantic revolution failed to develop.[1] I shall return to this significant point. In January 1957, on the occasion of his seventieth birthday, Salâma Mûsâ added a final chapter to his *Tarbîya*, one of the most moving books in modern Arabic literature. He offered the younger generation a secular humanism, and even more important, the example of a life of integrity, of hope maintained despite tragic failures and semi-obscurity. His 'Address to Youth'[2] is instinct with lucidity and sincerity. Paradoxically, this old revolutionary reproaches the younger generation with having lost the thread of the past. So radical are the changes of regime and setting through which they have passed that they no longer recognize any historical or logical connection between past and present. Now the construction of the future implies an objective criticism of the past, in which the sociologist and the psychologist must collaborate, together with the philosopher, who proclaims that faith is the suicide of reason. There is so much to reform! The sumptuary extravagance of weddings and funerals, the pedantic ostentation that sets the acquisition of diplomas above true education, the crude attraction of the American cinema, the selfish superstition of girls' virginity, sexual anomalies due to frustration, etc.

All these evils arise from a mistaken interpretation of 'old' and 'new'—the quarrel between the *qadîm* and the *jadîd* which had been obsessing the Arab world for the last three-quarters of a century. Salâma Mûsâ would seek remedies in total liberation, in the sphere of politics, feelings and senses; in a culture which would escape the tyranny of mandarinism and go resolutely to the masses; in woman's right to work. Fundamentally, the remedy for everything would consist in becoming natural again. 'The world is good. I bless life', were the old man's dying words.[3] And in his mind this total liberation must be counterbalanced by an equally total assumption of responsibility.

[1] Salâma Mûsâ, *Tarbîya*, 2nd edn., 1957, p. 44.

[2] *Aḥâdîth ilâ'l-shabâb*, Cairo, pp. 5, 7, 14, 54, 59, 99, 150.

[3] He was quoting Rimbaud. Eastern rationalism is profoundly linked with a poetic renewal of sensibility.

Humanism and the Sense of Guilt

Of course we cannot isolate these movements either from the Western trends whose influence they rightly recognize, nor from certain Eastern trends that pervade Islam, and that have been shrewdly analysed by H. A. R. Gibb. But let us continue the evaluation.

The key word is responsibility, which is subtly connected, in Arab minds, with the suffering brought on them by so many conflicts and changes. And it scarcely matters whether it assumes a Socialist significance in the message of Salâma Mûsâ, or whether al-Wardî inserts it into his justification of sectarian shî'ism, while Muḥammad Khâlid bases it on the strangest mixture of Azharist preaching and crude materialism. The essence of all these positions consists in the equation proposed between various terms: change, dissatisfaction, enfranchisement, pain, anxiety, search, revolution, consciousness, responsibility. It is not surprising that a poet felt more keenly and expressed more vividly than any other these mysterious connections which, long after him, the historian could only describe in clumsy and distorting fashion.

Jubrân[1] was, first and foremost, an exile—in his life as in his work. He left his mountain village, which never ceased to be a lost Paradise to him; he left Boston, which initiated him into the West, and then he left Lebanon, where he really learnt his native tongue. Having introduced into Arabic poetry a romantic idealism of European type, he then abandoned Arabic for English verse, into which he introduced what seemed an Oriental inspiration. He expressed with the intensity of a myth what he had known in his own life: the enrichment, the denaturation of self through deep contact with the outside world, as experienced by other Arabs at the same time as himself. The mist that his poetry so frequently invokes[2] is not only that *ghaṭaiṭa* that clouds the valleys of his native land on autumn mornings; it represents the cloudy limbo of a world in process of becoming, the haze of uncertainty. In contrast with the formidable clear-cut divisions of traditional ethics and life, these minds, these societies that are undergoing transformation feel a sense of limitless potentiality.

This is indeed the same romanticism sought at the same time by that good materialist Salâma Mûsâ, although without knowing Jubrân and in a wholly different spirit from his. But Salâma Mûsâ longed for the

[1] There is much valuable information in the unpublished thesis of Anṭûn Ghaṭṭâs Karam.

[2] *Al-Makshûf*, no. 164, p. 5.

advent of an Arab Faust, whereas Jubrân merely experienced in life and expressed in rhythmic prose the chiaroscuro of romanticism: an unheard-of innovation in an Eastern world of black shadows and violent light. And peace almost always eluded this explorer. Barely perhaps did he enjoy it in a certain sort of music, which granted him access to *sakîna*, remission. He sought this also from Nature, which he discovered for his compatriots. 'Thou art myself, O Earth.'[1] But if he invokes Nature it is because he has lost her. One of his own paintings, to be seen in the museum of Becharré, serves as illustration to his quest and its too prompt frustration: a young man is seen lying exhausted beside a female centaur, whom he loves, but whom he cannot possess.

The Arab *angst* of today is all too ready, as we have seen, to lay the blame on others. This is indeed its crudest form. But beyond the stage where denunciation of colonialism reflects self-hatred, another contest is taking place between moral suffering, bitterness and a sense of guilt. This is surely the historic significance of a remarkable book: 'The City of Wrong,' *Qarya ẓâlima*, by Dr. Kâmil Ḥusain.[2] The root *ẓ.l.m.* figures in the Koranic lexicon. Its etymology suggests 'disadjustment', being out of place; the contrary of what is suggested by the Greek word *cosmos*. But from the beginning the Arab term assumes a moral sense also: an injustice harms its perpetrator, because to be unjust is to be incomplete and ugly, and thus to suffer.[3]

The book, constructed round this word, consists of a series of essays in dialogue form, reminding us of Renan's later work.[4] Kâmil Ḥusain examines the death of Christ from various points of view: from that of the Mosaic law, from that of Rome, from that of the Apostles. 'The crime was committed by religious people imbued with a sense of faith and law.'[5] What a lesson in relativism! It would be too simple to accuse the proud Sadducees, or the hypocrites, or the authorities, or Pilate himself; each had his own arguments. Now the crime was none the less committed. Darkness, baffling to science, covered the earth. Why were all these learned men, all these 'responsible' people misled? Why do all men share the blame, which goes far beyond their own faults? In fact,

[1] Id., *al-Majmû'a al-kâmila*, vol. i, p. 55.

[2] Cf. important article by Father Qanawâtî in *M.I.D.E.O.*, no. 2, pp. 71 ff., from which I have borrowed fragments of translation; reception speech by Ibrâhîm Madkûr at the Arab Academy in 1952, and Dr. K. Ḥ.'s reply; articles by Ḥusain Haikal and particularly by Ṭaha Ḥusain on the book.

[3] Cf. *M.I.D.E.O.*, no. 4, p. 253.

[4] Dr. Kâmil Ḥusain was for a time influenced by Renan.

[5] *Qarya*, pp. 22, 23.

only the seer, the *magus* can understand the reason, perhaps because alone of his sort in the book he eludes any social or national conditioning. He comes from the East; that is all we know about him. He knows that the legalistic murderers of Jesus made a criminal attack that day on the *ḍamîr*, the ethical conscience of the world. 'This conception of conscience', the author comments, 'is clearly distinct from intellect and reason; it is the law which makes man aware of what is wrong, of what he must not do. But it is also the summit of all laws, the culminating point of a universal biological law. . . .'

Dr. Kâmil Ḥusain is primarily a great surgeon, an exact scientist. Another of his books throws light on this earlier one. Its title, *Waḥdat al-ma'rifa*, might be translated: oneness of knowledge. It opens with an assertion of optimism. There is an order reigning throughout being and throughout mind. Knowledge bridges the gap between them. It unifies them. But on different, superimposed levels, with gaps between them: the level of matter, then that of life, then of animal being, then of man. The author offers scientific proof of this discontinuity, which is both epistemological and ontological. Each upper level stands in relation to the one below as 'omnipotence and fate'. The break, the gap, *fajwa*, which separates them results from a different law of being. The author, insufficiently explicit on this point, calls this the law of inhibition, *kabḥ*. Each higher order rises from the lower one by a sort of leap. This is particularly apparent at the point where consciousness comes in. The ascent, rising thus not by degrees but by continual leaps, continues thus up to that something which is beyond man and which for man represents 'omnipotence and fate'. Inversely, being is reflected back, stage by stage, down to the stage of matter; and perhaps having gone down through all these steps we might find the initial Creation of religious teaching. . . .[1]

Thus Dr. Kâmil Ḥusain offers us a humanism based on a sense of guilt; but he clearly distinguishes it from Christianity. The latter is still dominated by the shock that the Apostles felt on the day of iniquity. Hence it lays 'more stress on abstention from sin than on doing good: on the fear of injustice than on the love of justice; on the dread of hell than on the desire for heaven; on forbidding evil than of commanding good'. Now in Islam the struggle against evil and the incitement to good, *amr bi'l-ma 'rûf wa nahy 'an al-munkar*, go together. The positive impetus is merely circumscribed by prohibitions. Moreover these must yield to necessity, according to the strictest jurists, perhaps because all

[1] *Waḥda*, pp. 2, 10, 71, 77 ff.

necessities, ethical and material, spring from the same source as that impetus. The Muslim thinker discerns in his ethical creed a surge of natural life whose principle seems to him contradicted by the tragic element in Christianity.

An Attempt at Interpretation

True, a concept such as this goes far beyond religious controversy. It is a noble acknowledgement of the Other,[1] and a willingness to share responsibilities, even metaphysical responsibilities, with the Other. But sharing does not impy adhering. The curious lines I have quoted contradict many accepted opinions about Islam and Christianity. Perhaps they confirm the interpretation I have myself tried to construct, factor by factor, during the course of this study.

By what paradoxical reversal has that Christianity, whose rejection of the world is stressed by Dr. Kâmil Ḥusain, led its supporters to activity, expansion, industrialism, whereas Islam, for all its acceptance of Being, withdrew into its inner world? Mediterranean history during the last century, which had the strongest and the deepest influence on the Muslims, may perhaps enable us to solve the riddle; and the political analysis in the previous chapter suggested a definition to which I should now like to return.

If, for Christian ethics, the inner stimulus is more important than external prohibition, it is because Islam and Christianity, the East and the West, envisage man's development in different ways. Western man makes an initial withdrawal from the world, of which the events on Calvary, according to the author, offer a symbolic motivation. But having thus stepped aside from the world, Western man fulfils himself through it and in conflict with it. His ethical rule is deliberately an inner one, because he builds up his personality from the outside inwards.[2] The West does not dissociate objectivity from sincerity. It has set up an interrelation between the outer and the inner world of whose fertile strength many nations were to become aware during the imperialist era.

The reverse is true of traditional Islam. Here, we must reiterate, man's personality is based on transcendence, as regards the Deity, and on a sort of immanence, as regards his own behaviour. Man

[1] Dr. K. H.'s reception speech at the Cairo Academy admirably expresses the attitude of the honest Arab intellectual, as free from opportunism as from resentment.

[2] We cannot here develop the suggestions offered by this idea towards a new type of character-study of 'Eastern' and 'Western' man.

adheres to the cosmic. Thus he escapes much anguish and many problems. He enjoys happiness through conformity, *taufîq*. His crisis only begins after consciousness of 'guilt'. But this is not original sin. Neither is it the death of a God. If 'God is dead',[1] as Nietzsche said, or rather if he is in danger of dying, it is for quite other reasons, in the Arab world, than in our own. Guilt, for them, is the other aspect of the defeat inflicted on their system by the intrusion of a technological and imperialistic civilization. The man whose attitude to the world was one of transcendence and adherence is now replaced by a man who knows separation and anxiety, but who has learnt criticism and action. At the end of his ordeal, he will have gained access to nature and to history. But his being will have lost something of its plenitude.

Kabḥ, inhibition, *kabt*, repression, *kaẓm*, repression with effort: these three terms, one translating the learned hypothesis of Dr. Kâmil Ḥusain, the other two phenomena of social psychology now popularized by the press, are derived from the same image. Already the etymological analysis of a word as contemporary as that of *qalaq*,[2] the 'modern Arab *angst*', suggested the image of walls whose content is slipping from them, of a solid body in which cracks are forming. And let us also note the term *fajwa*,[3] which denotes these gaps. If we might pursue this image to its end, we should evoke that total plenitude of traditional Muslim man, as he was before contact with the West, with the machine, with analytical thought. 'Man is like a sphere in which each fragment yearns nostalgically for the whole, towards which it strains with all its vital force.'[4] And we can see how, thenceforward, in that Arab world yearning for its lost immanence, it is through analysis, through division, at the cost of the most dispersive activity, that each fraction—man, nation, class—strives to close the cycle by recovering its unity.

Aspiration towards Completeness

This return to completeness may take many forms. That for instance of a restoration of Islam, which, as al-'Aqqâd[5] clearly saw, offered believers a system with no 'cleft', *fiṣâm*, and apparently no division of

[1] Cf. the exegesis of this picture by Heidegger, *Arguments*, no. 15, 1959.

[2] *Lisân al-'Arab*, q.v.

[3] *Waḥda*, p. 99. The word and the image also remind us of Plato's 'cave' and that of the Seven Sleepers, of which L. Massignon has given a universal interpretation.

[4] *Sand and Form.*

[5] 'Abbâs Maḥmûd al-'Aqqâd, *al-Islâm fî'l-qarn al-'ashrîn*, 1957, pp. 22 ff., 28 ff. But the theology and philosophy of this author are somewhat inadequate,

labour. The bulk of the nation has retained its faith: the politician may be greatly tempted to resort to this favoured form of integration. The risk, with this hypothesis—and the parties that claim allegiance to it have indeed succumbed thereto—is to mistake the path of the past for that of moral authenticity and of sociological exactitude. Lack of realism leads nowhere. More and more, in the Middle East today, meanings are assuming concrete form. A symbol, to retain its vitality, must correspond to men's needs and to the laws of life. And many ancient attitudes are now repudiated as being forms of evasion, mystification and alibi. It is hard for Islam, as for any other religion, to project itself into a material future while still clinging to its transcendentalism. This can only be achieved at the cost of a new *ijtihâd*, an 'effort' at doctrinal innovation as well as social modernization; it is in this sense that Islam must revive the message of Shaikh ʿAbduh.

The scientific optimism of many others takes a contrary direction. Its merit lies in setting synthesis at the end of long progress, with and not against the stream of concrete history. And since the latter also represents the evolution of the rest of the world, the Arab countries would thus recover both their own individuality, freed successively from all shackles, internal and external, and a solidarity with the rest of mankind. This is the twofold promise made to the Arabs by a socialism whose power the West has failed to realize, attributing it either to Soviet successes in this 'zone' or to the upsurge of self-assertion. True, these phenomena play their part. But their coincidence is not yet an established fact. Indeed it suffers from certain time-lags which are not purely accidental. There is inevitable confusion. Almost everyone professes adherence to Socialism in the Middle East. Now Marxism, which is the most experimental and the most doctrinaire form of Socialism, derives the major part of its strength in these countries less from a 'philosophy of poverty', or from its doctrine of action, than from its grasp of totality. It is here not so much a method of struggle against social or national dispossession as a hope of plenitude: of a plenitude to be looked for at the term of its history, not at its beginnings or in some realm above. The ultimate success of socialism will depend on its capacity to restore wholeness to man.

CHAPTER XIV

The Arabs, the World and Ourselves

If this is indeed the case, the problem of the Arab East becomes one with the problem of all mankind today: how to preserve its identity, or rather its manifold identities amidst the formidable transformation, and the no less formidable uniformity entailed by technical progress. From a leisurely, many-coloured world we are all being swept away together towards a world that is being constantly levelled out and renovated. The rich spatial variations to be found in humanity from one country to another, from one province to another, are giving way to variations in time, that is to say to mutations within themselves. This means that each original entity must lose that which differentiates it from others, and thus in many respects what makes it itself, in exchange for the right to survive. Must the cost be so high?

True, the infinite variety of men subsists everywhere; it displays itself furthermore by a wild diversity of attitudes and solutions. In this study I have tried to examine a single case and moment of this diversity. But the problem remains identical, whether we are considering Arabs or Europeans. For them, as for ourselves—there as here—the conflict is between human personality and the world, and consequently between material progress and values. Eastern thinkers have put it thus, with extreme lucidity. They feel impelled to respond to the urgent necessity, as well as to the lure of modernization by establishing relations between themselves and other nations on the one hand, between the individual and his surroundings on the other. And most of them, despite the prestige of a past and a faith more potent than our own, do not seek a solution in some return to a golden age supposedly immune from the laws of technical evolution. Belief in material progress, the urge to surpass oneself, direct men's efforts, inspire their courage, there as here. But the resemblance goes no further. If the problem is one and the same, conditions, rhythms, patterns and meanings are different.

What is the Arab East?

Let us once again envisage the Arab East, with its thousand-year-old loyalties, suddenly soaring towards the future. The second part of *Faust* contrasts the thesis of the Neptunians with that of the Vulcanians. According to the former, *being* proceeds through accumulation: according to the latter, through eruption. No doubt this antithesis confronts the two extremes suggestively rather than convincingly. However, if in Europe the Revolution itself takes its stand on a patient determinism, among the Arabs it bursts forth like a prophecy. Whence so many misunderstandings between the two worlds. Misunderstandings at all levels and in every category, since the forces of conservatism as well as those of revolt are different on the two sides. And yet the same language, the same ideologies, the same way of behaving, eating, dressing, making war and making love are gradually spreading over the whole face of the globe. This assimilation, superficial though it may be, has its effect in depth. It ends by creating the realities it apes. The Arab world is striving towards an image of itself which needs textiles, metallurgy, the manufacture of machines. Meanwhile it effectively acquires generalized attitudes of production. Our quest began with an investigation of differences; we glimpse, at the end of it, the common ground underlying idiosyncrasies. It leads us, finally, to recognize the unity of man. But was not that its initial hope?

If then our analysis correctly reduces the contrasts between our own reality and that Arab reality, which is akin and yet hostile to it, to mere variations of form and rhythm, it is because we have learnt from direct observation. For the immediate contains the truth, if we are ready to listen. The Arab East, synoptic in its landscapes, its men and its events, strikes us with all the power of an image, a desire, and with the gravity of an archetype; its hunger for the earth is alternately redeemed and frustrated by its invocation of values. It suffers from a conflict, it enjoys a coalition, which are peculiar to itself, between the prestige of a heaven-sent past and the mediocrity of the present. Or else, on the contrary, between the restrictions which that past can still impose, and its fresh powers of renewal drawn from social and mental strata hitherto unexplored.

The Arab East is Abraham, no doubt, but Abraham rejuvenescent;

somewhat as in that picture of Mantegna's which shows an old tree-trunk, rotted by time, suddenly burgeoning into green branches with shouting faces on them. The wretchedness and the greatness of the Arab East lie in its mingling of contrasts, and in the way it seeks from their association a remedy to present ills. Hence the warm vibrant emotion, the touching charm, but also the disproportion between words and deeds, between intention and practice, and in general the conflict, exacerbated by the colonial epoch, between justice and efficiency.

This makes for weakness and incoherence, no doubt. But also for mediation. Suhrawardi and, following him, Henri Corbin,[1] interprets the words Middle East (in a different sense from that of the Foreign Office!) as that zone of being suspended between the human and the divine. A more prosaic but not so very different analysis would discover that everything in Arab countries plays a mediatory part, in spite of the disruptive effect, experienced by them as by ourselves, of suddenly becoming part of history. Mediatory, because in every sphere there is constant intersection between values and things, and constant reference from one to the other. This is a land where things are for ever bearing witness to ideas, and ideas to things; where things and ideas, alternately and simultaneously, are exalted and humiliated.

One purpose of this study has been to determine how far these images reflect an exact truth and can serve to distinguish a historic instance under a pattern of landscapes and attitudes; and it is also one of its conclusions. One of the Arabs' most original characteristics is undoubtedly their power to make the immediate valid. In their case, there are surely other than phenomenological reasons. The cause of this constant shift from act to essence, from abstract to concrete, lies in their yearning for completeness. The Arabs intend, against all classifications and divisions, to maintain or re-establish unity. Hence their propensity to symbolism, and the fact that a study of their economic activity, such as I have sketched in the central chapters of this book, has to take into account so many correspondences between the most material facts and the spirit that lies behind them. And we must not see this merely as a somewhat primitive attitude of 'participation', but also, and above all, as the attachment of what we may call the Arab genius to such correspondences. It does not merely cultivate these correspondences; they are part of its very being. The closeness and warmth of the relationship between the material and the spiritual, the involvement of the senses with the

[1] H. Corbin, *L'imagination créatrice dans le soufisme d'Ibn Arabi*, Flammarion 1958.

Absolute, constitute undoubtedly, despite all the misfortunes of this time, one of its most enduring factors, in any case that which it rightly holds dearest.

This unifying energy,[1] whose content is so much more living than that assigned to it by politics or theology, added to a spirit of revolt against others and against themselves and to an ardent desire to rediscover Nature, constitute the essential features of the Arabs of our time. And if, indeed, there is no category or fact in their existence, no collective or individual personality among them, no social or mental level, which does not reflect this threefold character, on which it does not cast fresh light, perhaps I may also be entitled to accept this invitation to synthesize, to recall divers aspects and to infer from partial analyses a vision of the future. But although it may be legitimate to generalize and to forecast, I cannot do so without making a preliminary choice between two hypotheses, one optimistic, the other pessimistic. For the heart may here reassert its rights, and assessing extremes, consider them as good or evil.

The Two Hypotheses

In the pessimistic view, the Arab, victim simultaneously of conformism and resentment, alienates his original personality by adapting himself to a world which he indicts and yet submits to. The alteration of his own nature does not secure him a place in the sun among other nations. The after-effects of his history, both national and colonial, the considerable impoverishment, both material and moral, which these have inflicted on him, jeopardize his success even on the plane of a pragmatism which he is increasingly determined to adopt. Already the distinction between developed and under-developed countries is no longer confined to inequalities of achievement, but to a disparity in the rate of growth. An under-developed country is one which develops more slowly than the rest. Eventually, there would be an increased difference between recently emancipated countries and those that

[1] From the same important root are derived words as charged with meaning and emotion as *waḥda, tauḥid, ittiḥâd.* At the Congress on Political Science at Beirut, 5–7 Nov. 1959, Dr. Suwailim al-'Umarî pertinently contrasted the words *waḥda* and *ittiḥâd.* I might speak here of *Muslim* humanism, as does Louis Gardet (*La cité musulmane*, 1954, pp. 273–322) did I not prefer to stress, as has been seen, a certain *Arab* type of behaviour, which has been felt, in different ways and to different degrees, by Lawrence, Louis Massignon and Bishr Fâirs. Cf. A. Faure, 'La chevalerie islamique', *Revue de la Méditerranée*, 1959, pp. 45 ff.

were formerly dominant.[1] Inequalities between nations or zones, even more terrible than those which imperialism has exploited and generally aggravated, would extend so far that we should be confronted by a future of dizzying contrasts and frantic competition between the strong to appropriate the weak.

Such prospects impart an ever-increasing bitterness to the attitude of the former dependants towards their former overlords. There is a growing tendency in Arab countries, as in all those of the 'Third World', to reject not only the authority but the values of the Great White Powers; to borrow nothing even from their science save its laws, or rather its recipes and materials. A Western world thus reduced to the provision of equipment and processes, become—by an ironic twist—'raw material' for its former vassals, without hope of being understood, let alone loved, would repress its potential influence, withdrawing into dangerous egotism. It would confine itself to cultivating its capacities for purposes of destruction or for lucrative negotiation. It is obvious already that a certain type of 'technical assistance',[2] prolific of fine phrases and high salaries but poor in efficiency, engenders a sort of exploitation. True, today's inequalities do not, like those of the earlier phase, reveal the immoral attitude of the overlord. But they are clearly evident in so-called trade agreements. Mercantilism between nations,[3] even when qualified by 'assistance', is likely to bring no greater moral satisfaction or even positive results than the feudalism of the colonial epoch. By putting the two partners in the relation of dispossessor/dispossessed, of deceiver/dupe, they would lead to the crushing of one by the other, their mutual detestation, and the withering-away of the hateful victor.

But must we take so gloomy a view?[4] In its extreme form, this contingency is only to be apprehended if all mankind's hopes should fade in face of some mechanical concatenation of material events. Or, in

[1] The fear of this is expressed by K. M. Panikkar, *Problèmes des états nouveaux*, 1959, pp. 126 ff. This pessimistic view has since been confirmed by statistical estimates with respect to nations in the process of development. Correlatively, these nations display ever-increasing suspicion with regard to technical assistance.

[2] This is intended as a criticism of contemporary pharisaism, and not as a reference to the many valuable efforts of international institutions, which no one is less anxious to minimize than myself.

[3] By a curious transposition, a century later, of what had been, after the Declaration of the Rights of Man, the development of mercantilism between individuals in the form of liberal economy or bourgeois democracy.

[4] The Algerian nation, by realizing the synthesis to a minor extent in Mediterranean Islam, may constitute a historic test of great interest.

other terms, if analysis should cease to be sincere, if action should cease to be clear-sighted. If I expose the danger, it is because I hope to see my fellow-Europeans avoid it, by a victory not merely of generosity over avarice but of reason over unreason, of right judgement over delusion. And reciprocally I believe that the Arabs' history is destined, by its own logic, for a happier issue both for themselves and for others: the two are inseparable.

According to the optimistic hypothesis, the Arabs' quest, and their increasingly active participation in that contest for which formerly they merely provided the stake, will suggest to them solutions corresponding to their innermost nature, and not proceeding from ready-made data. They will see ever more clearly that history cannot move upside down, that progress, by arousing ever humbler strata of reality, is better in the long run than successful evasion. They know from experience that liberty must not only be won but must be deserved. Now the way to deserve it is to build it up: and for this no recipe will serve, only laws, and, even more than laws, the scientific and moral values that underly them. The Arabs have already come to realize, and have begun to act upon their realization, that they must find their own solutions; and above all through social analysis, through self-criticism. For deterioration is the gravest form of dispossession. Correspondingly, it is essential for them, no less than for ourselves, to discard what is out of date.

Certain signs, beneath the surface tumults, suggest that the process has begun. As I have already said, the quest for, and above all the practice of liberty involves, against all appearances, adherence—perhaps too ready an adherence—to the Alien's system. A gradual assumption of responsibilities, in which the field of conflict will shift and will gain depth, may perhaps cause the two partners of the colonial epoch to be relegated to some museum of antiquities, while their place is taken by something that is hostile to both of them and yet partakes of the best qualities of each.

Of course the future will be more commonplace. It will never coincide with either of the two extremes, but will take shape somewhere between them, depending on the time and place, on nations and individuals. And yet I am entitled to raise this alternative, precisely because it is to a large extent unreal and yet colours our assessment of the future with those violent feelings which the Arabs' historian has neither the right nor the power to ignore. And moreover, were I to remain unmoved, should I reach a different conclusion?

When M. de Lesseps, under Sa'd and Ismâ'îl, dug his canal, he did not consider the fate of those thousands of fellahs he had forcibly recruited and whose death resulted from his undertaking. Nor did the Universal Company concern itself with their memory. The ruthless virtues of that time, the engineer's daring, the one-way traffic in power, the dictatorship of money, relegated into oblivion for almost a century the sufferings of men who were potential citizens. The affair of 1956 abolished the old Company, replaced Anglo-French capitalism by State enterprise and overthrew the statue of Lesseps. Its violence parallels that of the famous consul; it relegated him, as he had relegated his workers, to oblivion. In the same way the phase of emancipation overthrows and outrages the heroic deeds of the colonial phase, as the latter had those of its immediate predecessors. But history is more than the story of men's enthusiasms. The destiny of the masses who had dug the Canal was not wiped out when Suez shares soared on the Stock Market; equally enduring are the results of that expansion which brought uniformity to the world and inaugurated the demiurgic seizure of Nature by man.

It is true that for the Arabs this phase was one of humiliation, which today they abjure with all their strength. Man changes his heroes because he needs to renew his symbols. He renews his moral attitudes as well. These have a contagious effect. Detestation of the colonial epoch discredits even its creative aspects. Having justifiably rejected its governing idea, which meant exploitation and depersonalization, they less justifiably condemned many elements in that epoch which did not merely serve that governing idea but sometimes contradicted it, or redeemed it. Was the crime so great as to contaminate all the human reality affected by it? This is unlikely, for such a verdict would misleadingly confuse historic with metaphysical truths, the relative with the absolute. Herein lies, in any case, one of the problems of our day. Truth to tell, it concerns the Arabs, who were never strictly a colonial people, less than it concerns others. But on its solution depends, in many respects, the evolution of their relations with ourselves and the evolution of the world as a whole.[1]

Will the two partners learn to rise above themselves? Each of them must exorcise within himself old appetites and old angers. We must ourselves liquidate, as fast as possible, the residue of old hegemonies, were it only to allow the other side to choose and to acknowledge what may have been creative about them. On the other hand the Arabs have

[1] Cf. the lucid synthesis of A. Abel, 'Psychologie et comportement', in *Le monde musulman contemporain, Initiations.*

to demoralize the moral element from their judgement, considering facts and men separately, and restoring to the earlier period its dignity as a phase of their own history; their prehistory perhaps, but not a metaphysical nightmare.

This will require enormous efforts, and relentless revision, for them as for ourselves! And yet we shall have to make these efforts if we, and they, wish to avoid two fatal errors: ours, to consider them as an ever-ready prey, an ungrateful victim; and theirs, to reject the West *en bloc*, in other words to condemn efficiency through hatred of injustice because we committed injustice in the name of efficiency.

From Misfortune to Favour

This study has tried to reduce many of the contrasts which strike us between the southern and the northern shores of the Mediterranean, and more broadly between two entities vaguely but expressively termed East and West,[1] to variations in form and in rhythm. And meanwhile, however, we have followed the teaching of this synoptic region of the world by indulging in a certain confusion of epochs and disdain of chronology. There were many reasons for this. For many places, many periods of the Arab East elude any sort of regularity. If I have sought to discern progress or symmetry therein, it has been for the sake of simplification, and by superimposing the logic of types on their sequence in time.[2]

And yet if I look still further afield, I can recognize over the whole extent of the Arab world, in the course of the hundred or so years since the beginning of the *nahḍa*, certain concordances between this typology and historical events. Better still, perhaps: if not the possibility of a choice between the optimistic and pessimistic hypotheses for the future, at least the basis for an approach, and thus for a choice between one and the other.

The Arab East, considered from the point of view of its vast mass and its long existence, appears to have travelled a considerable way along the road leading from almost total frustration to an ever more positive

[1] I must point out that the 'West' here referred to, strictly and directly in relation to the history of the Middle East during the last century, is the representative of technical progress and industrial expansion, of which the U.S.S.R. is today one of the most dynamic champions. Since these lines appeared in the French edition of this book (1960) the Sino-Russian conflict and ensuing controversies have strengthened the Middle Eastern view of the U.S.S.R. as part of the 'West'.

[2] But is this not every historian's problem?

reconquest. The shock of machine civilization had been severe, for it was inflicted by alien powers and proceeded from no internal preparation. Its modernity, originally inflicted rather than acquired, none the less produced in it the same constructive ravages as everywhere else, but with psychological and social effects which at first were wholly different, indeed contrary. For the Arab East the industrial revolution did not coincide with possession of the planet, nor with the corresponding deepening in feeling and sensibility, in the aesthetic sense, in the quest for liberty.

On the contrary, the Arabs were for a long time the objects rather than the subjects, the victims rather than the beneficiaries of an expansion which severed their connections with history and nature. At the time when they thus felt the full force of others' development they were in a plight worse than dispossession: they were mutilated, intercepted, withdrawn into themselves, devoid of hope, having moreover lost their own soul. The French Revolution sent Bonaparte into Egypt. The conquest of Algeria went hand in hand with the Romantic movement. Victorian Imperialism, the excitement of great investments and great machines found aesthetic expression in Kipling. And the East endured all this. Its colonial era represents the inverse side of Romanticism, Revolution and Imperialism. Its hollowness implies the swelling greatness of others.

For its own revolutionary effectiveness it had to wait for a greater or lesser period of time, according to the country and the men involved, without anywhere, as yet, achieving its aim. But in its entirety it has entered on to the long march leading, by bitter stages, from lost plenitude to a combined recovery of nature and history. True, archaism survives in many places, in these countries' institutions, in their collective or individual psychology. But it cannot be denied that a considerable distance has been covered, although still unevenly. More than an almost general transition from dependence to independence, what must strike one is the change which has broadly begun to take place in the threefold relationship of the Arabs with the world, with other nations and with themselves.

The Arab is reappropriating to himself the essential part of his world through political reintegration. But also by the hold over Nature—emotional and also active, which he is now developing, following the example of European Romanticism. Once dispossessed and intercepted, he is now learning, or relearning, to make objects, and, soon, machines. Economic reconstruction now appears to him as a basis which his national revolt had opportunely, but at its peril, neglected. In other words, he must set his revolution on its feet.

In this obligation lies his great opportunity in modern times. By a reversal of the old misfortunes which, owing to technical backwardness, had reduced him to dependence, he is now favoured above his former conquerors by the very fact that the machine, for him, means a return to nature. Whereas we are faced with so many 'human problems due to industrial mechanization',[1] and fear lest our power should denature us, access to industrialism offers this late-comer, this prodigal son of efficiency, not only a rise in the standard of living and the power of man over things, but a revivifying immersion: the literary discovery of nature, the scientific discovery of the world, the moral discovery of woman, the humanistic discovery of the foreigner.

New powers provide new spells. The old Arab genius, restored after its long eclipse, is not going to re-establish its interdicts and its formulae. It will have burst its own bonds as well as those of the Alien. For the swiftness of a movement provoked by external forces, while depriving it of the wisdom gained by experience and the benefit of a slow maturity, has left it both its impatient youthfulness and the privilege of its aspiration to the global.

Whereas in so many more 'advanced' countries the machine dissociates man from nature and imprisons him far from the green shade of the tree of life, in the gloomy landscapes of artificiality, the Arab can, through the machine, recover nature and become natural again. Even the very suddenness of his contemporary history may serve him, after having burdened him; it has not left him time to forget his unifying mission. He has overleapt our bourgeois centuries.[2] To the modern world, divided and hard pressed, the beneficiary and victim of analysis, he will be a harbinger of freshness through the completeness of his attitude to life.

If this vision is realized, if the power of hatred on both sides does not triumph, then the Arab, by means of and in spite of material progress, and the fratricidal conflicts of the age of steel, will have formed a sound companionship with us. He will have ratified that alliance between the Alien, the world and himself, whose savour he has not forgotten. No longer that of Abraham *al-Khalīl*, 'the friend of God'. But that of Heraclitus, the friend of things, and our common father.

[1] I have in mind the work of G. Friedmann, which stands in opposition to Marxist scientific optimism.

[2] And been spared their tragic dissensions.

Glossary of Arabic Words and Expressions

We have collected here, for the benefit of the non-specialized reader, the Arabic words and expressions used or mentioned in this book, accompanying them with a rough translation, valid for their context and necessarily arbitrary. Such terms are here given in italics—in transliteration. A circumflex (ˆ) denotes a long vowel, an apostrophe (’) the glottal stop, and an inverted apostrophe (‘) the laryngeal fricative. Consonants with dots beneath them (ḍ, ṭ, ṣ, ẓ,) are emphatic.

abaḍây: swashbuckler (Syria, Lebanon).
abnâ’ al-dhawât: aristocracy.
abûdîya: an Iraqi song.
âdâb: belles lettres.
‘âdî: ordinary.
adîb: man of letters.
ahl al-dhimma: ‘protected’ minorities in the Muslim state: Jews or Christians.
ahl al-khâssa: the élite, the initiated.
aḥyâ’: districts (sing. *ḥayy*).
‘ajâ’ib: wonders (of the world).
âla: instrument, tool, machine.
‘alâma: mark, index, emblem, boundary-mark.
âlî: mechanical, material.
‘amîd al-usra: head of the family.
‘âmil, pl. *‘ummâl:* workman.
amr bi’l-ma‘rûf wa-nahy ‘an al-munkar: religious precept enjoining well-doing and the struggle against evil.
anghâm: musical modes.
‘aql: reason.
‘arabîya wusṭâ: ‘median’ Arabic, the contemporary language of the Press.
ardib: measure of capacity (Egypt).
‘aṣabîya: esprit de corps, agnatic solidarity.

asâs: basis (pl. *usus*).
aṣwât fikrîya: spiritual voices.
auqâf dhurrîya: pious foundations transmitted within the family.
âya: sign, punctuation in psalmody, whence verse of the Koran.
ayât rajul: a man's personality.
'azba: farm surrounded by large estate.

badawî: Bedouin.
bâdiya: desert, nomads.
bak: lord, bey.
bâmya: Greek horn (a vegetable, an Egyptian national dish).
baqqâl: grocer.
ba'th: resurgence, renaissance.
bawâdir: first fruits.
bayân: sign denoting an epiphany (Sudan).
biṭâla: unemployment.
buḥḥa: huskiness of the voice.

dabbâgh: tanner.
daghdagha li'l-shu'ûr: titillate feelings.
ḍamîr: conscience.
ḍarb: street, lane.
dhâtî: essential.
dîma: kind of striped stuff (Syria, Lebanon).
dîwân: collected works of a poet.
dullâb: indefinite recurrence of a musical theme (lit. tourniquet).
durr: sort of archaic music.
duwwâr: great house (Egypt).

Effendî: gentleman, Mr.

faddân: Egyptian measure of area = 0,4200 hectares, feddan.
fâ'ida: interest.
fajwa: crack, cranny.
fallâḥ: peasant, fellah.
fann: kind, modality, branch, bough, art, industry.
fannan: O wonder!
fannî (pl. *fannîyîn*)*:* artisan, artist.
fatât al-darb: the local beauty.
fiqh: law, jurisprudence.

fiṣâm: fissure.
fitiwwa: swashbuckler (Egypt).
fitna: troubles, conflict, sedition.
fiṭr: breaking of fast.
fiṭra: innateness, natural disposition, intuition.
fûl: beans.
furqân: demarcation.

ghammâza: woman who makes herself understood by signs.
gharar: risk.
ghaṭaiṭa: mist (Lebanon).

ḥadîth: tradition relating the acts of the Prophet.
hâjât bilâdi-nâ: the needs of our country.
ḥakawâtî: popular story-teller (Egypt).
ḥalâl: permitted.
ḥalâwa: sweetness.
ḥallâj: cotton stripper.
ḥarâm: forbidden.
ḥarmal: sort of plant.
ḥarraka: to set in movement.
ḥasab: personal nobility.
hijâ': satire.
ḥîla: subterfuge, ruse.
ḥisba: police control of markets, moral censorship.
ḥishma: decency, self-restraint.

ibn al-'amm: father's brother's son. Fem: *bint al-'amm.*
ifâḍa: effusion.
ihtizâzât: starts, quivers.
ijâza: permission.
ijmâ': consensus of the learned.
ijtihâd: definite effort.
ikhtalaṭat al-dhât bi'l-mauḍû': the essence, or subject, has mingled with the object.
ilâ takwîn râ's al-mâl: for the formation of capital.
ilzâmî: obligatory.
intâj: production.
'iqâl: Bedouin's head-veil.
irâdîya: voluntaryism.

iṣlâḥ zirâʿî: agrarian reform.
istikhâra: practice of augury, based on the Koran.
istiʿmâr: colonialism.
istirbâḥ: pursuit of gain.
ittiḥâd: union.
izdiwâj: split personality.

jadâwil: canals (Iraq).
jadîd: new.
jallâb: one who buys small quantities of cotton to make up larger processed lots (Egypt).
jumla: whole, phrase.

kabḥ: inhibition.
kabt: repression.
kalâm: recitative (in Eastern music).
kaẓm: repression.
khabîr: expert.
khadamât: social equipment, services (Egypt).
khajjaʿa: to produce a repetitive guttural sound conducive to incantation and spell-binding.
khaṭîb: preacher.
khawâjâ: resident European (Egypt), gentleman (Lebanon).
khiḍr: intercessor.
khiṭaṭ: narrative, literary form.
khurâfât: legends.
khurda: scrap-iron (Egypt).
kilîm: carpet, rug.
kitmân: intimate withdrawal.
kullîya: school, faculty.
kullîyat al-hindasa: engineering school.
kutla: bloc, gathering.

laḥan (or *laḥn*)*:* barbarism, or song (according to vocalization).
lugha: language (here the Classical Arabic language).
lugha thâlitha: third language.

mâdda: material.
madhhab: theme, refrain, doctrine.
madîḥ: panegyric.

maḥâfil: social and literary parties.
Mahdi: leader of the Sudanese revolt in the last century.
mahjar: emigration. Poetry of the *Mahjar:* literary school created by Syrian and Lebanese émigrés in America.
mahr: matrimonial gift, formality of Muslim marriage.
mandûb: delegate commissionary.
markaz: centre.
mauḍû'îya: objectivity.
mawwâl: a species of popular poetry and music.
mdemmes: braised beans, popular Egyptian dish.
mîkânîkî: mechanics (machinery).
milk: property.
min aghwâr anfusinâ: from the depths of ourselves.
Mîrî: regalian tenure; literally: prince's land.
Miṣr sâmi'a: listening Egypt.
mlukhîya: gombo, a prized ingredient of Egyptian cookery.
mu'allim: master, boss.
mu'assasa: institution.
mudîr: governor.
mudîrîya: governorate (Egypt).
mughâzala: flirtation.
muhâjara: exile, emigration.
muhandis: engineer.
muhandis ma'mârî: town-planning engineer.
mulklah: title borne by certain religious officials (especially in non-Arab Islam).
munaẓẓama: institution.
muqâwil: jobbing workman, entrepreneur.
muṣawwir: home-worker.
muta'ahhid: contractor.
muthâqqafîn: cultured people, intelligentsia.

nadî (pl. *andiya*)*:* literary coterie, club.
nahḍa: revival, renaissance.
naḥwa: towards.
nasab: genealogy, nobility of birth.
niẓâm 'ashâ'irî: tribal order.
nudhûr: votive celebrations.
numuw: growth.
nûr: light.

qadarîya: fatalism.
qadîm: ancient.
qaisârîya: trading districts (especially for imported fabrics).
qalaq: anxiety, anguish.
qanṭâr: Egyptian unit of weight.
qânûn: theorbo, regulation.
qarawî: villager.
qarrâdî: popular poetry (Lebanon).
qarya: village.
qaṣîda: piece of verse.
qaumîya: nationalism, patriotism.
qibla: direction of Mecca.
qunâq: pavilion, kiosk (Syria).
Qur'ân: the Koran.
qurr: hut.
quṭnî: relating to cotton.

rabḥ: profit.
râ'id al-ḥaraka al-ta'âwunîya: pioneer of the co-operative movement.
rajul râmiz al-ra'î: sage speaking in allusive maxims.
rajulun bi-fannin: virtuoso.
rammâza: woman who makes her meaning clear by signs.
ramz: meaning almost devoid of material basis: whisper, allusion, symbol.
ri'âsa: headship, leadership.
riḍâ: approval.
rûḥ: spirit, soul.
rûḥ al-takattul: committee spirit.
ruḥânîya: religious idealism.
rustâq: rural area including villages.
rûth al-ḥayawân: animal excrement.

ṣabr: patience.
ṣaḥâfî: journalist.
sakîna: remission, peace.
salafîya: school or system preaching recourse to doctrinal precedent and the cult of ancestors.
salaf jârr naf'a: loan with interest.
salsabil: artificial waterfall (Aleppo).
ṣamt al-ḥikma: sapient silence.
ṣarîfa: hut made of mats (suburbs of Baghdad).

ṣawwara: to represent or fashion.

sayyid: lord.

sha'b: people.

shai': thing.

shaikh: master, head of tribe.

sha'r: hair.

sharîf: (fem. *sharîfa*)*:* noble, descendant of the Prophet.

sharwâl: loose trousers.

shâwish: policeman (Egypt).

shi'âr: sign, slogan, war-cry.

shighâr: exchange of fiancées (illicit practice).

shûrâ: canonic consultation.

shu'ûbîya: historically, antagonism between the two principal ethnic elements, Persians and Arabs. By extension, any national antagonism.

shu'ûr: consciousness.

shwâl 'oṭn: sack of cotton.

sima: sign, character.

sîrân: country outing (Damascus).

sirdâq: dais.

sirr: secret.

ṣiyâgha: goldsmith's work.

sû' al-tanẓîm: bad organization.

sunna: law, tradition.

sûq al-aurâq al-mâlîya: Stock Market.

ta'akhkhur: inadequacy, backwardness.

ṭaba'a: to print.

tabaḥḥur: total immersion.

ṭabî'a: nature, character.

tadbîr manzilî: domestic science.

tahayyaj min hiyâj al-nâs: he was carried away by the general enthusiasm.

taḥrîm: denoting something as forbidden (*ḥarâm*).

taḥṭîb: dance of 'the sticks' (Egypt).

ṭâ'ifîya: religious sectarianism (Lebanon).

tâ'ih: wandering.

tajdîd: renovation, renewal.

takhalluf: under-development.

takht: orchestra for traditional music.

takhṭîṭ: plan (Egypt). In Lebanon, *taṣmîm.*

talḥîn al-Qur'ân: intoned psalmody of the Koran.

ta'mîm: nationalization.
tanzîl: descent from Heaven to earth (Koran).
taqâwî, ta'âwi: seeds (Egypt).
taqlîd: traditionalism.
ṭaraba: to arouse joy or sorrow, to stir.
ṭarâwa: freshness.
tarbîya: education.
tasalsul: chain, series.
taṣnî': industrialization.
taṣwîr: representation.
taufîq: success granted by God.
tawassul: intercession.
thâ'r: vengeance.
thaura: revolution.
tiknîkî: technical, technician.

'uḍwî: organic.
'ulamâ' (sing. *'âlim*)*:* learned men, doctors, *ulema.*
'umda: village chief (Egypt).
umma: the Muslim nation, Islam.
ummî: (pl. *ummîyîn*)*:* illiterate.
'urûba: Arabism.
ustâdh: professor, Mr.
uṣûlî: fundamentalist.

waḥda mujamma'a: polyvalent centre (Egypt).
wa'î: consciousness.
walâ': allegiance.
waqf: mortmain.
waqi'î: realistic (*waqi'îya:* realist school).
warsha: workshop, factory (Egypt).
wasîm: thoroughbred.
wasm: mark.
waẓîfî: functional.
wijdân: life-pulse.
wukalâ' (sing. *wakîl*)*:* mandatories.

zahhâr: merchant buying cotton in flower (Egypt).
za'îm: chief, leader.
zakât: legal tax.
zâr: magical practice of 'dispossession' (Nile Valley).

List of Author's Works on Related Subjects

Les Pactes Pastoraux Beni Meskine: Contribution à l'étude des contrats nord-africains; La Typo-litho et J. Carbonel, Algiers, 1936

Études d'Histoire Rurale Maghrébine: Éditions internationales, Tangier, 1938

Les Nawazil Al-Muzara 'a du Mi'yar Al-Wazzanî: Étude et traduction de l'arabe; Moncho, Rabat, 1940

Essai sur la Méthode Juridique Maghrébine: Rabat, 1944

Aperçu sur l'Histoire de l'École de Fès: Tiré à part de la *Revue historique de Droit*; Sirey, Paris, 1949

Al-Ma'dani, Tad'mîn Aç-çunna': Bibliotheca arabica de l'Université d'Alger; J. Carbonoel, Algiers, 1949

Structures Sociales du Haut-Atlas: Bibliothèque de sociologie contemporaine; Presses Universitaires de France, Paris, 1955

Histoire Sociale d'un Village Égyptien au XXe Siècle: Le monde d'Outre-Mer, passé et présent, III: Études; Mouton et Cie, La Haye, 1957

Al-Yousi, Problèmes de la Culture Marocaine au XVIIe Siècle: Le monde d'Outre-Mer, passé et présent, II: Études; Mouton et Cie, La Haye, 1958

Les Arabes: Texte d'un album de l'Encyclopédie essentielle; Delpire, Paris, 1959

La Maghreb entre Deux Guerres; Éditions du Seuil, Paris, 1962

Dépossession du Monde; Éditions du Seuil, Paris, 1964

Index